Race, Class, and Community Identity

Radical Philosophy Today

The Proceedings of the
Radical Philosophy Association National Meetings

RADICAL PHILOSOPHY TODAY
VOLUME ONE

Race, Class, and Community Identity

Edited by
Andrew Light and
Mechthild Nagel

Humanity
Books

an imprint of Prometheus Books
59 John Glenn Drive, Amherst, New York 14228-2197

Published 2000 by Humanity Books, an imprint of Prometheus Books

04 03 02 01 00   5 4 3 2 1

Library of Congress Cataloging-in-Publication Data

Race, class, and community identity / edited by Andrew Light, and Mechthild Nagel.
    p.   cm. — (Radical philosophy today ; vol. 1)
    Proceedings.
    Includes bibliographical references.
    ISBN 1–57392–816–X
    1. Philosophy—Congresses. 2. Radicalism—Congresses. I. Light, Andrew, 1966– II. Nagel, Mechthild. III. Series.

B65 .R24 2000
335.4'01—dc21
                                       99-058011
                                           CIP

Printed in the United States of America on acid-free paper

For Bob Stone, with many thanks.
Coordinator, Radical Philosophy Association, 1982–1996.

Contents

PART II. PAST, PRESENT, AND FUTURE OF CLASS ANALYSIS

PART III. COMMUNITY IDENTITY, VIOLENCE, AND THE NEOLIBERAL STATE

Introduction

Andrew Light, Mechthild Nagel, and David Roberts

PURPOSE OF THE SERIES

Since the early 1970s radical philosophers in the United States have been organizing themselves in a range of ways, from small discussion groups to larger forums, for theoretical labor as well as occasions for practical engagement. The current principal manifestation of these efforts is the Radical Philosophy Association (RPA), an organization started in the early 1980s, having evolved out of the Radical Caucus of the American Philosophical Association (APA). The RPA continues today as one of the most diverse and active philosophical organizations in existence. For more than fifteen years the RPA has organized sessions meeting in conjunction with the Eastern, Central, and Pacific divisional meetings of the APA, as well as more specialized meetings such as the annual Socialist Scholars Conference. The group has regularly scheduled conferences and study sessions abroad, most notably in Cuba and Mexico, as well as pushed the philosophical community as a whole to take a stand on pressing issues of the day. Most recently, the organization's Anti–Death Penalty Project successfully lobbied the Eastern, Pacific, and Central divisions of the APA to vote on a referendum opposing the death penalty. Strong versions of this referendum passed in the Eastern and Pacific divisions. As a result of the passage of this referendum, the Eastern division wrote a letter to President Clinton, going on record as "opposing the use of the death penalty and calling for an immediate end to all executions in federal and state prisons."

But with all of this activity, it is again the diversity of this organization that is most impressive. On any given RPA program, one is likely to find a variety of concerns and perspectives represented—critical race theory; feminism; lesbian, gay, and bisexual theory; Marxism; radical political ecology—and a host of topics covered—ethics, politics, economics, health care, pedagogy, community identity, nationalism, public planning, and so on. Add to this a variety of critical perspectives on important figures and movements in the history of philosophy, and the array of topics covered and views represented outstrips most other philosophical organizations affiliated with the APA, which tend to focus on either one figure in the history of philosophy or even one narrow set of philosophical questions. Indeed, if one were to judge the health of a form of philosophy by its representative organization (and that organization's activity) then the broad array of what counts as "radical" philosophy is one of the healthiest branches of philosophy today.

As is the case with many larger philosophical organizations, the RPA decided in 1994 to begin hosting its own stand-alone meetings. Accordingly, the first National RPA Conference was held in November 1994 at Drake University in Des Moines, Iowa. The RPA's first foray into organizing its own meeting was a dramatic success, drawing several hundred people and resulting in a number of new initiatives, including a focus for the group on mentoring and coaching leftist graduate students in philosophy for the job market, and an attempt to draw the attention of the APA to the growing plight and abuse of adjunct teachers.

With the success of the Drake meeting, a second national conference was scheduled and held two years later in November 1996 at Purdue University in West Lafayette, Indiana. Again, the meeting was a rousing success, resulting in several new initiatives, including the continuation and strengthening of the Anti–Death Penalty Project and the Latin America Solidarity Group. Importantly, the Purdue meeting also resulted in the reorganization and extension of the association's publications. The organization's principal publication, in addition to its newsletter, the *Radical Philosophy Review of Books*, which had been edited with vitality and distinction for nearly ten years by Joe Walsh, was expanded to include the publication of invited and refereed articles and recast as the *Radical Philosophy Review*, under the editorship of Lewis Gordon. Additionally, the association signed a contract to begin publishing selected papers from its national conferences in an annual form. The result is the new series, Radical Philosophy Today, of which this collection is the first volume. The series is coedited by Bat-Ami Bar On and Andrew Light, and supported by a distinguished editorial and advisory board. Editors of particular volumes will change with each national meeting.

In addition to producing volumes dedicated to highlighting some of the best papers read at the RPA national meetings, Radical Philosophy Today hopes to serve as a window for the larger philosophical community on the current focus and interests of philosophers working in a broad range of leftist orientations. Our hope is that in turn, this publication will begin a new conversation about the future of radical philosophy in the next century. Whereas in the past, much of the conversation about radical philosophy has occurred inside the community of leftist scholars, this series and its allied journal may also broaden this discussion to the larger philosophical and leftist community.

CONTENTS OF THE VOLUME

In recent years, critical race studies in the United States have increasingly turned to the problem of "whiteness." Questions ranging from "Is white a race?" to "Is white a color?" have started to turn the study of race and racism to problems of white privilege and white supremacy. Such analyses are now found in the fields of education, political and legal theory, psychology, anthropology, and areas studies (gender/women's studies, ethnic studies, and even environmental studies). Philosophy, however, has been remarkably resistant to theorizing race and whiteness. In part I of this volume, "The Production of Race and Ethnicity," the essays by Charles Mills, Richard Peterson, and Steve Martinot speak to this concern and attempt to broaden and deepen the discussion of race in philosophical terms.

After noting that most white Anglo philosophers have neglected serious discussion of race, despite its continued and central importance to both non-white philosophers and society in general, Mills offers an investigation into the "metaphysics of race." He seeks out the meanings and implications of the incredulous question posed to a person of mixed race ancestry, "But what are you *really?*" Mills begins with a thought experiment, positing a category—"quace"—that is analogous to race in that it is inscribed into our identities at birth, much like sex and national origin. Quace could be determined biologically, by physical characteristics, or perhaps even arbitrarily. The disanalogy to race is that quace is a neutral, or "horizontal" category; there is no vertical hierarchy that might institutionalize quacial discrimination. In this scenario, one would find it odd to be pressed on the question, "But what quace are you *really?*" The question is odd because there is no vertical dimension to quace, and thus no deeper meaning to the question—other than perhaps the hypothetical possibility of having been assigned a mismatched quacial identity in a census. Racial identification, on the other hand, places one within a vertical, hierarchical system, a system that is laden with deep ideological implications and justifications, thus giving force to the question that frames the essay. Mills looks at the objectivist theories of racial realists and racial constructivists and at a range of antiobjectivist theories such as relativism, subjectivism, and error theory. He maintains that an objectivist, constructivist position avoids the metaphysical pitfalls of treating race as a biologically based characteristic (as in racial realism), an arbitrary social category like quace (as in relativism), or a simple cognitive mistake (as in error theory), and is therefore better equipped to deal with the question of passing and mixed race identity. Mills clarifies his metaphysical position through an examination of nine problem cases drawing on the following categories: bodily appearance, ancestry, awareness of ancestry, public awareness of ancestry, culture, experiences, and self-identification.

Where Mills focuses on the present American racial hierarchy and the metaphysics it implies, the two essays that follow focus on the historical and cultural dialectics of racial formation. Richard Peterson draws on the work of Hegel, Sartre, and W. E. B. Du Bois to develop a relational view of race based on recognition. Like Mills, Peterson rejects subjectivist error theories, which assert either that race does not exist or that racial conflicts are reducible to gender or class struggles. Peterson uses Hegel's notion of recognition to underscore the extent to which identity is a function of social relations. He notes that five different aspects play a role in recognition relations: (1) agency, i.e. affirmation or denial of selfhood, (2) reciprocity, (3) conflict, (4) the conceptualization and maintenance of conflict, and (5) principles of freedom and justice. Each of these aspects are explicated, via their treatment in Hegel. However, Peterson contends that two aspects of Hegel's philosophy make a straightforward application of Hegelian dialectics to questions of race difficult: Hegel's emphasis on the singular rather than social aspects of the idea of the self, and the teleology of Hegel's system.

To make his critique of Hegel more concrete, Peterson turns to a historical discussion. There are three ways, he says, in which race is historical. First, it emerges in history; indeed, it can be argued that it is a specifically modern concept. Second, race exists in different and changing forms. Historically specific conceptions of race contribute to social conflicts and are themselves altered by extra-racial social conflicts. The third sense in which race is historical is that it provides social understandings to a group of their historical predicament; in this sense, race can be constructive as well as destructive, but it is always social, never a function of the singular subjectivity. Peterson draws heavily on DuBois's philosophy, in particular DuBois's famous notion of double-consciousness. He concludes by gesturing at some possible political implications of this conception of race as a matter of recognition relations. First, that both blacks and whites should be concerned with the reconstitution of a separate black public sphere, and second, that philosophers (especially white philosophers) should set about reconstructing the public sphere in order to expose tacit and implicit justifications for racial oppression.

Steve Martinot begins his essay by criticizing the tendency of white philosophers to reduce questions of race to questions of class, ignoring the possible ways that racialization itself conditions class relations in the United States. If it is true that racialization serves as a precondition for the formation of class structures in the United States—implicating the construction of "whiteness" in oppression— then attempts by white philosophers to open a space for class-consciousness may paradoxically reinforce another form of hegemony.

To give credence to his historical thesis, Martinot turns to a historical study of the construction of whiteness, focusing on the early colonialization of America, specifically Bacon's Rebellion in 1676. His narrative makes clear that the racial categories of "Negro" and "white" were not in place prior to colonization, much less a sense of antipathy or superiority between the races. In fact, racialization came slowly, and only became identified with biology and heritage later in American history. However, the response of land owners to Bacon's Rebellion was a large step in the racializing process of African slaves. Martinot claims that racialization was bound up with oppression and hegemony, a feature that cannot be dropped easily by well-meaning white liberals. Our goal should be to unravel cultural narratives, not to work from within them.

But of course, a radical critique of the academic approach to racial questions cannot stop at critiques of liberal approaches. Self-critique is also required. Another danger which the white Western Left is subject to is the universalization of gender or economic struggles at the expense of ethnic particularism and diversity. This section closes with Xiarong Li's critical discussion of two Western feminist perspectives that have too often theorized on the basis of a monolithic, ahistorical picture of "Chinese women." While it is true that many political and economic gains were achieved by women under Maoism, Marxist feminists, for the most part, fail to recognize the extent to which these gains were defined and controlled by male party leaders. Marxist feminists often fail to see the ultimately damaging extent to which the party prioritized its class struggle over the struggle for gender equality. To achieve equality, women were instructed by the party to abandon femininity, to dress and behave more like men. Furthermore, what gains there were for women under Maoism were subordinated to the goals of the party and thus quickly sacrificed in situations where the party's goals were threatened. In their exclusive focus on class struggles, Marxist feminists have failed to see women's issues as on par with, and worthy of being pursued in tandem with, socialist goals. In particular, they valorize the "Chinese woman" under Maoism, overlooking the real gender inequalities remaining in, and indeed constitutive of, Communist China.

That said, just as Marxist feminists have given excessive priority to class struggles at the expense of the more particular struggles of culturally situated women, liberal First World feminists prioritize what they conceive of as "universal" women's struggles against patriarchal oppression, thereby papering over and occasionally damaging the culturally specific struggles of women in China. For instance, they have overlooked Chinese women's high degree of participation in state affairs (as compared to surrounding Far and Near Eastern countries); also, their focus on the "universal" need of women for birth control causes them to neglect the fact that rural Chinese women often face forced, violent, and oppressive birth control through China's population policies. Li urges that feminists in general pay more attention to context, that they avoid generalizing the struggles of, for instance, "Chinese women" at the expense of attending to the unique and particular needs of real, flesh-and-blood Chinese women, whose problems and struggles in fact diverge in many important ways.

Often, white U.S. leftists are guilty of uncritically valorizing Marxism on the one hand, and romanticizing the class struggles of distant Third World peoples on the other. The contributions to part II, "Past, Present, and Future of Class Analysis," tack against this trend in two ways: First, they take a hard critical look at Marxism with an eye toward adapting it more carefully to contemporary use; second, they center their analyses on the First World, specifically the United States, and show that Marxism is relevant here as much as in the Third World. But certainly, Marxism in America must grow and change in order to achieve viability, if only as a form of social critique. The essays at the end of this section address this concern by expanding the boundaries of Marxist analysis.

The first two essays in this section, the first by Patrick Murray and Jeanne Schuler and the second by Tony Smith, show the continuing relevance of Marx's *Capital* in demystifying notions of wealth, surplus value, and technological rents. Their analyses are particularly helpful in countering some of the postmodern, post-Marxist, and neo-Ricardian positions on the capitalist mode of production. In "Recognizing Capital," Murray and Schuler discuss the uses and abuses of the term "capital," why it is frequently misapprehended, and what makes it difficult to adequately theorize. They assert that capital is a social form. Of course, "forms" are in ill repute in some postmetaphysical philosophical circles. This is unfortunate, the authors tell us, for it is precisely capital's formal properties that give the notion its power. Also, capital manifests as material wealth, which leads to the temptation towards "wealthism," though wealth, a mere byproduct of capitalism, only gives capitalism a thin self-justification. Furthermore, capitalists themselves encourage the "illusion of the economic," which focuses on wealth and the exchange of consumer goods, diverting attention from the systemic, formal, social nature of capital.

Murray and Schuler single out Nancy Fraser's paper "From Redistribution to Recognition: Dilemmas of Justice in a Post-Socialist Age" as falling prey to many of these misconceptions about capital. The authors make three critical observations about Fraser's paper: First, its conception of capital, focusing on "redistribution," is more left-Ricardian than Marxist; second, Fraser's analysis of capital and the politics of identity is dualistic and demarcationist, emphasizing that these spheres are intertwined, yet her framework fails to clarify how these spheres are mutually constituting; and third, Fraser's dualism with regard to redistribution (capital) and recognition (identity) is a direct result of her failure to adequately conceptualize the essentially social nature of capital. The authors then present their alternative conception of the unity of capital and identity and conclude by pointing out several barriers that remain to adequately theorizing capital.

In the next section, Tony Smith scrutinizes the notion of "technological rents," or surplus profits generated by monopolies on technological innovations. This notion, not explicitly named by Marx but heavily implicated in his work, has traditionally been interpreted as simply one part of the process whereby prices of production center the flux of market prices. Smith begins his careful and detailed analysis by tracing Marx's theory of capital from its broad outlines in *Capital* volume 1 to its more specific applications in volume 3. Technological rents enter in volume 3, allowing us to distinguish between "weak competition" and "strong competition," a "struggle unto death" in which technological innovation plays an integral role in the future of capital. However, most Marxian theorists have characterized technological rents simply as an aspect of the determination of prices of production, not something that transforms its very dynamic.

In contrast, Smith argues that technological rents define a distinct stage in the dialectic of industrial capital. Profits and prices are "transformed" through technological rents. In defending this alternate conception, Smith draws on the work of Giovanni Dosi, a leading Schumpeterian, and his notion of "technological trajectories" within technological systems. Since different technological sectors have different "warranted rates of growth," technological innovation is uneven. As such, the mobility of capital investment tends to lead to uneven rates of growth in the economy. Smith concludes by gesturing at some political opportunities that emerge from this conception of technological rents, pointing to the inherent tension between those rents and capital fetishism, a tension that opens up opportunities for socialist awareness and reform.

While the previous two essays point up the continuing strengths of Marxism in exposing the contradictions of capitalism, John Brentlinger in "What's 'Left' of Our Spirituality?" instead critiques what he takes to be a crucial weakness of Marxism: its failure, both in its "real existing" and theoretical forms, to offer a spiritually enriching alternative to what the early Marx called the "soulless conditions" of capitalism. Marxism's antispiritualism has made it unable to answer the needs of the world's oppressed groups, who tend overwhelmingly to rely on religious values and institutions. Focusing on two case studies—the squatter movement in Puerto Rico and the Sandanista revolution in Nicaragua—Brentlinger demonstrates the crucial role that spiritual and religious values play in cohering and strengthening the will of oppressed groups struggling for survival. Brentlinger proposes a noninstitutional spirituality that emphasizes the connectedness of people to one another and to the land. He claims that Marxism can accommodate such a spirituality, in contrast to the views of Cornel West, dismissing Marxism as inherently antireligious. Brentlinger also critiques Michael Lerner's *The Politics of Meaning*, which suffers from a "center-outward" model of spiritual change that focuses unduly on First World, privileged, middle-class white liberals. While Brentlinger advocates the separation of religious and political institutions in a democratic socialist state, he urges that this separation not be achieved at the cost of completely excluding religious and spiritual values in policy making, education, and other areas of social life.

In the final essay in this section, Joel Kovel reminds us that despite our hopes, we must not forget the immense power of capitalism to subvert criticism and defuse ideological resistance. Kovel's focus is the power of capitalism in its relationship to the environment. Far from an epiphenomenal or remediable side-effect of capitalism's global expansion, ecocatastrophe is part and parcel of the logic of the expansion of capital, a fact whose sheer breadth and immense consequence has stunned many critics into silence. Just as Brentlinger urges us to integrate spirituality into socialism, Kovel urges us to imagine a socialist mode of production that not only accommodates our environmental concerns, but which is fundamentally ecological.

Kovel notes that the Left is stuck in a dogmatic antagonism between "green" (ecocentric) and "red" (anthropocentric) positions; both lack an empathetic and imaginative identification with the other's concerns. Kovel discusses a notion of dialectic that will allow both sides to "negate" their negations of the others' concerns, a dialectic that will allow synthesis rather than antagonism. The Marxism that results from such a dialectic could move past the instrumental view of nature implicit in Marxism's own past as well as in capitalism, while retaining its essential concern for class consciousness and economic liberation.

The final section of the book expands beyond discussion of specific forms of radical critique to take a broader look at the neoliberal state. Thomas Jeannot begins by turning our attention to the untapped radical potential of the communitarian critique of liberalism. Most leading North American communitarian theorists, such as Michael Walzer, Charles Taylor, and Robert Bellah, are reformers rather than revolutionaries. In their critiques of Rawlsian liberalism they tend to draw on traditions that are less than radical. Jeannot begins by charting the communitarian terrain, finding one communitarian critic, John Dewey, whose insights are closer to Marx's than Dewey himself acknowledged, and certainly closer than those of Walzer, Taylor, and Bellah. In the second part of the selection, Jeannot points out the affinities between the "postmodern self," with its "hostility to meaning," and the form of subjectivity that results from capitalism, claiming that the two are virtually identical, thus making postmodernism impotent with regard to a radical critique of liberalism. Finally, Jeannot confronts what he takes to be standard communitarianism's central failure: its refusal to confront directly the greatest roadblock to real democracy, the logic of capital itself. But the insights of Dewey, fortified with the radical critique of Marx, can complete the communitarian critique and fulfill its radical potential. Indeed, for Jeannot a left communitarianism, democratic socialism, may have the potential to move us beyond "liberal anguish," lamenting the loss of identity and community but lacking the resources to do otherwise.

Of course, beyond this broader critique, we need an understanding of the specific characteristics and institutions of liberalism. The following two essays, by Frank Cunningham and Stephen Hartnett, discuss the insidious nature of violence in relation to and service of contemporary state forms of systematic oppression. In "Antioppressive Politics and Group Hatreds," Frank Cunningham looks at a particular and troubling form of violence, namely that of group hatred. In searching for an explanation for group hatreds, he rejects neo-Hobbesist accounts which claim that tribal antagonism is inherent in human nature. Rather, according to Cunningham, we should view these hatreds as historically and culturally constructed. The question is, why and how are these hatreds constructed? Cunningham rejects the rational-choice view put forth by Russell Hardin, who claims that group identification is natural and group antagonism is "accidental," that is, a response to contingent and entirely avoidable historical circumstances. This view, Cunningham contends, dismisses the significance of intense animosity which is generated in group conflicts, as well as the systematic relation such animosity has to structural (and thus not accidental) oppressions.

Cunningham's alternative strategy is to theorize the connections among group animosities, group conflicts, and group oppressions without prioritizing any one of them. Cunningham imagines a triangle, "involving antagonistic conflict between ethno/national groups, attitudes of animosity on the part of their members, and oppressive relations within and between groups," each side mutually supporting the others. The final parts of the essay propose a "democratic fix," again in the tradition of John Dewey. Cunningham asks us to look beyond a political or procedural democracy, to democracy in cultural and economic spheres as well. By getting clear on the mutually supporting relationships among structural oppressions and group hatreds, we can begin to take steps to avoid both.

Stephen Hartnett begins his essay, "Prisons, Profit, Crime, and Social Control," by pointing out the obvious systemic failures of the industrial-correctional complex and proposing a question in response: On what grounds can society legitimate prison? Such a question cannot be answered only through recourse to judicial or criminological premises, since prison is demonstrably ineffective at deterring crime. Rather, Hartnett proposes this startling answer: The modern penal system was created to contain certain volatile forms of violence so that other more productive forms of violence could proceed. The essay is divided into four sections, each of which address the question from a different perspective. The first is philosophical, drawing on Rousseau's *Discourse on Inequality* and Arendt's *On Revolution* and "On Violence," each of which examine the relationship between property, the state, and violence. The second is criminological, drawing on Beccaria's *On Crimes and Punishments*, which points out the connection of early-modern criminology to the Enlightenment. The third is economic, drawing on Linebaugh's *The London Hanged*, a historical study that shows how the rapidly changing imperial needs of eighteenth-century Britain led to a dramatic change in notions of property, worker's rights, crime, and state-sponsored violence. These perspectives, taken together, provide ample support for the claim that prisons have historically been used to reinforce hierarchies of class privilege and political power. Hartnett concludes with the story of a prisoner, Big Will, and the ways that he has been forced to resort to irrational violence in response to prison culture, demonstrating that, far from being an unanticipated side effect, violence in prison between inmates and between inmates and guards is an inherent structural feature of the modern penal system. The modern trend of privatizing prisons, says Hartnett, far from being a new phenomena, is in fact a continuation of a long tradition of prisons serving to enforce oppressive hierarchies.

Finally, Gabriel Vargas Lozano closes the section with a challenge to the thesis that neoliberalism is the only viable political state formation, focusing his critique on the strongest defender of that thesis, Francis Fukuyama. Fukuyama's thesis, that humanity's theoretical evolution has culminated in liberalism and need proceed no further, is open to two obvious objections. The first is that all past experience, which is filled with theoretical and ideological upheaval and development, counsels us to be suspicious that such upheaval is at an end. The second and more trenchant objection is that liberalism and democracy are anything but coextensive. In fact, the relationship between liberalism and democracy is and has always been conflictive. Fukuyama treats the antidemocratic and violent events engendered by liberalism as "merely empirical," epiphenomenal historical contingencies that do not result from structural features of liberalism itself. This contention, says Vargas, verges on the perverse. As Norberto Bobbio has pointed out, liberalism has always had "two souls," one which seeks political freedom and one which seeks material accumulation, and the two are inherently in conflict.

Vargas further criticizes Fukuyama for an interpretation of Hegel that is highly contentious and an interpretation of Marx that is flatly false. Fukuyama claims that Hegel's dialectic supports the end-of-history thesis when in fact, Vargas claims, Hegel's theory of history was much more likely open-ended, despite gestures towards culmination in the form of the Prussian state. Marx, as Vargas demonstrates with an extended analysis of Marxism's historical theory, also thought of history as irregular and open-ended. The esssay concludes with some general remarks on why Fukuyama's theory and others like it have retained any credibility.

Taken together, the contributions to this volume help to demonstrate the continued and dynamic character of radical philosophy today. Older models of analysis have been informed with new life and new challenges while older problems continue, like Marx's specter, to haunt us. But despite the intransigent nature of philosophical puzzles concerning race, class, gender, community identity, and nature, radical philosophers today push on in hopes of contributing to the development of a viable alternative politics.

PART I
The Production
of Race and Ethnicity

1

"But What Are You *Really*?": The Metaphysics of Race[1]

Charles W. Mills

Race has not traditionally been seen as an interesting or worthy subject of investigation for white Western philosophers, though it has of course been the *central* preoccupation of black intellectuals in the West.[2] Such sporadic discussions as have taken place in "white" Anglo-American philosophy have usually revolved around moral issues, for example the debates from the 1970s onward about the rights and wrongs of affirmative action. But race raises interesting "metaphysical" issues as well, in terms of who and what we are, that can also properly be seen as philosophical, and that deserve more analysis than they have usually received. The modern world has been profoundly affected by race for several centuries, not merely in the United States and the Americas, with their history of aboriginal expropriation and African slavery, but more broadly, through the shaping of the planet as a whole by European colonialism. In a sense, then, this neglect by Western philosophy has been an evasion. That race *should* be irrelevant is certainly an attractive ideal, but when it has *not* been irrelevant, it is absurd to proceed as if it has been. So a philosophy that consistently abstracts away from race, as Western philosophy does, is obviously problematic for a *world* that has not abstracted away from race. There is a growing body of work—at this stage largely by nonwhite philosophers—on such issues as slavery and colonialism, race and racism, culture and identity, bi- and no-racialism, Pan-Africanism and Afrocen-

---

A version of this paper was published in Charles W. Mills, *Blackness Visible: Essays on Philosophy and Race* (Ithaca: Cornell University Press, 1998).

trism,[3] and with the projected demographic shift in the United States over the next century to a majority nonwhite population, we can expect philosophical interest in these matters to increase. This paper is a contribution to this emerging literature, attempting to elucidate what could be termed the "metaphysics of race" that underlie the question "But what are you *really?*"

I

Before talking about race, let me begin by describing a hypothetical contrasting system that we could term "quace." Imagine a nation in which at birth, or at naturalization, all citizens are assigned a code Q1, or Q2, or Q3, that indicates their "quacial" membership. This code is entered on their birth certificate, naturalization papers, passport, state ID, driver's licence, etc. So all citizens have a quace. But the assignation is done by a randomizing device. There is no connection between quace and individuals' morphology (skin, hair, facial features) or genealogy. It is not the case, in other words, that we could tell a person's actual or likely quacial membership just by looking at her, or that parents of a given quace will automatically have children of the same quace. Nor is there any correlation between quace and historic patterns of exploitation and systemic discrimination. There are no Q1/Q2/Q3 ghettoes; no prohibitions, juridical or moral, on intermarriage between Q1s/Q2s/Q3s; no domination of the state or the corporate sector by representatives of a particular Q group; no embedded structural differentials in property ownership between the various Qs; no quacial division of labor; no trumpeting of the superiority of Qx culture; no calls to maintain Q1 purity or heart-wrenching accounts of the existential trauma of being a Q2. The designation comes down from some long-forgotten practice and is now maintained by cultural momentum.

Now in such a society, if someone were to ask us what our quace was, we would, if we are truthful (and it means so little there would be no motivation to lie), just report what it said on our passport, let us say "Q3." But suppose the person persisted, and asked, "No, but what are you *really?*" In such a society the question would barely be intelligible. "Really" contrasts with "apparently," but here there is no ontological depth, so to speak, to separate one from the other. We might wonder whether she thought our code had originally been filled in incorrectly (the randomizing device actually generated "Q1," but the computer was on the blink, or the recording clerk was recovering from the previous night's debaucheries, so that "Q3" was entered instead). But the question would have no deeper significance, and this is precisely because quace has no significance to the lives of the people in that society beyond bureaucratic irritation. "I am a Q1!" has no metaphysical ring, no broader historical resonance to it, any more than our declaration of our passport number has any metaphysical ring or broader historical resonance to it. And this is, of course, in sharp contrast with declarations of *racial* membership, which in the United States and many other countries *have* historically had deeper reverberations and significances.

Let us try to get at the root of these differences by now imagining an ideal racial system, a system of race rather than quace.[4] One could distinguish *horizontal* and *vertical* racial systems as contrasting types. In a horizontal system, race has no present or historic link with political power, economic wealth, or cultural influence: The races are randomly distributed in the social order. So though race here is not like quace in that it is morphologically/genealogically grounded, it is like quace in being completely disconnected from patterns of discrimination. Whether such a society has ever actually existed seems unlikely, but the question need not engage us, since this abstract possibility has only been mentioned for the sake of the contrast with our real focus of interest: a vertical system. Here, the polity and the economic order are expressly structured on a hierarchical axis in which $R1>R2>R3$. The functional goal of the system is to privilege the R1s and to subordinate the R2s and R3s. To this end, the R1s are designated as the superior race. Different criteria are possible, but usually the most important dimensions of this metric of assessment will be intellectual/cognitive and characterological/moral; that is, the R1s will be seen as more intelligent and of better moral character than the other races.[5] We could speak of this as an R1-supremacist system, since the R1s are systemically privileged over the other races.

An ideal vertical racial system would then have rules to regulate its internal structure and guarantee as far as possible its reproduction. Such a system should be complete. That is, every person in the system should have a racial designation, R1, R2, R3 . . . , and if there are people for whom that designation is R0, this would be the outcome of the system's rules themselves (as against being the result of confusion over where the person fits). The system should also be *well-formed*, that is there would be clear-cut, unambiguous principles determining to which race the products of intermarriage between Rs would belong. (And this would have to be recursive to take account of what happens when those offspring themselves intermarry.) Unless it is a closed system (no immigration), it should also have rules for allocating new arrivals to the appropriate racial slot. The extent of the R1 privileging (for example in deciding public policy) should be *determinate*, whether through the stipulation of a strong "lexical" ordering of R1 interests vis-à-vis R2 and R3 interests (R1 interests as carrying infinite weight), or some weaker principle (R1 interests as finitely weightier). Finally, it should be nationally *uniform*, in the sense that there should be no local variations in the rules according to state or region.

Now it is obvious that in such a system, by contrast with a system of quace or the horizontal racial system, one's racial designation *will* have immense significance, since it will be an indicator of one's social standing and will profoundly affect one's life. And it is because the United States and many other nations *have* historically been vertical racial systems of this kind that race has significance. They have been *non*ideal systems because the rules have not usually been complete, well-formed, determinate, or nationally uniform. Moreover, many of those in the privileged race of R1s have opposed the system ("race traitors"/"white renegades"), refused to abide by its prescriptions, and supported the R2s and R3s in their efforts to change it. Nonetheless, it has been sufficiently successful that—to take the United States as an example—more than two hundred years after the system's founding, people still think of themselves as raced, American cities are more segregated now than they were at the turn of the century, there is little intermarriage, blacks are still—by conventional economic measures—near the bottom of the ladder, and some leading black intellectuals are now speaking despairingly of "the permanence of racism."[6] So this, I suggest—as against the system of quace, or the horizontal racial system—is the background against which the metaphysics of race need to be examined, and from which the question "But what are you *really*?" gains its ontological import.

II

The phrases "social ontology" and "social metaphysics" (I will use the terms interchangeably) have a certain intuitive transparency, being obviously meant to refer to the basic struts and girders of *social* reality in a fashion analogous to the way in which "metaphysics" *simpliciter* refers to the deep structure of reality as a whole. So there are basic existents that constitute the social world, and that should be central to theorizing about it. Thus, one would readily understand what would be meant by saying that the social ontology of the classic contractarians was an ontology of atomic individuals; that for Karl Marx it was classes defined by their relationship to the means of production; that for radical feminists it is the two sexes. In pre-post-modernist times, these categories would have been confidently put forward as part of foundationalist and theoretically exhaustive explanatory schemas: history as class or gender struggle. In the present, more cautious period, greater theoretical circumspection is wise. Note, then, that I am certainly not claiming that race is the only principle of social hierarchy, or that racial struggle is the comprehensive key to understanding history, or that individuals' racial ontology is in all circumstances the most important thing about them. I am simply saying that systemic racial privilege has been an undeniable (though often denied) fact about recent global history, and that exploring an ontology of race will contribute to (though not exhaust) our understanding of social dynamics. There are other systems of domination beside race (class, gender), that overlap and intersect with it. But in the United States (and elsewhere) race has correlated strongly with civic standing, culture, citizenship, privilege or subordination, and even designations of personhood. What race you are categorized as being has been taken as saying a great deal about what and who you are more fundamentally. So it is upon this that we will focus. To what extent and in what ways is race "real" and how deep is this reality?

My suggestion will be that terminology developed elsewhere can illuminatingly be drawn upon to map some representative positions on the ontology of race. As we all know, philosophers of science and ethicists have an elaborate vocabulary for demarcating contrasting views on the reality of scientific entities and the metaphysics of moral value, for example realism, constructivism, conventionalism/relativism, instrumentalism, subjectivism, noncognitivism, nihilism/error theories, and so forth. I think that some of this vocabulary can be usefully appropriated to clarify debates on race. The correspondences are not exact, and should not be pressed too far; moreover, some terms have no plausible "racial" equivalent at all. There is the danger that too many qualifications and epicycles may so muddy the homology as to vitiate the whole exercise. I hope this will not be the case, and that sufficient similarity emerges that the appropriation can be enlightening.

Let us distinguish, to begin with, between *objectivism* and *antiobjectivism* as umbrella categories of theories about the reality of race (see Fig. 1). "Objectivism" is itself used in different ways, but usually has the connotation of independence of what we choose, what we believe. I suggest there are two main kinds of objectivist position: realist and constructivist.

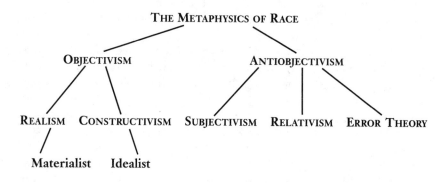

FIG. 1

In metaethics and philosophy of science, "realism" is standardly used to denote the view that acts have value or disvalue and the entities postulated by natural science exist or do not exist independently of human consensus or dissent. So, for example, killing the innocent is objectively prima facie wrong even if a certain community has no prohibitions against such actions, and electrons objectively exist even if nobody knows about them.

What, by analogy, would be "realism" about race? A "racial realist" in the most minimal sense will be somebody who believes it is objectively the case—independently of human belief—that there are natural human races, in other words, that races are natural kinds. In the stronger, more interesting sense, a racial realist will also believe that the differences between races are not confined to the superficial morphological characteristics of skin color, hair type, and facial features, but extend to significant moral/intellectual/characterological/spiritual characteristics also, that there are "racial essences."[7] Anthony Appiah argues that such a view (which he designates as "racialism") needs to be distinguished from *racism* proper, though the latter presupposes it, since these traits may be thought to be distributed in such a way across the population that there is no clear-cut hierarchy among races.[8] Historically, however, it is the case not merely that all racists have been realists, but that most realists have been racists. For the past few hundred years, realism has in fact been the dominant position on race, that is, people have believed there are natural biological differences between races and that these run deeper than mere phenotypical traits.

Such views of race are often hostilely characterized as "essentialist," and this term coheres nicely with the "realist" categorization insofar as we think of realism in philosophy of science as being associated with a belief in natural kinds with defining essences. One way of making the theoretical commitments here vivid is to think of the issue in terms of transworld identity. For racial realists, people categorizable by their phenotype in our world with its own peculiar history as belonging to a particular "race" will continue to have the same "racial" intellectual and characterological traits in another world with a radically different history. For those racial realists who link culture to genotype, this implies, for example, that black American culture would still be basically the same even if Africans had come here as voluntary immigrants and never been enslaved. And to the extent that intergroup relations between those identified as races are also explained in these naturalistic terms, relations between white and black Americans would still have the same antagonistic character.

Racial realism, whether in its racist or merely racialist versions, thus runs directly against the gathering consensus of the last few decades of anthropological and biological research. It is not merely that racism (the natural biological hierarchy of races) is false; it is not merely that culture, psychology and intergroup relations are far more convincingly explained on the basis of contingent histories than "natural" racial traits; it is that the very categories we use to identify "races" are themselves significantly transworld relative. Indeed, as commentators standardly point out, the U.S. "one-drop rule" for determining membership in the "black" race is practically unique even in *this* world.[9] Many of those categorized as "blacks" in the United States would be categorized as "browns"/"mulattoes" or even "whites" in the Caribbean and Latin America. And one could easily imagine a parallel universe of the type beloved of science fiction writers, where—as a result, say, of the overrunning of Dark Ages Europe by an Islamic army of Moors and black Africans—an inverted racial order is established in which the one-drop rule is applied in reverse, and any discernible "white" blood relegates you to membership in the conquered and despised tribe of native European "savages."

But from the fact that racial realism is false, it does not follow that race is not real in other senses; this is the point of developing "objectivism" as an umbrella category broader than realism. Many white liberals (and indeed historically many white Marxists also), aware of the verdict of science on race, are puzzled at black intellectuals' retention of race as a significant social category; they wish to move from the falsity of racial realism to global claims about the unreality of race in general, and the corollary political mistakenness of race-centered political discourse such as one finds in black nationalism, Pan-Africanism, Afrocentrism, and so forth. But part of the point of my taxonomy of metaphysical positions is to show that there is conceptual room for a view of race as *both* real and unreal, not "realist" but still objectivist. This position is *racial constructivism.*

In metaethics and philosophy of science, constructivism is a kind of epistemically idealized intersubjectivism; for example, hypothetical moral agreement behind Rawls's veil of ignorance or in Habermas's ideal speech-situation, or scientific consensus on what theory best explains the phenomena. Values and scientific existents are "objective" in the qualified sense of being independent of particular agents' *actual* judgments, but not their hypothetical *ideal* judgments. As such, constructivism contrasts both with realism as a fellow-objectivist view and with relativism and subjectivism as antiobjectivist views. In David Brink's words, "[Nonrelativist constructivism] agrees with moral realism that there are moral facts and true moral propositions but disagrees with realism about the nature or status of these moral facts and truths. . . . [It] holds that there is a single set of moral facts that are constituted by some function of our beliefs, often by our moral beliefs in some favorable or idealized epistemic conditions."[10]

Now radicals, whether the depleted class of Marxists or the thriving tribe of postmodernists, standardly speak of the "social construction" of race, so that the term is already in use, and I see this as more than a serendipitous homonymy.[11] What they mean is, to begin with, that there are no "natural" racial divisions between different human groups, but rather a continuous spectrum of varying morphological traits. The fact that the lines of demarcation, the categorical boundaries, are drawn here rather than there is a social decision, and one which creates the reality in question. There is no independent, "objective" perspective from whose standpoint one could say that these racial categorizations are *wrong*, for the resultingly racialized world is in part theory-dependent, constituted by these very beliefs. Under other circumstances, in other worlds, or even in our same world at different times, different lines of demarcation could have been drawn. This point is not in itself particularly radical, since, as noted, it is in fact a view shared by most anthropologists.[12] The additional claim that distinguishes the radical view is a political one, that the decision as to where to draw the line is politically motivated, to serve the ends of establishing and maintaining the privileges of particular groups. So, for example, the motivation for using the one-drop rule to determine black racial membership is to maintain the subordination of the products of "miscegenation."

However, there are obvious differences between "constructivism" in this sense and the standard use of the term. The intersubjectivist agreement in moral and scientific constructivism is a *hypothetical* agreement of *all* under *epistemically* idealized conditions. Racial constructivism, by contrast, involves an *actual* agreement of *some* under conditions where the constraints are not epistemic (getting at the truth) but *political* (establishing and maintaining privilege), so that the "idealization" is pragmatic, instrumental to the best way of achieving this end. Nevertheless, the semantic virtue of retaining the same term (apart from the fact that it is already in use) is to highlight the crucial similarity, viz. that an objective ontological status is involved that arises out of *intersubjectivity*, and that—though not naturally based— is real for all that. Race is not foundational—in different systems, race could have been constructed differently, or indeed never come into existence in the first place; race is not essentialist—the same individuals would be differently raced in different systems; race is not "metaphysical" in the deep sense of being eternal, unchanging, necessary, part of the basic furniture of the universe. But race is a *contingently* deep reality that structures our particular social universe, having a social objectivity and causal significance that arise out of *our* particular history. For racial realism, the social metaphysics is simply an outgrowth of a natural metaphysics; for racial constructivism, there is no natural metaphysics and the social metaphysics arises directly out of the social history. Because people come to think of themselves *as* "raced," as black and white for example, these categories, which correspond to no natural kinds, attain a social reality. Intersubjectivity creates a certain kind of objectivity.

Finally, it should be noted that constructivism comes in different varieties depending on the background theories of social dynamics presupposed. "Materialist" theories ("materialism" here as a claim about patterns of social causality, not ontology), preeminently Marxism, will see this dynamic as economically driven, related to the structure of capitalism and the projects of the bourgeoisie, and embedded in (though not reducible to) class.[13] "Nonmaterialist" theories will either deny any causal preeminence at all (pluri-causality with no dominant sector) or attribute it to culture/ideas/"discourses."[14]

We turn now—more briefly—to the umbrella category of antiobjectivist theories of race. Of the variety of antiobjectivist positions in metaethics and philosophy of science, I think the ones relevant for our purposes are subjectivism, relativism, and nihilism/error theories. (Noncognitivism and instrumentalism have no plausible racial equivalents.) (1) Subjectivism in ethics is the view that what makes an action right or wrong is the agent's opinion. Subjectivism about race would be the view that since racial designations are arbitrary (as constructivists would agree), one can choose one's race for oneself. Subjectivism would therefore imply a kind of voluntarism about race, which is, of course, what makes it an antiobjectivist position. For constructivists, by contrast, the arbitrariness of racial designation is rooted in a particular social history, and cannot be overturned by *individual* fiat.[15] (2) Ethical relativism and scientific conventionalism make the truth of moral and scientific claims dependent on actual (nonidealized) community agreement. An epicycle is required here, since racial constructivism does *itself* necessarily involve an element of relativism (the reality/objectivity of race is relative to the particular racial system concerned). So this would need to be distinguished from racial relativism proper. The latter would imply that within the ("objective") constructed global racial system, which is, let us say, coextensive with the nation, it is possible to change race through the decisions of a subcommunity of like-minded people within the larger population. (3) Finally, error theories of ethics, such as, famously, John Mackie's, deny that moral terms refer to anything.[16] A corresponding error theory about race would deny not merely (as racial constructivism does) that races have biological reality but also that they have reality as *social* entities. As earlier noted, many liberals, and those Marxists committed to an explanatory class-reductionism, could be said to have an error theory about race in this sense. Traditional Marxist debates about race and class, or race versus class, can then be seen, from this perspective, as often being debates over whether racial error theories or racial objectivist theories (realist or constructivist) are correct.

Now it should have been obvious from my characterizations that I myself am most sympathetic to a constructivist position on the metaphysics of race, a position that is objectivist while being antirealist and antiessentialist. I see this as most congruent with the actual historical record, where race has not been an arbitrary social category like quace, nor an innocent designation as in a horizontal system, but has functioned as a real marker, if imperfectly, of privilege and subordination in a *vertical* system. In such a system, racial subjectivism, racial relativism, and racial error theories are, in my opinion, mistaken positions; the metaphysics of race is an objectivist if antirealist metaphysics.

III

I want to turn now to the question of the possible criteria for determining racial identity, and what happens when these criteria conflict. So these are puzzle cases, what could be regarded as cases of racial transgression. I will assume throughout a nonideal vertical racial system, where R1s are the privileged race.

Consider the more familiar philosophical debate on *personal* identity. In the literature on this subject, going back to Locke's classic discussion in *Essay Concerning Human Understanding*,[17] it has usually been assumed that there is an answer to the question "Who are you *really*?" that is not necessarily the same as the answer to the question of who the person is *taken* to be. The whole point of the soul-transmigrating, brain-transplanting, memory-loss examples is to get at this difference. The idea is that there is some kind of metaphysic objectively there—who the person *is*—and that we have intuitions that point at it, even if only fuzzily. Through problem cases we can draw on these intuitions, sometimes refining and reformulating them, sometimes giving them up altogether, in the attempt to capture the essence of personal identity, if not in terms of necessary and sufficient conditions, then perhaps in some looser formula that can at least handle most situations. Moreover, personal testimony, while it is given some weight, is not taken as indefeasible (e.g., cases of implanted memory), so that though in some respects the person herself has a privileged first-person viewpoint, it is allowed for that this viewpoint may on occasion be mistaken. The question will be whether people's race, similarly, is an objective "metaphysical" fact about them, so that by considering "puzzle" cases where the standard criteria conflict rather than agreeing, we can sharpen our intuitions as to what "race" really inheres in.

I want to distinguish seven possible candidates for racial self- and other-identification, not at all necessarily mutually exclusive since they usually function in conjunction with one another. The interesting issue will be to see what happens when this conjunction begins to disintegrate. They are: (1) bodily appearance, (2) ancestry, (3) self-awareness of ancestry, (4) public awareness of ancestry, (5) culture, (6) experiences, and (7) self-identification (see Fig. 2).

FIG. 2: "BUT WHAT ARE YOU REALLY?": RACIAL TRANSGRESSIVES

"RACIAL" CRITERIA

	1	2	3	4	5	6	7
BODILY APPEARANCE	W	W	W	B	W*	W	W
ANCESTRY	B	B	B	B	B	W	W
SELF-AWARENESS OF ANCESTRY	YES	YES	NO	YES	YES	NO	YES
PUBLIC AWARENESS OF ANCESTRY	NO	NO	NO	YES	NO	NO	YES
CULTURE	B	W	W	W	W	B	B
EXPERIENCE	W/B	W	W	W/B	W	B	W/B
SELF-IDENTIFICATION	B	W	W	W	W	B	B
Person is:	?	?	?	?	?	?	?

W = white; W* = artificially white; B = black

Case 1:   Conscious episodic passing (natural whiteness) for strategic reasons
Case 2:   Conscious passing (natural whiteness) for ultimate assimilation
Case 3:   Unconscious passing (natural whiteness)
Case 4   Mr. Oreo
Case 5:   Mr. Oreo and the Schuyler Machine (artificial whiteness)
Case 6:   Unconscious "passing" as black
Case 7:   White renegade
Case 8:   ("Black") White renegade
Case 9:   "Biracials" (self-identified)
Case 10: "No-racials" (self-identified)

(BACKGROUND: U.S. Racial System)

When these all coincide in pointing to a specific racial designation, R1/R2/R3, then we experience no hesitation in identifying the person as a particular R, and the person does not either. But since, as mentioned, the United States is a *non*ideal racial system, with rules that are occasionally less than clear-cut, we may experience difficulty in knowing how to decide when the criteria conflict. Moreover, the problems in any decision procedure are compounded by the fact that some of the criteria are themselves somewhat fuzzy, and not subject to precise stipulation. There is also the question of whether R1/R2/R3-ness is a discrete, on-off affair, or whether there is on occasion allowance for degrees of R1/R2/R3-ness. This is separate from the question of whether there is an *intermediate* category; the idea rather is that one could be seen *as* an R1 or an R2 or an R3, but in a somewhat qualified (sometimes grudging?) fashion, not *whole-heartedly* or *full-bloodedly*—to use biological metaphors, though the basis for the judgment need not itself be biological—an R1 or an R2 or an R3. It may also be that there is a partial gender asymmetry, so that what holds true for men in situations of criterial conflict does not always hold true for women. Finally, it may be that the fact of racial hierarchy (R1s being systemically privileged) carries over into the criteria for racial identification; that is, that in certain circumstances the rules for adjudicating the racial identity of R1s are different from the rules for R2s or R3s.

(1) *Bodily appearance*: Bodily appearance, the so-called eyeball test, is the criterion we all use to make summary judgments about race, since information about the others is not usually immediately known to us. Historically, this has been true not merely for lay but for "scientific" judgments about race also, since before the advent of genetics there were earnest attempts to ascertain racial membership on the basis of skin color, skull measurements, hair texture, and so forth. However, in some racial systems, the appearance of R-ness is neither sufficient nor necessary for actual R-ness—though it will generally be a good evidential indicator—as some people may be able to "pass." Appearance is then the generally (but not always) reliable visible manifestation of a deeper essence, that is taken to inhere in ancestry.

(2) *Ancestry*: In the U.S. racial system, ancestry is usually taken as both necessary and sufficient for racial membership. (Elsewhere, for example in some Latin American countries, appearance is more important, so that siblings of different colors may be assigned to different races despite having the same genealogy.) The rules for ancestral adjudication will themselves, of course, be system-relative. In a bipolar system, consisting exclusively of R1s and R2s, there is no social and conceptual space for a third category, R3s, that would explode the binary opposition, so that the offspring from "miscegenation" are assimilated either to the R1s or the R2s. Where blacks and whites are concerned, U.S. policy has historically been to

classify them with the R2s on the basis of the one-drop rule; that is, that any black blood makes you black. This is what the anthropologist Marvin Harris calls the rule of "hypodescent," normative descent from the "lower" race.[18] So entrenched has this been until recently in national folkways and popular consciousness that it seems obvious, "natural," when in fact, of course, it is simply the result of a conscious public policy decision.[19] The alternative policy of social *elevation* to R1 status is not merely an abstract possibility, but was actually followed at certain times in the Dutch East Indies; that is, the children of Dutch males and Asian women were counted as Dutch.[20] Finally, in a tri- or multileveled racial system, such as obtains in the Caribbean and Latin America, there are formally recognized intermediate racial categories. (In the case of racial combinations, we may sometimes just be satisfied with the less exact judgment "non-R1"; that is, even if the details of the racial mixture are not clear to us, we at least want to know whether the person would count as an R1, a member of the privileged race, or not.)

(3) *Self-awareness of ancestry*: I have separated this (and "public awareness," below) from "ancestry" itself in order to provide a conceptual entree for some of the puzzle cases I want to consider later. It might be thought that this is an epistemological rather than an ontological issue, that whether or not we *know*, or others know, if we are an R1 or an R2 is not relevant to the substantive metaphysical question of whether we actually *are* an R1 or an R2. However, as this is one of the very claims I want to examine, it seems better to leave it open rather than conceptually foreclosing it.

(4) *Public awareness of ancestry*: "Public awareness" as a criterion is itself fuzzy because one may be officially classed as an R2 (e.g., on ancestral criteria), but, because of one's appearance, seem to be an R1, so that—unless one remains in a small community where one's genealogy is known to all—one's ancestral R-status may be on the record but not generally known.

(5) *Culture*: Traditional racial theory, committed to racial realism, sees culture as an emanation of biological race, so that invoking it as an *additional* criterion would be otiose (except perhaps as confirmation in contested cases of "mixed" ancestry). If culture stems from genotype, then for R1s/R2s to adopt the cultural traits of R2s/R1s should either be impossible (the strong version of the thesis), or should at least involve considerable psychological strain (the weaker version), so that one's "real" biological self is always immanent within the borrowed clothes of the alien culture waiting to assert itself. For nonrealist theories, on the other hand, whether constructivist, relativist, or subjectivist, culture is seen as adoptable with greater or lesser degrees of fluidity, and is detachable from biological "race," so that it may play a role in racial identification. Sometimes there is a tacit or overt normative premise of a moral/political kind presupposed, that those identifiable

by other means as R1s/R2s should exclusively or predominantly embrace the culture associated with R1s/R2s. Failure to do so then makes one racially inauthentic. Note, though, that use of culture as a criterion presumes that there are relatively clear demarcating traits in differentiating R1 from R2 culture. But even if a clear genealogy of origins can be traced (not always the case), the constant intermingling of peoples means that patterns originally associated with one group can be adopted by others and, over time, transformed so as to be recognizably "theirs." There are unacknowledged Native American and African roots to many Euro-American cultural practices, while on the other hand the syncretism resulting from slavery makes dubious the dream of some Afrocentrists of recovering an uncontaminated African essence.

(6) *Experiences*: Like culture, "experience" has an unavoidable fuzziness, but it is important since, in the vertical racial systems we are considering, it is seen as part of the core of what it is to *be* (with all its metaphysical overtones) a member of a particular race. Thus in the United States, we naturally think of whiteness as being associated with the experience of racial privilege and of blackness as being associated with the experience of racial oppression. Since, as pointed out above, criterial divergence is possible, so that R2s who look like R1s and are not publicly identified as R2s will escape racism, it may then be alleged of these R2s that they are not "really" R2s, insofar as the essence of being an R2 is the experience of oppression *as* an R2.

(7) *Subjective identification*: Finally, there is subjective identification—what the person *sees* herself as. This needs to be conceptually separated from self-awareness of ancestry, since the person may refuse to recognize the validity of this criterion for racial membership, and from culture, since the person could still identify herself as an R1/R2 while embracing R2/R1 culture, and finally from experience, since the person could have experiences characteristically taken to be definitive of the R1/R2 experience while denying that these experiences should be seen as definitive of who she is. As a further complication, while self-awareness of ancestry is an either-or affair (either one knows or not), subjective identification lends itself to degrees of variation, in that one can weakly or strongly identify oneself as an R1/R2, so that this is less or more significant to one's sense of oneself and one's life-projects.[21]

IV

I now want to explore what happens when these criteria conflict with one another, that is, when through naturally occurring or artificially devised problem cases individuals are produced whose racial ontology is not immediately, or maybe not even indefinitely, clear. As with the parallel personal identity discussions, the strategy will simultaneously involve drawing on some intuitions and overturning others. At this point I will simply drop the abstract R1/R2 vocabulary and focus specifically on the U.S. situation, where R1s and R2s are whites (Ws) and blacks (Bs), respectively. The justification is that mobilizing our intuitions in any useful way requires contextualizing them in a situation where the background is familiar to us.

Refer now to the table of "racial" criteria (fig. 2). Standardly, we assume there is uniformity down the line: People who look respectively white/black, are descended from ("pure") whites/(some) blacks, are aware of their descent, have public recognition of their descent, embrace the culture typically associated with whites/blacks, have experiences taken to be characteristic of the white/black experience, and identify themselves as white/black. These individuals are thus uncontroversially white/black. In the table, we alter some of the criteria so as to be inconsistent with the others, and then see what our intuitions say. We will consider both "natural" and "artificial" cases, where one expressly sets out to try to change one's race. (We might think that this is impossible, that race for an individual is permanent, but this is one of the intuitions I am going to try to undermine.)

Throughout the following discussion, particularly in the latter set of cases, I would like us to bracket the moral/political question of whether one *should* try to change one's race, or at least one's apparent race. The motivation for such actions has often been seen as ignoble: the desire to enjoy the privileges of the dominant race, while distancing oneself from the fate of the oppressed. But I see this as a separate issue, certainly of interest in its own right, but distinct from the metaphysical one. So we should try to avoid the kind of cognitive interference that comes, say, from thinking that because it is morally/politically *wrong* for a black person to try to become white, he cannot succeed in doing so—that the (moral) "inauthenticity" of the decision somehow carries over to infect the metaphysical status. (One would then be not a white person who is inauthentic, but an inauthentic white person.) Unless, of course, it is true that a case can be made for such a connection.

Problem Case 1

Consider first the case of someone with a body naturally white because of the genetic lottery, who knows his black ancestry (i.e., that he has at least one black ancestor) but deliberately sets out to "pass." This is one of the most famous themes of the African American experience, and has been the subject of numerous stories, novels, and movies.[22] Let us begin with what I will call "conscious episodic passing." Here the person leads a bifurcated life, passing for the purpose of taking advantage of differential economic opportunities in a segregated workplace, or a better residential area, or for investigative ends, and so forth, but continuing to think of himself as black and maintaining contact (cautiously, if necessary) with the black community. (For example, the head of the NAACP from 1931 to 1955, the ironically named Walter White, had what was judged to be only one-sixty-fourth black ancestry. Socially categorized as black but with blond hair and blue eyes, he describes in his autobiographical *A Man Called White* how he often posed as a white man—that is, a man called white—so that he could investigate lynchings in the South.[23]) The public will not generally know he is black, so that he will not have many of the negative encounters characteristic of the black experience. Nonetheless, I suggest that in such cases we would generally conclude that these individuals, identifying with and acculturated by the black community, are indeed "really" black. Nor would we, I think, regard the person as sometimes white and sometimes black; rather, we would say that she is always black but sometimes pretends to be white.

Problem Case 2

Now contrast this with a different kind of case, which I will call "conscious permanent passing." Here the goal is not conjunctural advantage but ultimate assimilation: The person wants to be taken for white. Maintaining contact with black relatives, childhood friends, neighborhood acquaintances, will obviously jeopardize this, so it will be necessary to move away from them, sever all relationships, and give one's children a highly pruned version of the family tree. Similarly, to avoid betrayal by "black" cultural traits, the person will consciously steep himself in white culture. Let us assume this act of assimilation and acculturation is successful. (Historically, there were in fact tens of thousands of U.S. blacks who did take this step annually. One famous, recently exposed example is the prominent New York literary critic, the late Anatole Broyard.[24]) The person is accepted by his white neighbors as white, there is no public awareness in his social world of his black ancestry, he does not experience racism, and though he is naturally initially nervous for the first few years, he gradually comes to relax and be confident that his deception will never be discovered.

Now clearly such an individual has changed his *apparent* race—that should not be controversial—but why shouldn't we go further and say he has changed his *actual* race? For racial realists, this is ruled out, since they identify race with biological criteria (ancestry, in the U.S. system). It might be that they also imagine that biological race will continue tendentiously to manifest itself—one will be sitting tuxedoed in the symphony hall listening to Schubert and suddenly get an uncontrollable ancestral urge to start boogeying. But even without these bio-cultural claims, it might still be felt that the person is still *really* black. Once we accept a constructivist view of race, in what sense is this person still black? He looks white; is socially categorized as white; embraces white culture; has white experiences. Why can't we say that he has successfully changed his race and become white? (Note that accepting this description does not undermine commitment to an objectivist metaphysic. Constructivism about race implies that there are objective criteria to being a member of a race, and what we have done is to respect that objectivity by taking measures to meet these criteria. We cannot change our actual ancestry, but we can change awareness of it. And we can also change culture and experience. So a subjectivist view, according to which it would be a mere matter of will—one could just decide to be white without doing anything about it—is wrong, as is an error theory that denies the social reality of race.) The point of the example is to test the strength of our commitment to ancestry ("objective") as a definitive criterion. I suggest that if our intuitions are now somewhat tugged the other way, this indicates that intersubjective criteria (awareness of ancestry) are more important.

Nevertheless, it might still be insisted that there is a basis other than the ancestral one for still attributing the label of blackness, and that this is because the person (unless he has self-induced amnesia also) will still be aware of his black ancestry, and cannot avoid thinking of himself as a black person pretending, even if very successfully, to be white. Moreover, it might be argued, to describe the person's experience as "white" is question begging, since by definition experience is a subjective internal affair, not merely the third-person external description of events happening to an agent. It is true that neither the average white person nor this particular individual will experience white racism, but the crucial difference, it will be argued, is that the average white person will never even think about this possibility (why should she?), whereas for the individual in question, there will be the watchfulness that comes from anticipating exposure as black, even if it never happens. So there will be a phenomenological difference between the consciousness of the "real" white person and the "apparent" white person which is alone sufficient to show that the person cannot *really* be white but is still black.

I think there is definitely something to this. It could, of course, be replied that while this nervous consciousness is admittedly likely to be present in the earlier period, it would quickly dissipate if, by hypothesis, the charade is successful, so that appearance would then become reality.[25] But let us grant this point of differentiation, and move on to a case where it is no longer present.

Problem Case 3

In both the above examples, the person was still aware of his nonwhite ancestry. Suppose we now remove this condition, so that the person thinks her ancestry is white. If the two previous cases come under the heading of "conscious passing," these are cases of "unconscious passing." Again, there are many literary treatments of this theme in American fiction. One classic discussion is Mark Twain's *Pudd'n-head Wilson* (1894), where a slave mother switches her own light-skinned baby for the master's child at birth, so that her son grows up as her white master while the master's child is taken for her slave son.[26] A real-life example is Gregory Williams' *Life on the Color Line*, subtitled "The True Story of a White Boy Who Discovered He was Black."[27] In the problem case 2–kind of examples, as discussed, part of our hesitation in classifying the person as white—even apart from realist sympathies—may be because we imagine a kind of psychic tension, the awareness that one's presented persona is not the same as one's internal one. One is playing a role, one is performing an act, one is pretending to be something one is "really" not. But eliminating the condition of awareness of ancestry removes this feature of the situation: The person now thinks of herself as white. So if this obstacle is no longer present, what is the objection now to saying that the person is "really" white? Note, by the way, that demographers estimate that millions of officially "white" Americans actually fall into this category; that is, that they have black ancestry unknown to them, so that by their nation's rules they are "really" black.

One way to think of the issue is as follows. In determining racial identity, there is an interesting combination of objective, subjective, and intersubjective factors at work. For a constructivist as against a realist theory, ancestry is crucial not because it necessarily manifests itself in biological racial traits, but simply, tautologically, because it is *taken* to be crucial, because there *is* an intersubjective agreement (originally in the dominant R1 population, later embraced by the R2s) to classify you in a certain way on the basis of known ancestry. As a result of this classification, you will typically think of yourself in a certain way, identify with a certain culture, and have certain kinds of experiences. But if the intersubjective classification is mistaken, then you will *not* think of yourself in that way, *not* identify with that culture, *not* have these experiences. The tendency is to see these as cases of *mistaken* racial attribution; thus in the Williams book, the narrator "discovers" he is black. His blackness is supposed to be a fact about him that continues to obtain even in the absence of the other features with which it is usually linked. But why not the alternative description: He was white, and then became black? (Indeed one chapter title is

"Learning to be Niggers.") If we say that he was really black all along, are we doing anything other than repeating the uncontested assertion that his ancestry was black? What other ontological freight does this "really" carry?

Here's another way to think about it. The point of starting off with the story about the quace society was to get a foil for our actual society. In the quace society, there is never any difference in the answer to the questions "What are you?" (how are you classified?) and "What are you *really?*" because how you are classified, whether as a Q1/Q2/Q3, makes no difference to your life. The adverb "really" introduces a notion of ontological import, metaphysical depth, signifying something that *makes a difference* in some fairly profound way. But quace does not do this, hence there is no room for the added emphasis; it can be put in the sentence, but nothing answers to it. If you do find that you were misclassified, you would barely give it a moment's thought. Race, on the other hand, can overturn your life, as with people in apartheid South Africa who found themselves reclassified to nonwhite, as with Gregory Williams. Making the ancestral criterion the sole arbiter fails to capture this metaphysical dimension, because we are then reduced to saying that race is just how you are classified. Whereas the reality is that it is the *import* of this classification that, through subjective internalization and intersubjective recognition, is doing the metaphysical work. So once you set up an example where this classification is made wrongly, it opens it up for us to see what our intuitions are really responding to. We focus on ancestry because in this world ancestry and the others usually go together, but once we peel them apart we can see that ancestry is not really the important thing. The important thing is really the intersubjective/subjective criterion of what ancestry is *thought* to be.

But this might then give rise to the following objection: You began by distinguishing objectivist and antiobjectivist "metaphysical" positions on race, and endorsing constructivism as an objective but nonrealist view of race. But it now seems to be turning out that your view is not really that sharply distinguished from antiobjectivist positions. Realists about race can assert that race will continue to manifest itself in the same way through different possible histories, that it has an enduring transworld quality. But your position now seems to be that race is just what we think it is. And how can this be a variety of objectivism? How is this different from the subjectivist and relativist positions on what is supposed to be the other side of the metaphysical fence?

The answer is complicated by the nonepistemic character of this "constructivism" and the fact that, as mentioned, it does contain a relativist element. But it *is* distinguished as follows. The construction is intersubjectivist (not individual), state-backed, and usually crystallized both in law and custom. Subjectivism about race would seem to imply a kind of voluntarism, that merely being determined to deny race, or to think of yourself as differently raced than you are classified, can change your race.

Problem Case 4

Consider, as an example, the case of someone we could call Mr. Oreo. Mr. Oreo can *not* at all "pass," being quite dark with clearly black African features, and with known black ancestry. But he is unhappy with his racial designation, so he fills in "white" on bureaucratic forms, identifies himself as white, rejects black culture, and so forth. Will this make him white? There is a standard negative moral judgment about such people in the black community, that is of course signified by the name. What is presupposed is some notion of racial authenticity, and a normative judgment that this kind of repudiation is morally contemptible. It would be interesting to explore the values that underlie this judgment—after all, if race is constructed, what gives it moral significance?—but as I said at the start, my focus is on the metaphysics rather than the ethics. And the term "Oreo" clearly has a metaphysical as well as a moral dimension since its implication is that the person is divided, black on the outside but white on the inside. Does this mean that for lay consciousness the person *has* succeeded in changing his race, insofar as the spatial metaphors of inside and outside standardly correspond to essence and appearance? In some contexts, after all, it *would* critically be said of Mr. Oreo that "he's really white." But I think this is really a statement about values and identification, and that if pressed people would deny that Mr. Oreo *actually* becomes white. Rather the sense would be that he is a black man pretending, or trying and failing, to be white, so that the moral opprobrium arises from the attempt, not the success of the attempt.

Now why do we not think the person has succeeded? For lay consciousness, which will typically be realist, the simple answer will be that race inheres in ancestry, appearance, and so forth, so that it cannot be changed. But racial constructivists would also deny that race changing in this fashion is possible, seeing this as an untenable racial subjectivism, voluntarism. And one central reason for their claim will be that Mr. Oreo will still be socially *categorized* as black, especially by the crucial population, the white one, so he will still experience racism, and as such will still be black insofar as the experience of white racism is definitive of the black experience. When followed around in department stores, stopped by the police in white neighborhoods, mistaken for the waiter in restaurants, Mr. Oreo might protest, with a reassuring laugh—"No, no, you don't understand, I'm not one of *them*. . . "—but this is not likely to be effective. (Note, though, that this opens the possibility of a more liberal, "cultural" racism, where people could be prima facie black, but gain at least a virtual, courtesy whiteness by passing the appropriate cultural tests, and thereby being distinguished from unreconstructed blacks.) So if racial subjectivism is a mistaken position on the metaphysics of race, Mr. Oreo will still be black.

Problem Case 5

But suppose Mr. Oreo comes to understand this, and is a sufficiently determined fellow. Let's give him the option of a technological fix, introducing to that end the Schuyler Machine. The well-publicized cosmetic transformation of Michael Jackson raises the possibility that advances in plastic surgery techniques, or even genetic engineering, may make it possible one day to transform one's skin, hair, and facial features so that one looks completely white. In George Schuyler's neglected satirical classic, *Black No More*, a black scientist invents a machine that can do just that, with the result being that within a few months all the blacks in the United States vanish, having seized the opportunity to transform themselves into apparent whites.[28] Let us call this device the Schuyler Machine (in the book it has no name).

Suppose individuals like Mr. Oreo, whose bodies are *not* (as in the first three examples) naturally white, make use of this device, and then go on to assimilate as above. Does the fact that in these cases their bodily appearance is now artificially rather than naturally white support the doubts of those who question whether one can really change one's race? Why? What would the basis of this judgment be? Compare another kind of physical transformation, that of bodily physique and strength. If a machine were invented that could transform ninety-eight-pound weaklings into massively muscled supermen capable of pressing hundreds of pounds (call this the Schwarzenegger Machine) without the tedium of years of special diets and weight training, would we say that the person only *looked* strong but had not really *become* strong? Obviously not: His new body, new physique, new strength, are real. So what is the difference? (The question here is not the deep ontological one of whether an apparently white body makes you really racially white, since we have already seen that—at least by itself—it doesn't necessarily do this. The question here is the shallow ontological one of whether an apparently white body is any the less really apparently white because the whiteness is artificially engineered rather than natural. So we are dealing here precisely with an ontology *of* appearance, *of* surfaces.)

Is the difference that we think of the first three persons' surface whiteness as real (because genetic) while Mr. Oreo's is unreal (because artificial)? In the first place, of course, the Schuyler Machine may work through genetic manipulation, so the etiology would still be genetic, though not hereditary. If we then insist on the whiteness coming from parental genes, then is this not just a repetition of the ancestral criterion, whereas we began by agreeing to consider them separately? In the second place, even if the whiteness is artificial, why is it any the less real? "Artificial" does not necessarily contrast with "real"; it just contrasts with "natural." An artificial heart is real enough, and can sometimes do the job just as well as (or better than) a real heart. Moreover, it is generally the case, of course, that technological advance, and the general mediation of the natural by the social, makes the distinction itself increasingly problematic. Or is it another kind of objection, that we are thinking of the "whiteness" as somehow merely surface, a kind of full-bodied "whiteface" that corresponds to the "blackface" of nineteenth-century minstrels, but underneath which there is the original black-skinned person? But by hypothesis, the pertinent bodily parts really are transformed; it is not that the skin acquires a white sheen, which—for example, if one goes out in the rain, or if one scrapes oneself by accident—will come off. Rather, the change is in the skin itself (and hair texture, facial features, etc.). Or is it that we are unconsciously thinking of physiological "whiteness" as something that permeates the whole body, inhering not merely in skin color, facial features, hair texture, but sparking in the synapses of the brain, pumping through the bloodstream, dripping through the pancreas? If so, it is a revealing indication of how, despite ourselves, lay conceptions of race affect us. In fact, scientists have shown that the morphological differences between those classed as white and those classed as black are minor ones— even apart from the fact that in the U.S. case, many "blacks" will have largely "white" ancestry.

My suggestion is, then, that whether the apparent whiteness is natural or artificial should make no difference to its "reality"; in both cases, the person is "apparently white." So the point of the exercise is to further undermine our intuitions about the "natural" basis of whiteness, and the location of its ontological depth in the biological. Race *is* ontologically deep, but its depth lies in intersubjectivity, and a body that appears to intersubjective judgment to be white is all, I am arguing, that is necessary here. (The alternative would be to introduce another level and speak of bodies that "appear white" while other bodies "appear to appear white.") A case can be made, then, that Mr. Oreo succeeds in changing his race, especially if he moves to a part of the country where nobody knows about his black past, though admittedly, if he marries a white woman, having children will be a challenge.

Problem Case 6

Consider now the case of "unconscious passing" from the other direction: The white child in the Twain story raised as black. So this is someone with a genetically white body and all-white ancestry who, unaware of his actual parents, grows up as black, thinks of himself as black, is culturally black, and is categorized by the community as black. If the ancestral criterion is the overriding one, then we have to say that this person is still "really" white. But what does the "really" mean other than the tautology that his ancestry is white? In the ending of the actual novel, the deception is discovered, and the biologically white young man resumes his place as rightful heir (though never to feel at home except in the kitchen), while the unconscious impostor, who has been a miscreant in various ways, is sold down the river as partial payment for estate debts. But suppose the switch had never been discovered? Would it still have been true that in some deep sense, the biologically white boy was "really" white? Or should we just say that he became black, so that his race was changed?

Problem Case 7

In a vertical racial system, those of the subordinate race who assume the privileges of the dominant race are usually morally condemned, as discussed. Correspondingly, those members of the racially privileged who support and identify with the racially oppressed usually gain our moral approbation, if not that of their peers. Can this identification extend to race-changing? The hostile phrase "nigger-lover" often carried with it the threat that if one persisted in one's subversive behavior, one might end up being treated in the same way as blacks, but could this actually amount to an ontological shift? There are a number of terms from the American and colonial experience that seem to register such a possibility: the "white Injun" of the frontier period, the European explorer who "goes native," the general notion of the "white renegade" or "race traitor" who is seen as not merely betraying his race, but in some sense *changing* his race. A recently established U.S. journal, *Race Traitor*, calls on white Americans to self-consciously repudiate their whiteness. (Norman Mailer wrote a famous 1950s essay on the hipsters as "White Negroes"; their contemporary descendants are "whiggers" or "white niggers," suburban white kids who affect the clothing, language, and musical styles of black inner-city youth.)

Imagine such a contemporary "white renegade" who sets out to support and identify with black struggles, steeps himself in black culture, joins nonseparatist black political organizations, and is on occasion targeted for differential treatment by the hostile racist authorities precisely because of this. Now sometimes, of course, whites who do this are working out personal problems, indulging in some kind of "exoticism," "slumming," and so forth, but presumably this need not always be the case. It might be that this individual's sincerity so impresses the black community that he is even regarded as an "honorary" black. In this kind of case, unlike the case of Mr. Oreo, our moral judgment is likely to be favorable, but is this relevant to the metaphysical issue? Could it perhaps be argued that since the metaphysics depends in part on some kind of subjective decision, the moral "authenticity" of giving up racial privilege translates into, or becomes, a kind of metaphysical authenticity? I'm not sure about this, but I think we'd tend to feel that the person is at most politically, or maybe culturally, but not *really*, black. After all, there will certainly be many situations in which his assumed identity will not be known, and he will just be treated like a regular white guy. And in any case, we might feel, he can always have a change of heart and jettison his assumed identity, which in a world without a Schuyler Machine, blacks in general cannot do. (But suppose the community is a small one, and there is an official policy on the part of the racist authorities to penalize such transgressors by publicizing their identity and formally and permanently changing their racial standing. Consider the real-life case of the white author John Howard Griffin, who, in a reversal of the Schuyler Machine process, had his skin treated to darken it, and on the basis of his experience wrote the bestselling *Black Like Me* in 1959.[29] If Griffin had done this in a society small enough for everyone subsequently to have been informed about his "crime," and to treat him accordingly, might we not want to say that he really would then become black?)

Problem Case 8

But let us agree that the white renegade above would not really become black. Now consider four variations on this theme: (a) unknown to the white renegade, he actually *does* have black ancestry, but neither he nor anybody else ever finds this out; (b) he discovers this, makes it public, and is officially recategorized as black; (c) he discovers this, but chooses to keep it secret, wanting to "earn" his blackness through his own efforts, so that his official categorization remains white; (d) he makes the same discovery and announces it publicly, thereby being recategorized, but in fact the "discovery" is erroneous, and the supposed black ancestor is really white, though this is never found out. In all cases, let us say, he identifies with black culture and supports black struggles to the same extent, so that whether public or secret, real or mythical, his ancestral blackness makes no difference to his actions. What do we judge the metaphysics of race to be in each case?

Problem Case 9

Let us turn now to the case of biracialism. The U.S. racial system has historically mainly been polarized between white and black, with blackness, as noted, being demarcated through the one-drop rule. An intermediate mulatto category has occasionally or in particular locales been officially recognized, and within the black community itself, there are traditional shade hierarchies,[30] but this has been the basic division. By contrast, in the Caribbean and Latin America there is a more variegated spectrum of statuses. In part because of the growth in intermarriage and resulting "mixed" children, there is now a movement afoot in the United States to introduce a multiracial category on census forms to accommodate the experience of people who reject the bifurcation into black and white.[31] The young golfing star Tiger Woods, for example, identifies himself as "Cablinasian"—Caucasian, black, Indian and Asian. There has been moral and political opposition to this, since some blacks feel that this is merely another way for those with visible European ancestry to differentiate themselves from the "pure" black population. Historically, browns/mulattoes/mestizos have been seen as superior to the "unmixed" blacks, if not as good as whites, and as such have been privileged in various ways in mainstream white society. (This is recognized in black American popular discourse in the old rhyme: "If you're white/You're all right/If you're brown/Stick around/If you're black/Stand back." Moreover, within the black American population in certain cities, there were somatically exclusive clubs—e.g., the blue-vein or brown paper bag clubs—from which dark-skinned blacks were excluded.)

However, as before, our focus is on the metaphysical question. The question is not whether such a tri- or multipolar racial system is possible, because the Latin experience shows it is, and one could imagine a United States with an alternative history that had evolved with such a system. If racial constructivism is correct, then by definition the same human population can be demarcated and constructed into different "races" in many different ways. The question is whether, in the face of majority white resistance to such a revision, subgroups within the existing bipolar system can successfully construct themselves *as* biracial. I have throughout endorsed constructivism, predicated on a uniform national system. But it might be argued that under certain circumstances, a racial relativism could be true, in which particular subcommunities could reject official categorizations and construct their own identities. So this is not individual voluntarism (racial subjectivism), but the notion of a group decision to challenge dominant conceptions. And the question would be whether such a hybrid self-chosen identity can be sustained on the basis

of local endorsement in the face of majoritarian adherence to the traditional principle by which any black blood makes you black. Would they really become
another race, or, because of their interactions with the larger society, would they
really just stay black?

Problem Case 10

Finally, there is the interesting challenge posed by philosopher Naomi Zack, the
argument that the admitted absurdity of racial classifications should push us to
endorse neither race 1, nor race 2, nor even bi- or multiracialism, but rather no
race at all: the simple repudiation of racial categorization. "The concept of race is
an oppressive cultural invention and convention, and I refuse to have anything to
do with it. . . . Therefore, I have no racial affiliation and will accept no racial designations."[32] Whereas bi-/multiracialism has some objectivist base, though a local
rather than global one, this position seems to me to be a nonstarter, and ignores
the fact that in a racialized society people will continue to have racialized experiences whether they acknowledge themselves as raced or not.

V

In conclusion, then: I have tried to show that there are issues pertaining to race and
racial identity that are well worth the time of philosophers to address, and that
will doubtless become more pressing as the nation's racial composition shifts.
Western philosophers have mostly been white, and have taken their racial standing
for granted, not seeing how it enters into their identity and affects their relationship with the universe. Race may not be real in the sense that racial realists think,
or would even like, but it is real enough in other senses. The metaphysics of racial
identity is thus a metaphysics well worth investigating.

NOTES

1. My title is indebted to Anthony Appiah's "'But Would That Still Be Me?' Notes
on Gender, 'Race,' Ethnicity, as Sources of Identity," *Journal of Philosophy*, vol. 87, no. 10
(Oct. 1990): 493–99.

2. As simply illustrated, for example, by the title—*Being and Race*—of novelist
Charles Johnson's book on recent black American fiction. Charles Johnson, *Being and Race:
Black Writing since 1970* (Bloomington and Indianapolis: Indiana University Press, 1988).

3. See, for example: Howard McGary Jr. and Bill E. Lawson, *Between Slavery and Freedom: Philosophy and American Slavery* (Bloomington and Indianapolis: Indiana University Press, 1992); Kwame Anthony Appiah, *In My Father's House: Africa in the Philosophy of Culture* (New York: Oxford University Press, 1992); Naomi Zack, *Race and Mixed Race* (Philadelphia: Temple University Press, 1993); Naomi Zack, ed., *American Mixed Race: The Culture of Microdiversity* (Lanham, Md.: Rowman and Littlefield, 1995); Lewis R. Gordon, *Bad Faith and Antiblack Racism* (Amherst, N.Y.: Humanity Books, 1995); John Pittman, ed., *African-American Perspectives and Philosophical Traditions* (New York: Routledge, 1996); Lucius T. Outlaw Jr., *On Race and Philosophy* (New York: Routledge, 1996); Lewis R. Gordon, ed., *Existence in Black: An Anthology of Black Existential Philosophy* (New York: Routledge, 1997).

4. "Ideal" here, of course, has no moral connotations, just meaning "model," a system that has the virtue of being well-designed to carry out its designated end. In that spirit, one could speak about an ideal concentration camp, or an ideal instrument of torture.

5. Physical and aesthetic criteria may also be employed, and have certainly been of great historical significance. As late as the 1936 Berlin Olympics, for example, Hitler's intention was that Aryan superiority be demonstrated by German domination of the games (an intention defeated by the four gold medals of black American sprinter Jesse Owens). But in a modern technological society achievements of strength and speed become increasingly less important, so that the subordinate races may be granted higher standing on this dimension, indeed as a positive indicator of their closer proximity to the animal kingdom.

6. Andrew Hacker, *Two Nations: Black and White, Separate, Hostile, Unequal* (New York: Charles Scribner's Sons, 1992); Derrick Bell, *Faces at the Bottom of the Well: The Permanence of Racism* (New York: Basic Books, 1992); Douglas S. Massey and Nancy A. Denton, *American Apartheid: Segregation and the Making of the Underclass* (Cambridge, Mass.: Harvard University Press, 1993); Donald R. Kinder and Lynn M. Sanders, *Divided by Color: Racial Politics and Democratic Ideals* (Chicago: University of Chicago Press, 1996).

7. See the very useful discussion in Appiah, *In My Father's House*, chap. 1.

8. Appiah, *In My Father's House*, p. 13. In part, the issue is simply about how we're going to use words, and the fuzziness of "racism" as a term. Certainly, it could be argued that *any* differentiation in presumed moral/intellectual/characterological/spiritual traits among human "racial" groups counts as racism, even if R1s' greater intelligence is supposed to be counterbalanced by R2s' deeper spiritual capacity (as in nineteenth-century "romantic racialism," for example). The issue does not usually arise because most racists have judged their group to be superior on all the important dimensions of appraisal, or at least those seen as characteristically mental and thus paradigmatically human. (As earlier noted, physical ability in the inferior race—strength, speed, reflexes, natural rhythm—is less threatening.) But certainly it is possible to imagine a group being stigmatized as more intelligent but of dubious character: Think of some traditional racist representations of Jews, for example.

9. See, for example, F. James Davis, *Who is Black? One Nation's Definition* (University Park, Penn.: Pennsylvania State University Press, 1991).

10. David O. Brink, *Moral Realism and the Foundations of Ethics* (Cambridge: Cambridge University Press, 1989), pp. 19–20.

11. Michael Omi and Howard Winant, *Racial Formation in the United States: From the 1960s to the 1980s* (New York: Routledge and Kegan Paul, 1986); Theodore W. Allen, *The Invention of the White Race: Vol. 1, Racial Oppression and Social Control* (New York: Verso, 1994); Ian F. Haney Lopez, "The Social Construction of Race" and "White by Law," in *Critical Race Theory: The Cutting Edge*, ed. Richard Delgado (Philadelphia: Temple University Press, 1995).

12. See, for example, Frank B. Livingstone, "On the Nonexistence of Human Races," (1962), reprinted in *The "Racial" Economy of Science: Toward a Democratic Future*, ed. Sandra Harding (Bloomington and Indianapolis; Indiana University Press, 1993), and the special issue of *Discovery* magazine (Nov. 1994), "Race: What Is it Good For?"

13. See, for example, David Roediger, *The Wages of Whiteness: Race and the Making of the American Working Class* (London: Verso, 1991).

14. See, for example, many of the essays in Dominick LaCapra, ed., *The Bounds of Race: Perspectives on Hegemony and Resistance* (Ithaca: Cornell University Press, 1991).

15. However, I will later argue that there are circumstances where individual choice *does* make a difference, though certain "objective" prerequisites have to be met first.

16. J. L. Mackie, *Ethics: Inventing Right and Wrong* (Harmondsworth, Middlesex: Penguin, 1977).

17. John Locke, *An Essay Concerning Human Understanding*, ed. Peter H. Nidditch (New York: Oxford University Press, 1979).

18. Marvin Harris, *Patterns of Race in the Americas* (New York: W. W. Norton, 1964).

19. In a course on African American philosophy I taught some years ago, it became clear to me that my black students saw this as a testimony to the superior strength of blackness. In other words, "black blood" was viewed as a kind of superconcentrated solution, any drops of which would remain triumphantly undiluted even by gallons upon gallons of the feebler white stuff. What had been intended as a stigma, "pollution," had been inverted, redefined as "power."

20. George M. Fredrickson, *White Supremacy: A Comparative Study in American and South African History* (New York: Oxford University Press, 1981), pp. 96–97.

21. Robert Gooding-Williams makes the useful distinction of "thin" and "thick" senses of "black" to differentiate these degrees of self-identification for African Americans.

22. For example: Charles W. Chesnutt, *The House Behind the Cedars* (1900; reprint, New York: Penguin, 1993); James Weldon Johnson, *The Autobiography of an Ex-Colored Man* (1912; reprint, New York: Penguin, 1990); Nella Larsen, "Passing," in *Quicksand and Passing*, ed. Deborah E. McDowell (1928, 1929; reprint, New Brunswick, N.J.: Rutgers University Press, 1986); Langston Hughes, "Passing," in *The Ways of White Folks* (1933; reprint, New York: Vintage Classics, 1990); the whole "tragic mulatto" literature, some made into films, e.g., "Pinky" (1949), "Imitation of Life" (1934, 1959).

23. Walter White, *A Man Called White: The Autobiography of Walter White* (Bloomington: Indiana University Press, 1948).

24. For a fascinating account of Broyard's life of deception, see Henry Louis Gates Jr., "White like Me," *New Yorker*, 17 June 1996.

25. And it poses the following puzzle: Consider two individuals of different temperaments who both pass successfully over the course of their lifetimes, but with one person having experienced apprehension all throughout the masquerade while the other, more self-confident, never gave the possibility of discovery a moment's thought. Would their achievement/nonachievement of whiteness then turn on this phenomenological difference?

26. Mark Twain, *Pudd'nhead Wilson* (New York: Bantam Classic, 1981).

27. Gregory Howard Williams, *Life on the Color Line: The True Story of a White Boy Who Discovered He was Black* (New York: Dutton, 1995).

28. George Schuyler, *Black No More: Being an Account of the Strange and Wonderful Workings of Science in the Land of the Free, A.D. 1933–1940* (1931; reprint, Boston: Northeastern University Press, 1989), with a foreword by James A. Miller. Schuyler was one of the leading lights of the Harlem Renaissance.

29. John Howard Griffin, *Black Like Me*, thirty-fifth anniversary ed. (1961; reprint, New York: Signet, 1996). The jacket copy claims sales of ten million copies.

30. See, for example, Kathy Russell, Midge Wilson, and Ronald Hall, *The Color Complex: The Politics of Skin Color Among African Americans* (New York: Harcourt Brace Jovanovich, 1992).

31. For a collection of writings on the subject, see Zack, *American Mixed Race*. Linda Alcoff gives a personal and philosophical exploration of the issue in her "Mestizo Identity," in Zack, *American Mixed Race*, pp. 257–78.

32. Naomi Zack, "An Autobiographical View of Mixed Race and Deracination," *APA Newsletter on the Black Experience* 91, no. 1 (spring 1992): 9.

2

Race and Recognition

Richard Peterson

In recent years race and racism have received increasing philosophical attention, but there has been little clear agreement or even sustained debate over how we should understand the idea of race. Anthony Appiah's work is often cited for its arguments against a biological basis for racial distinctions or for the social and cultural characteristics that racists have associated with racial difference, but his conclusion that race therefore does not exist has not been widely accepted by philosophers writing on this subject.[1] The biological evidence indicates that patterns of genetic makeup correlate only very slightly with socially drawn race distinctions and that these patterns have nothing to do with cultural and social differences associated by racists with skin color and other physical characteristics like hair texture and facial structure.[2] Nonetheless Bernard Boxill argues for a physical or biological basis for race on the grounds that such characteristics are cited by racists.[3] Perhaps Lucius Outlaw has a similar claim in mind when he argues that race has a biological component which is at the same time historical.[4] In any case, Boxill's view may not contradict Appiah's since Boxill goes on to describe the racist view as "irrational."[5] Race, then, could be biological in Boxill's sense and still be a social invention. That is, race could be seen as a function of historically emerging and evolving practices in which claims are made about biological attributes as having practically relevant social and cultural consequences.

Such an approach to race as a social rather than biological reality plausibly begins from racism (and its false assumptions). But definitions of race in terms of racism risk leaving out an important part of the historical reality of race. In the United States, for example, race has not only figured in racist attempts to justify slavery and later forms of inequality and oppression inflicted on black people; it has also figured in a politics of resistance in which racial ideals have been promoted against racism. Ideas of racial solidarity, identity, and authenticity have been developed in a politics that rejects biologically conceived racism in favor of historical understandings and practical projects which in some cases inform a separatist or nationalist perspective and in others inform a pluralist and democratic perspective. The work of W. E. B. Du Bois is an important example of this attempt to develop the idea of race for antiracist purposes. The intensity of the controversy around Appiah's argument against the reality of race was undoubtedly fueled by his choosing Du Bois as the target of his criticism.

Undoubtedly there are political as well as analytical issues at stake in debates over the idea of race. Perhaps this justifies thinking that race is an "essentially contested concept."[6] In any case, recognizing the constructive as well as critical uses to which the idea is put should lead us to explore the ways in which race is a distinctively social reality. Otherwise there is the danger that denying the biological existence of race will lead to an exclusively psychological treatment. Such a subjectivizing seems implicit in Appiah's treatment of racism as a "cognitive error." A parallel subjectivizing can be found in accounts of racism as matters of irrational prejudice or covert economic calculation (for example, by those who see racism primarily as buttressing or expressing the economic self-interest of racists, as in some accounts of white working-class racism). While the mistakes, passions, and interests of racists must figure in an adequate conception of race, the fact that race has to do with inequalities, power relations, and conflicts throughout society indicates that a subjective focus on the racist (or antiracist) is insufficient. Rather, we need a properly social conception, that is, one that conceives of race in its distinctively relational character.

In what follows I will argue for the fruitfulness of the idea of mutual recognition for the purpose of developing a relational view of race. I don't claim that race can be fully treated in terms of recognition relations, but that this idea is helpful for reflection on general features of the social reality of race, on important features of the historical evolution of race relations, and on a democratic response to racism today. My discussion will start with references to the classical theorist of recognition, Hegel, though it will also draw from Sartre's revisions of the idea. For thinking about the historical reconstruction of race in these terms, I draw most from the work of Du Bois, whose career can be seen as in large part concerned with recognition issues.[7]

RECOGNITION THEMES

Philosophical conceptions of recognition have played an important part in thinking about race. Hegel's dialectic of "Lordship and Bondage" seems directly to have influenced Du Bois,[8] and at least indirectly to have influenced Fanon and many others by way of Kojève and Sartre's existential reworkings of the theme.[9] Regardless of philosophical influences, it is not surprising that many intellectuals concerned with racism have thought in terms of recognition, since racism's biologizing rejection of the full humanity of its targets is directly a refusal of recognition, or, more precisely, a refusal of adequate recognition. The significance of this denial has figured within debates over the politics of race. The controversy over Booker T. Washington can be seen in this light insofar as his critics, like Du Bois, argued that his provisional acceptance of the color line in effect conceded an insult to the dignity of black people.[10] The failure of nineteenth-century feminism, the labor movement, and socialists to develop a consistent antiracism can also be seen not only as a readiness to defer the race question, but to treat it as in some way functional to or resolvable by other objectives, thus ignoring the irreducible aspects of recognition. Similarly, ongoing debates over nationalism and various kinds of separatism, as well as over possible and desirable forms of integration, can be seen as conflicts over the terms and meaning of recognition. The same can be said for the discussion of the idea of mixed race categories,[11] and for the exploration of the tacit place of whiteness as identity and racial assertion.[12]

Later I will try to develop some of the practical implications of conceiving race as recognition, but first I need to make clear what this idea involves. We will see that there are many dimensions and forms of recognition, and that it can inform relations of domination and inequality as well as organize relations between equals. For this discussion I will draw from elements of Hegel's conception, but rather than provide a full exposition of his view, I will directly connect these themes to the issue of race.

First, we should recall that Hegel presents recognition as a precondition for individual agency. On this account, one seeks the acknowledgement of another as the affirmation of one's own freedom, which, to begin with, means the capacity to act effectively in the world. The reality of one's self is inseparable from the objectivity of one's willing, and this requires one's acknowledgement by others. What is to be recognized is both a matter of *who* one is (identity in the sense of the distinctive being of the individual) and of *what* one is (in the sense of qualities and capacities the individual displays in acting).

The corresponding vulnerability of selfhood and thus the potential for crippled agency is attested to in the phenomenologies of racism provided by such the-orists as Du Bois and Fanon as well as such novelists as Richard Wright and Ralph Ellison.[13] As a matter of prejudice directed at such physical characteristics as skin color and imputing underlying conditions of inferiority, racism is paradoxical. Although depersonalizing in its imputation of biologically conditioned inferiority, it is imposed on individuals in ways that penetrate the formation of their person-ality. Any notion of race that abstracts from this person-focussed denial of per-sonality, for example, in favor of ideas of a generalized hostility to the other or a tacit calculation of economic advantage, is phenomenologically inadequate. Missing the dynamic of denied or distorted recognition is to miss an irreducible sense in which racism is literally dehumanizing.

A second feature of recognition is its consisting of reciprocal relations. Hegel argues that one is simultaneously giving as well as receiving recognition, and that what each person receives in the recognition relation is affected by what she gives, and vice versa. The agency that emerges in recognition involves a mutual depen-dency in which one's capacity to grant recognition is inseparable from the recog-nition one receives. It is thus a relation of powers standing in what is at best always a provisional balance. Since recognition relations can hold between unequals, rec-iprocity is often asymmetrical.

While discussions of racism often focus on the recognition imposed on the victims of racism, emphasizing reciprocity points also to the recognition demanded by members of the racially dominant group. In the United States, we can infer a need to explore the resulting self and cultural understandings of whites as well as of blacks. Balibar notes more generally that the biologizing or natural-izing demeaning of the racial other goes with claims about the racist's own full humanity and biological vitality. Racism can take the form of nationalism that makes claims about authentic membership, purity of tradition, a shared value system, and so forth.[14]

The third claim about recognition is that this reciprocity in which agency takes shape is frequently conflictual. On Hegel's account, the mutual dependency of agents seeking their freedom is marked by inequality and hence results in rela-tions of domination. To save its life, the slave has accepted the dominance of the master and so the power relations between the two are in effect relations between the different and unequal powers that each acknowledges in the other. Conflict results because each agent is guided by the telos of freedom and the dependence each agent experiences in the other is oppressive because it denies or limits poten-tial freedom. This reminds us that recognition relations bear on self-under-standing, hence a reflexive relation to the existing state of affairs. Insofar as recog-nition relations are power relations they also contain the possibility of resistance.

Making use of these themes for analyzing race of course requires finding alternative terms to Hegel's idealist metaphysics. First we need to notice that the Master/Slave dialectic is not even posed in social terms since it is a dialectic of self-consciousness that pits a single individual against another. The individuals who experience and fight out racial conflicts exist within relations over which issues of identity and possibility arise. Moreover, restating this dialectic in adequate social terms requires an alternative to a metaphysics of history that structures conflict around the goals of self-knowledge and freedom, but doing so does not require excluding a telos of freedom altogether. Rather, an appropriate historical account needs to think of social practices and structures in which possibilities of freedom are couched in cultural and political terms that bind them to conditions marked by contingency and uncertainty, but also by rational possibility. The elements of such an account can be found in *The Souls of Black Folk*, where Du Bois supplements economic and sociological analyses with accounts of the cultural traditions in which ideals of freedom forged in the struggle over slavery are preserved and projected onto new circumstances.[15]

The fourth aspect of recognition analysis has to do with how these conflicts are to be conceived. Hegel treats mutual dependence in terms of enforced labor and the materially conditioned relations between master and slave that result. His dialectic of recognition presupposes the need to preserve life, but also connects freedom to transcending natural necessity. Labor is important for itself and as something to be transcended, or at least supplemented, by other kinds of freedom. Translating these ideas into historical and social terms requires the kind of differentiated treatment of activity found in the *Philosophy of Right*, though it must avoid the idealizing harmonization of practices that Hegel provides.[16] The conflicts proper to recognition relations can be explored across the whole range of practices whose control and potentials constitute the stakes of a democratic politics.

If the corresponding casting of race relations in recognition terms must avoid Hegelian teleology, it also stands in uneasy relation to Marx's analysis of modes of production. Race has to do with struggles over identity and capacities in practices throughout the whole of society. Besides being about who is really human or who is really an American, racism is about who gets to do what and under what conditions. As such it bears on the division of labor in the most general sense. Since race issues are interwoven with the complexity and differentiations of modern society, resulting claims about the self and agency must be sensitive to the differential and overlapping forms of recognition and the many different outcomes they can have.[17]

The fifth and final aspect of recognition connects the conflictual and material aspects of reciprocity to processes of learning which organize potential forms of

justice and freedom won in conflict. In Hegel, the struggle over recognition is correlated with a process of posited understandings and self-criticisms guided by a
telos of freedom and self-knowledge. Indeed, the recognition theme figures
prominently in Hegel's intriguing exploration of the problem of how humanity
has expanded and transformed its understanding and practices of reason from
within contingent historical settings. Habermas offers his communication theory
as a materialist philosophical approach to such learning processes.[18]

In the context of race discussions, thinkers like Du Bois preserve from Hegel
the argument that the evolution of our understanding of freedom is inseparable
from experiences gained in struggles against domination. Orlando Patterson
makes a similar claim in arguing that ideals of freedom emerged historically from
battles over slavery.[19] Du Bois also claims that exploring the reciprocal standing of
races can lead to a specifically democratic learning, in which the limitations of
American democracy can both be identified and challenged.[20] We will return to
this idea of democratic learning when we address contemporary forms of race.

Let me summarize what a recognition approach to race takes from Hegel. On
this approach, race has to do with reciprocal and conflictual processes in which
agency, that is, identity and capacities, is embodied in a variety of social practices.
The inequalities and power relations organizing these practices involve the imputation of biological or physical factors that limit or diminish the agency of those
subjected to racist recognition. But the conflicts which mark these relations have
the potential to challenge these imputations in a process whose liberating potential includes learning about the nature of society and freedom itself.

The rejection of Hegel's systematic perspective for thinking about race
implies not only the loss of his teleology for thinking about learning through conflict, but also the centering of the social process on the learning that emerges from
those conflicts. This makes the place of recognition issues within the social
process more of an empirical and practical matter than it is for Hegel. It also
deprives the concern with race of any reliance on assumptions about historical
progress, but accepting a tragic dimension to race conflicts does not diminish the
respects in which we might see race as bearing on general political questions. To
explore how these more systematic issues are to be conceptualized requires a
clearer alternative to Hegel than discussed so far.

Race as recognition relations thus provides a social rather than biological
concept of the reality of race and has the advantage of casting race in terms that
are open to historical analysis. To this historical dimension we can now turn.

THE HISTORICITY OF RACE

There are at least three important senses in which race is historical. First, it emerges in history. The term itself appears first in the sixteenth century and the biological conceptualization of race difference is developed in the latter part of the eighteenth century.[21] While one may find prefigurings of social discriminations along racial lines before the eighteenth century, this was not at first the main way of distinguishing the African slaves in the New World, but seems to have emerged with a confluence of factors including resistance by servants from Europe as well as Africa, new forms of social control, the debate over slavery that developed in Europe during the eighteenth century, and contradictions within the liberal nationality of the British colonies that came to a head with the founding of a new nation.[22] How we are to explain the emergence of race within this mix of slavery, science, nationality, and social conflict is an open question. For our present purposes, the main point is that there are grounds for arguing that race is not only historical but is specifically modern. Although my references are mainly to the historical experience of the United States, I am assuming that racialized thought and practice is a wider though quite diverse phenomenon in the modern world. Since my discussion focuses on the black/white racial divide, it sets aside a host of related issues, for example, the racial dimension of the treatment of Native Americans.

The second sense in which race is historical, then, is that it exists in different and changing forms. As a specific kind of recognition framework proper to relations of domination, race involves conflicts which contribute to changes that at the same time are influenced by social changes independent of specifically racial relations. We can, for example, distinguish race relations after the Civil War from those during slavery. Emancipation involved a fundamental transformation of recognition relations which in turn became the focus of bitter conflict. The Civil War amendments codified the recognition of full citizenship not just for the former slaves but for previously free blacks whose civil and political rights had typically been violated. But the reaction against Reconstruction led, with legal segregation and the blocking of the franchise, to a withdrawal of the recognition of full citizenship. The status of citizenship then became a major focus of black struggle until the victories of the civil rights movement.

By distinguishing the slavery period from the century after the Civil War, we draw a broad contrast between types and terms of racial recognition. While both periods illustrate race as earlier defined, they do so in importantly different ways. While the contrast can be drawn in legal terms, for example, between persons treated as property as opposed to citizens denied full property and political rights, we can also speak of social membership. Here the contrast is between denied membership to individuals who are an integral part of society and compromised membership for individuals who are explicitly recognized citizens. The contradictory character of the recognition relations after the Civil War are captured in Du Bois's classic statement of double consciousness:

> It is a peculiar sensation, this double-consciousness, this sense of always looking at one's self through the eyes of others, of measuring one's soul by the tape of a world that looks on in amused contempt and pity. One ever feels his twoness,— an American, a Negro; two souls, two thoughts, two unreconciled strivings; two warring ideals in one dark body, whose dogged strength alone keeps it from being torn asunder.[23]

Beside offering such striking formulations of recognition conflict, Du Bois's work explores the range of respects in which race relations were a matter of recognition during the post–Civil War period. I suggested earlier that his conflict with Washington can be read as being about both the irreducibility and the primacy of recognition issues. We can reconstruct Du Bois's emphasis in terms of the various kinds of rights that American society conferred on those who were granted full membership, namely civil rights (covering a private life that was not restricted to but included a range of property rights), political rights (including the vote, but participation rights more generally), and social rights (which at the time for Du Bois meant education, but assumed wider meaning with the expansion of the welfare state).[24]

With this emphasis on rights, and therefore on formal recognition of blacks as full members of American society, I don't mean to play down DuBois's concern with economic conditions or culture. Especially with his arguments for consumer collectives in the 1930s, he confronted existing material needs on the assumption that no short-term overcoming of racism was in sight. But even then he saw the formation of these institutions as an assertion of black identity and solidarity and as part of an ongoing struggle for full social membership.[25] Similarly, concern with culture was a matter of the evolution of a racial solidarity linked to racial accomplishments, a process he described early in his career as developing the distinctive message of the black race.

Although what he meant by this message remains a point of debate, his concern with racial achievements and solidarity illustrates the third main sense in which race is a historical reality. Race sometimes provides the terms in which groups come to identify themselves and their predicament in history. Racial identification may or may not be racist, so far as this implies evaluations based on imputed physical characteristics. Certainly it was an ongoing concern of Du Bois's work to find a nonbiological formulation of the conditions and aims of racial solidarity. Whether or not he succeeded in this regard, his efforts are instructive for thinking about the historical reality of race.

For Du Bois, racial solidarity was strategically necessary for overcoming racial oppression.[26] Given the weakness of blacks as a group and the persistence of racial prejudice, Du Bois thought it necessary for blacks not just to support each other but to forge a common project. In part this was a matter of effective resistance and pursuit of common goals, and in part it was a condition for effective alliances with sympathetic whites. In part it presupposed that whites were in the last analysis open to reasoned persuasion on the race issue, a presupposition Du Bois later came to doubt. But, in addition to all of this, racial solidarity was also an end in itself for Du Bois, since he believed in the unique qualities and promise of the black people, as these were rooted in experience and tradition rather than biology. The project of cultivating this promise, though not exclusively a strategic aim, nonetheless contributed to a higher goal than the race itself. Du Bois persisted in what today might be called a democratic multiculturalism. The accomplishments of the race were to benefit not only its members but a wider humanity and in particular were to contribute to a uniquely American democratic culture.[27] Here we see racial solidarity as linked to the aim of addressing white self-understanding, and as contributing to democratic learning.

This third respect in which race conceived as recognition is historical, namely as providing social understandings of the historical predicament of a group, bears on how we understand the second respect, namely race relations as evolving. In Du Bois we see how the idea of racial solidarity, identity, even mission, is conjoined with the specific recognition issues proper to full achievement of civil, political, and social rights. To draw out further what recognition issues amount to here, we can consider some of the political dimensions of this struggle for solidarity and the achievement of these rights. Achievement of political rights would mean full entry into the public sphere, the realm of public discussion among mutually acknowledged political equals. In the public sphere, each citizen deserves a full hearing and a reasoned response within a debate over policies and institutions, a process that leads to the formation of shared political understandings.[28]

The effect of the reaction against Reconstruction was almost entirely to exclude blacks from the public sphere. This not only involved the denial of constitutionally mandated political rights but also undercut the struggle for the implementation of civil and social rights. The extent to which racist recognition was centered on exclusion from the public sphere can perhaps be measured by the extent to which intellectuals like Du Bois worked to construct what Dawson calls a black counterpublic.[29] The idea of such a counterpublic is of interest to my argument since it illustrates the importance of recognition struggles and provides historical terms in which to think about the issues they pose. In Du Bois's day, the counterpublic included institutions like churches, schools, women's clubs, newspapers, and civic organizations and was animated by movements among students, women, workers, and local communities. Within this setting intellectuals (Du Bois's "talented tenth") could play a variety of mediating roles. The resulting complex of educational, religious, journalistic, and legal activities contributed to a political understanding and capacity for action that, despite Du Bois's own misgivings and frustrations, led to the victories of the civil rights era.

Before turning to the uncertain relation in which racial recognition stands today to this historical background, let me point out a paradox about the recognition that was achieved in the civil rights period. This has to do with the limitations of formal rights, but is different from, though related to, the familiar point that racial justice requires a material or economic component as well. The rise of a counterpublic amounted to a kind of political capacity that contributed to and was confirmed by the recognitions achieved in the civil rights struggle. But this capacity dissipated along with the counterpublic itself. In part this can be understood as a cost of the victories of the movement so far as the recognitions that were achieved provided the middle class opportunities which allowed its members to leave the segregated communities within which the black public sphere was rooted. Cornel West speaks of the resulting decline of independent black institutions, including the black press and black universities, and corresponding changes in the role of the black intelligentsia.[30] To be sure, the fate of race politics was a far more complex affair than these considerations capture, since, among other things, it was also affected by structural changes in the economic life of cities, including the loss of investment and the decline of industrial work.

In any event, one thing lost with the decline of the black counterpublic was a specific recognition demand on which the civil rights movement had made real headway. This movement did not only press for benefits for black people, but also demanded acknowledgment of the racial character of American society in general. In this respect it was a demand for self-understanding among whites. Had the race question more deeply and consistently penetrated the public sphere, the question of the racial dimensions of the society and culture would have had to be more fully explored. In the event, however, the achievement of rights by state action (the passing of the Civil Rights and Voting Rights Acts, among others) helped bring the movement to a close. It also aborted the emergence of a transformed public sphere that would necessarily have followed the intersection of the black counterpublic with the public sphere more generally. There were many causes for this failure, but the result was a one-sided recognition that could play into new kinds of racism in the following decades.

RECOGNITION AND RACE TODAY

Earlier I suggested that race is an essentially contested idea, that an analysis of race is inseparable from a political relation to racism. If this is so, then the idea that race is a matter of historical recognition relations should have specific political implications. To think about how to identify these we need to consider what has become of racial recognition since the civil rights period.

Perhaps most striking in this regard is the widespread denial that racism is today even a problem, or at least a political problem, in the United States. On this view, the implementation of civil rights legislation provided appropriate and adequate social recognition to black people. Accordingly, the persistence and even deepening of racial prejudice may be a moral, legal, or cultural problem, but it is not a political matter that would require making new laws or changing institutions. It is in keeping with this view to argue that patterns of racial inequality are largely matters of individual responsibility, and that social policies designed to overcome such inequality constitute reverse racism. Alternatively, some argue that inequality is not simply a matter of individual or cultural shortcomings, but has a basis in economic conditions and so remedies should take the form of class-oriented, but not race-oriented, policies. In any event, the analysis of race relations as recognition relations would on these views be at best an anachronism.

To show that the recognition approach is still fruitful, then, it is necessary to see how the victories of the civil rights movement have either left other recognition issues unaddressed or, in conjunction with other social changes, have given rise to new issues of recognition. Though arguments can be made for both alternatives, I will focus on new kinds of recognition issues. In particular, I want to develop my references to the evolution of the public sphere and how it converges with the ambiguous legacy of the civil rights era.

Any discussion of recognition relations in general and the public sphere in particular must take into account ways political discussion not only takes place through mass media, but avails itself of the devices of mass culture. In the following schematic discussion, I will begin with some claims about representations proper to race found in the mass media, and then will discuss how viewing these as matters of recognition leads us to directly political questions that have relevance to the idea of a democratic public sphere.

In turning to representations found not just in the statements of professional politicians, but in TV news, print journalism, opinion polls, and mass entertainment, we look to representations that articulate prevailing terms in which individuals and groups are recognized. Of course such mass media and mass cultural representations do not exhaust public discourse, but they constitute the most important form in which political understandings circulate in society. Identifying such representations is not the same as describing prevailing opinions, but it does establish the point of reference for choices, resistance, or withdrawal. First I will make some claims about the content of such representation as they bear on the recognition relations proper to race, then I will turn to the kinds of political processes in which such representations figure.

There are three kinds of representation to which I will refer: direct and indirect depiction, and displacement.

Among direct depictions of race we can cite the frequent representation of middle-class blacks, sometimes as major figures, but usually in the background, in roles that imply integration into mainstream America. In their study of *The Cosby Show*, Sut Jhally and Justin Lewis argue that such figures lose distinctive racial identity for most audiences.[31] This paradoxical version of racial invisibility goes with the respects in which these figures have been assimilated into the existing division of labor, assuming what were previously white roles and positions, albeit in idealized form. A contrasting representation can be found in the depictions of the black urban poor, either in entertainment or news, as socially problematic because of criminal activity, dependence on welfare, unstable families, and the like. In a setting in which the welfare state casts citizens as clients, black citizens are represented as bad clients, falling below the threshold of responsible citizenship.

Indirect representation takes place when race is tacitly a factor in the depiction of social issues. Crime can be tacitly made a race issue, for example, in the notorious Willie Horton campaign ad. Welfare, drugs, and teen pregnancy are often racially coded, linking what are taken to be pathological tendencies specifically to minority groups. Conversely, conventional or prescribed roles or norms (for example, "family values," the idea of "middle class" itself) can be tacitly coded as white and made the norm for all groups. The fact that such practices are normalized in this way doesn't give them an intrinsically racial character, but it contributes to a distinctly undemocratic relation of individuals to their social options and reinforces the tacit weight of racialism.

Displacement, the third kind of representation, takes place by way of indirect and direct depictions, but should be distinguished from them. This takes place when social issues that are not mainly or inherently race issues are associated with race and, given the downplaying of race, are distorted and often removed from serious discussion. When, for example, welfare is coded as a race issue, relevant questions of joblessness and poverty are removed all the more from public debate. Another example of displacement is the use of the idea of the underclass. As an ideological representation of the urban black poor, the idea of the underclass homogenizes and localizes social issues (drugs, welfare, teen pregnancy, etc.) in a specific group. This is despite the fact that these problems do not characterize all the inner city poor and are not the monopoly of black people. But the idea of the underclass crystallizes the various associations of these social issues in racial terms. In doing so it also contributes to a reduction of class issues about inequality to the imputed behavior of a racially identified and isolated minority.

In these respects, the evolution of the forms of racial recognition is closely linked to the evolution of political understanding generally. This should not be surprising since the race question has been a crucial part of American national and political identity from the very beginning. For thinking about some of the practical implications of the way this interconnection is playing out today, it may be useful to consider the intersection of the representations I have cited with the politics of the declining welfare state, itself an institutional expression of political uncertainties in the face of structural change. Today, institutionally respectable conservatives seem to mimic the ultra-right in attacking the state, though their alternative, that is, the promise of market forces, contrasts with the ultra-right's evocation of rugged individualism or simply being left alone. Both movements reject explicitly racist arguments, yet the focus of their attack is those features of the state which offer some remedy to racism, for example, affirmative action, welfare, and public education.

This feature of antistatist politics illustrates a kind of indirect relation to race as discussed above. But in doing so it articulates a problematic relation to politics and public life generally. This bears in part on the uncertainties of the state in globalizing capitalism, but also on the very basis of democratic understandings. In the United States, and perhaps elsewhere, race is not only one of many important political issues, it also shapes the relation of citizens to political life by organizing their understanding of political issues and what is at stake in them. As a result, recovering a sense of politics proper to a democratic project is inseparable from addressing the racially coded understandings of contemporary debates. Tracing some forms of contemporary racial recognition has, then, pointed us to new issues concerning the kind of political learning Du Bois conceived as connecting race issues with issues about democracy more generally.

We have been exploring the thesis that the social reality of race can at least in significant part be conceived as relations of recognition. Since politics itself is in part a matter of recognition, it should perhaps not be surprising that issues about race and about the quality of politics overlap, even though the depth and extent of this overlap is itself a historical matter. Establishing the connection between racial and political recognitions provides further support for the claim that the social and historical dimensions of race can be reconstructed in recognition terms, but it may only complicate questions about the relation of this to other dimensions of race and society.

Let me conclude this discussion with a more direct if still schematic reference to the political implications of a reconstruction of race in terms of recognition. One is a point made by many black intellectuals, namely that race issues today require the reconstitution of a black public sphere or counterpublic. Clearly the issue of a black counterpublic is in large part a matter for discussion by African Americans. But the context and evolution of such a public is not uniquely a black concern. Moreover, the logic of recognition relations should serve to remind us that white intellectuals have critical tasks specific to the racial side of the problem of the public sphere. These include reconstructing the very processes in which race becomes invisible, and thus unmasking contemporary ways the seeming neutrality of mainstream culture hides racial content.

This point holds for criticism internal to intellectual work as well. Philosophy in particular has been part of the construction of racialized understanding. This is apparent not just in the racist comments of thinkers like Hume, but in the construction of a scientific theory of race, as found in Kant, or in the turn to racial thinking in confronting problems of historicity, as in Heidegger. Philosophical criticism has much to do that bears on reconstructing and challenging tacitly racialized understandings, for example, as figuring in notions of humanity, tradition, and such collectives as nations and peoples.[32]

NOTES

1. Anthony Appiah, "Racisms," in *Anatomy of Racism*, ed. David Theo Goldberg (Minneapolis: University of Minnesota Press, 1990), pp. 3–17.

2. Richard Lewontin, Steven Rose, and Leon Kamin, *Not in Our Genes* (New York: Pantheon, 1984), pp. 162–67.

3. Bernard Boxill, *Blacks and Social Justice*, 2d ed. (Lanham, Md.: Rowman and Littlefield, 1992), p. 178.

4. Lucius Outlaw, "On W. E. B. Du Bois's 'The Conservation of Races,'" in *Overcoming Racism and Sexism*, ed. Linda Bell and David Blumenfeld (Lanham, Md.: Rowman and Littlefield, 1995), pp. 79–102.

5. Boxill, *Blacks*, p. 179.

6. Leonard Harris makes somewhat different use of this idea in "The Concept of Racism," forthcoming in the *Centennial Review*. The idea was earlier developed by W. B. Gallie, for example, in *Philosophy and the Historical Understanding* (New York: Schocken Books, 1968), chap. 8.

7. Richard T. Peterson, "Du Bois's Dialectic of Political Recognition," unpublished manuscript.

8. Shamoon Zamir, *Dark Voices* (Chicago: University of Chicago Press, 1995).

9. Frantz Fanon, *Black Skin, White Masks*, trans. Charles Lam Markmann (New York: Grove Weidenfeld, 1967); Jean-Paul Sartre, *Anti-Semite and Jew*, trans. George J. Becker (New York: Schocken, 1965); Alexander Kojève, *Introduction to the Reading of Hegel*, trans. James Nichols (New York: Basic Books, 1969); Lewis R. Gordon, *Fanon and the Crisis of European Man* (New York: Routledge, 1995).

10. W. E. B. Du Bois, "Of Mr. Booker T. Washington and Others," in The *Souls of Black Folk* (New York: Signet, 1969), pp. 79–95.

11. Naomi Zack, *Race and Mixed Race* (Philadelphia: Temple University Press, 1993).

12. David Roedinger, *The Wages of Whiteness* (London: Verso, 1991).

13. Richard Wright, *Native Son* (New York: HarperCollins, 1993); Ralph Ellison, *Invisible Man* (New York: Vintage, 1995).

14. Etienne Balibar, "Paradoxes of Universality," in *Anatomy of Racism*, pp. 283–92.

15. Du Bois, "Of the Faith of the Fathers" and "Of the Sorrow Songs," in *Souls*, pp. 210–25, 264–77.

16. G. W. F. Hegel, *Philosophy of Right*, trans. T. M. Knox (New York: Oxford University Press, 1967).

17. Michele M. Moody-Adams, "Race, Class, and the Social Construction of Self-Respect" and Howard McGary, "Alienation and the African-American Experience," *Philosophical Forum* 24, nos. 1–3 (spring 1992–93): 251–66, 282–96.

18. Jurgen Habermas, *Communication and the Evolution of Society*, trans. Thomas McCarthy (Boston: Beacon Press, 1979).

19. Orlando Patterson, *Slavery and Social Death* (Cambridge, Mass.: Harvard University Press, 1982).

20. Du Bois, "Of Our Spiritual Strivings," in *Souls*, pp. 43–53.

21. Michael Banton, *Racial Theories* (New York: Cambridge University Press, 1987), pp. 1–2.

22. Thomas F. Gossett, *Race: The History of an Idea in America* (New York: Schocken, 1965).

23. Du Bois, *Souls*, p. 45

24. Habermas reconstructs T. H. Marshall's distinctions in communications terms in *Between Facts and Norms*, trans., William Rehg (Cambridge, Mass.: MIT Press, 1996).

25. W. E. B. Du Bois, "A Negro Nation Within the Nation," in *W. E. B. Du Bois: A Reader*, ed. David Levering Lewis (New York: Henry Holt, 1995), pp. 563–70.

26. Du Bois, "The Conservation of Races" and "Separation and Self-Respect," in *A Reader*, pp. 20–27, 559–62.

27. Du Bois, *Souls*, p. 52.

28. Jurgen Habermas, *The Structural Transformation of the Public Sphere*, trans. T. Burger and F. Lawrence (Cambridge, Mass.: MIT Press, 1989).

29. Michael C. Dawson, "A Black Counterpublic? Economic Earthquakes, Racial Agenda(s), and Black Politics," in *The Black Public Sphere*, ed. Black Public Sphere Collective (Chicago: The University of Chicago Press, 1995), pp. 199–228.

30. Cornel West, "The Dilemma of the Black Intellectual," in *Keeping Faith* (New York: Routledge, 1993), pp. 67–85.

31. Sut Jhally and Justin Lewis, *Enlightened Racism* (Boulder: Westview, 1992).

32. This revision of earlier drafts has benefitted from the comments of Carolyn Loeb, Richard Schmitt, and Charles Mills.

3

The Structure of Whiteness, Its History and Politics

Steve Martinot

I n a paper on Martin Luther King, Gerald Early made the statement that King was "a black leader in a society in which there are no white leaders."[1] It was a somewhat surreal way of reflecting the American blind spot, and points to a central incommensurability in U.S. politics. White recognition of King as a black leader grants him cultural legitimacy, and at the same time withholds it by bestowing it through the assumed hegemonic power to grant cultural legitimacy in the first place. It confirms a hegemonics in the very act of presuming a non-hegemonic situation.

A similar situation obtains for other political issues. Affirmative action programs, for instance, were instituted to rectify (in small part) the effects of centuries of exclusion and discrimination against large groups of people (called minorities and women). They attempt to open a space of economic and political inclusion on the theory that social parity is a necessary condition for democratic participation. These programs have been attacked by conservatives for being forms of exclusion and "reverse" discrimination against white people. In thus forgetting the history to be rectified, such attacks render those prior forms of discrimination by whites as nonexistent as "white leaders."

Sara Diamond points out that a more general attack on black and Chicano communities has been in progress since the 1980s. It is part of a renewed racialization of the United States, whose aim is to rebuild what the civil rights movement had begun to dismantle or transform. No longer lurking in such things as redlining or a war on drugs, the disappearance of jobs or the abandonment of social programs, it is now located in a prison industry (a version of the mid-European ghettoes), the deployment of drugs (a version of the Opium Wars), and institutionalized violence (the Mark Fuhrmans are not anomalies or rogue exceptions).[2] Her concern is the ability of the new racist Right to harness grassroots energy, and promote itself as populist.

By fostering a "populist" repeal of affirmative action, the Right actually calls the democratic process into question. It transforms the necessary conditions for that process, namely, parity and participation, into ideologically contested issues to be decided within it. The real social problems of inequities or exclusions become unintelligible when transformed into ideological concepts, or (one could say) "ideologized" as issues. It is the political existence of people that is at stake in those inequities. To ideologize them is to turn people themselves into issues, to transform the subject of the democratic process into its object. This only reifies the exclusions, conceptually barring those people from real participation. Minority status itself is an example; it is brought into existence by a continuing act of exclusion whereby the excluding group creates itself as a majority. Or in the arena of civil rights, what white society takes for granted as part of its sociocultural (constitutional) environment must be continually approached as a political task and political struggle by African Americans, as a source of continual daily concern. When civil rights, as the foundation for dealing with all political issues, becomes itself the issue, then political participation is set out of reach in the distance. Again, a hegemonics is reconfirmed through the very channels presented as nonhegemonic.

A similar incommensurability appears in the politics of abortion, for instance. Abortion was legalized to give women greater control over themselves as women, against religio-political power that historically withheld that control. But to legalize it as a personal right, rather than as a medical procedure, is to disguise personhood and personal self-control behind an ideology of constitutionality, through which similar "rights of the unborn" could be defined. The abortion "issue" has become the contestation of an ideological fetus against the ideologized personhood of women. The integrity of a woman as an organism gets fragmented into "constitutional" functions over which the granting of privacy rights can be decided by others. In the name of nonhierarchical (ideologized) rights, the hierarchical control of both women and sexuality is both forgotten and confirmed.

The Right's rhetoric turns issues like abortion and affirmative action into icons that can be used against the very people who need them, silencing people by ideologizing their social being. And its grassroots success indicates the extent to which the mainstream finds this to be acceptable, to make sense. This raises the question, what makes an incommensurability that contradicts the foundations of democratic process appear democratic to the mainstream? Diamond describes at length the Right's obstructions and disruptions of the social movements for equality, justice, and social liberation, deflecting them from those goals to defense of past democratic gains. And she bemoans the left's apparent loss of initiative at the grassroots level.[3] The implication is that the Right relies on something more than simply rhetoric, and that the real foundation for the political process in the United States lies elsewhere. In noting that the Right equates traditional social norms and values with the sanctity of white society and the "white nation," she returns us to Gerald Early's terse marking of the white blind spot.

A critique of whiteness and its role in U.S. politics and class-consciousness has begun to emerge on the left.[4] But, for the most part, it focuses on class-oriented notions rather than on the process of racialization itself. The white left tends to explain racism through concepts of "divide and rule" and "white-skin privilege," for instance, immersing race and racial hegemony in questions of class. This begs the question by acceding to the nature of racial difference as given by whiteness and white supremacy; that is, as something with which to politically strategize; and it obviates seeing how racialization may have conditioned the development of class itself in the United States. Theodore Allen argues that racism and white supremacy were invented to establish social control over both rebellious poor whites and a racialized "other" (e.g., Native Americans, or African Americans, or the Irish). This may be true, but it remains in the realm of political instrumentality, even while Allen is arguing that English colonial racialization of the Irish conditioned the development of class relations in England. Neither "divide and rule" explanations nor the economism of "white-skin privilege" explain the many instances where the impoverishment of white workers in white solidarity had greater allure than the power or benefit of class solidarity. The question of racism's tenacity, the power of race discourses to withstand class struggle ideologies, goes deeper than the instrumentality of power. What the white left has perhaps not grasped about itself or the mainstream is not that it is white, but what that whiteness means.

To plumb the depths of this relationship will require a critique of whiteness and the dynamics of racialization which go beyond class-centered explanations of racism. I will argue that the source of the incommensurabilities so familiar in mainstream thinking lies in the structures of whiteness as an identity, a sociopolitical mode of identification, and a cultural process of racialization whose history can be traced concretely in the development of the Virginia colony in the seventeenth century.

The Structure of Whiteness

Let us first recognize that race is a social construct, and not a biological reality. In the United States, a person is black if he has one black foreparent, but is not white if he has one white foreparent.[5] That is, race is marked with an arbitrary purity condition for whiteness that is ideological and hierarchical. To say this another way, a white woman can give birth to a black child, but a black woman cannot give birth to a white child, not because of appearance but because of the way racial descent is defined. As Ashley Montagu has argued, the human characteristics by which so-called races are differentiated belong to continuous spectra of variation, with no inherent determinable dividing lines, and no two of which are in necessary association.[6] There is no natural criteriological basis for defining any particular racial distinction. Biology, then, is deployed to "naturalize" socially constituted differences and rationalize their hierarchy. Behind the biological mask, race resides as a social relation. This does not mean that "race" doesn't "exist"; it does exist, but as a social structure, and not as a biological fact. Rather than a biological fact, race is a system of social designations and meanings invented by Europeans and inscribed upon non-European bodies using color as its icon. In a word, racism itself is the source of race and racialization.

The first question, then, is, if race and white supremacy are social constructs, what is the inner structure of those constructs? Beyond their sociopolitical effects, how can they be understood as structures? Albert Memmi provides four criteria for racism: (1) "the insistence on a difference, real or imaginary" (which can be somatic, cultural, religious, etc.); (2) the imposition of a negative valuation on the other through that difference, accompanied by a positive valuation for the one imposing it; (3) the generalization of that valuation to a group; and (4) the legitimization of aggression or privilege through that difference.[7] For Memmi, the statement of a difference does not constitute racism; that difference has to be used against the other.[8] He adds that racism is "a discourse formulated by a group, which addresses itself to a group."[9]

Three discursive levels can be distinguished in Memmi's paradigm. The first is that of generalization. Race discourse defines in generality what is to be noticed about a person as racial, both physically and personally (who the person is). Physical difference exists, but it has significance only if pointed out and given a social importance. This act of pointing out already subordinates the individual to what is named to be noticed about him or her; it is already a generalization. Allen refers to this process as the de-differentiation of the "other," rendering the person a group instance rather than a proper individual. Yet because people present themselves only as individuals, such generalizations always remain underivable from experience. They must be imposed as prior concepts if they are to be noticed conceptually. But if a prior concept superimposes itself on the way a person is encountered, it will have already substituted itself for experience of that person. In other words, the act of generalization, as always nonempirical, effaces a person's self-presentation and, to that extent, obviates experience of that individual. Generalization renders other people wholly or in part unknowable. And as an alibi for that unknowability, racism resorts to the ostensible "objectivity" (i.e., determinism) of biology. Though Memmi couches his criteria in terms of individuals, the ability to notice a difference as something to which valuation can be given implies a prior discourse has already defined that difference. In its immanent self-referentiality, the act of generalization brings into existence what it is about. And a certain supremacy is already inherent in the self-arrogated power to define and give import to a difference in the first place.

But if the white supremacist is to be in some social relation (however hierarchical) with the unknowable other, then an alternate knowability must be constructed. The "other" must be endowed with a "racialized" subjectivity, an intentionality, a temperament and capability by which to be encountered. To this purpose, racism produces a vast system of narratives that reinvent personhood and subjectivity for the one generalized. This is its second, discursive level. These narratives are what link concepts of culture and character to an alleged biology. Because what is not renarrativized remains unseen or unheard, such narratives present themselves as originary. They emerge and impose themselves in spite of the individual they are about, while their "aboutness" is used to prove the involvement or participation of that individual in their content. From its very inception, for instance, the Virginia colony renarrativized the indigenous as always war-hungry and treacherous, especially in their friendly overtures and fair dealings, on which basis it rationalized its exclusionism. The nature of the narratives may shift over time, or in different circumstances, but their imposition will always be derogatory and self-referential, reflecting the presumption to define. As Toni Morrison puts it, "the fabrication of an Africanist persona [for and by whites] is reflexive, an extraordinary meditation on the self." And Simone de Beauvoir points out analogously that patriarchy says to women: We will paint your portrait so you can get started imitating it.[10]

Thirdly, because these narratives function as signs of racializing reference about the invented Other, they constitute the language of white discourse as white. Because the signifier "white" has meaning only in differential relation to other signifiers for color, a system of meanings for those other color signifiers must be generated before the signifier "white" can be apprehended as a social signification.

Though this narrative sign system ostensibly refers to the generalized "other," its real meaning is to function as white discourse as such, the speech by which whites proclaim themselves to be white. All discourse between whites as whites assumes and includes them through cliché, tone of voice, innuendo, and derogatory terms. It is by unendingly retelling the stories, and alluding to them, that whiteness reaffirms itself. Even when a white speaker is addressing a designated "nonwhite" person in this language, she is essentially speaking to other whites. This only reflects the fact that such a language is already hegemonic, since the social structures of exclusion will not work if the excluded are able to include their own story in the social discourse (hence, the tradition of an exclusionary literary canon). De Beauvoir points out that marriage is a relation between men for which women are the means; similarly, racism is a relation between whites for which nonwhite people are the language.

The psychic violence experienced by those subjected to such conscription as a language, to being rendered the means whereby whites institutionalize their relations to each other, remains practically indescribable. W. E. B. DuBois speaks of the double consciousness it produces, of "always looking at oneself through the eyes of others." It is to live a world that is at all times appropriated as a source of meaning for others (whites) who are always elsewhere and "here."

In sum, the racialization of whites comes about through the racialization of others. For white people to be white, they must have defined others as nonwhite. That is, others are defined as nonwhite in order for whites to define themselves as white. Or, as Ian Lopez puts it, whiteness is a double negative; it is what is not nonwhite.[11] Though such racialization is always associated with forms of domination and exploitation, it is the deployment of the dominated as a language that racializes, and which gives the exclusions, derogations, and oppressions to which they are subjected their special meanings. It is in this way that racism becomes the source of race, while the concept of race it generates then becomes the content of that racism.

As Michelle Fine has argued, "whiteness is actually co-produced with other colors," as fundamentally relational, and not merely in parallel.[12] A hegemonic white population can apprehend its own identity only in a situation that is racial. It needs to continually redefine a "nonwhite" other for itself through an ever-changing system of narrativizations in order to be privileged and to construct its boundary, which becomes its "fix," as she says, its sense of identity and belonging.

Conversely, if the definition of another as "nonwhite" is at the core of white self-definition, then to be white is to find the core of one's identity elsewhere, in the other. The other becomes the substance of that identity. This is the source of white obsession with the one excluded, the racialized other. The other is given to be noticed, yet thrust elsewhere; differential and exterior, yet interiorized. For whites, the "nonwhite" becomes at once nemesis, fascination, and self. Herein lies the stupefying nature of racism for the "white mind." At the same time, it is the source of its self-universalization. If the other must be both excluded as other and absorbed as self, the white identity which thus constructs itself of two elsewheres intuits itself as the universal human (that is, as unmarked) through that absorption. Or, as Fine puts it, social institutions are designed "as if" hierarchy, stratification, and scarcity were inevitable.[13]

Real violence is inherent in such a system. The other is both placed at the center of white identity and continually evicted from it. But because the operations are performed without the involvement or provocation of those they are about (however they ultimately respond), the violence and harassment are always gratuitous.

What is critical, however, is that the signifier "white" and the white identity it generates also remain wholly contingent on their affirmation by other whites. White people become white by coalescing around the language of whiteness as a symbol system, which prescribes the identity of the group. In effect, group identification becomes the real meaning of the "white" sign system; and whiteness, identification of oneself as white, constitutes the means of belonging to it. White identity becomes a membership card to that community. Yet it is a membership that must be continually renewed. It is to reaffirm membership in the white group that whites deploy gratuitous derogatory terms and racist violence, or tolerate it in others. Speaking the symbols, and the generalizing terms (as group icons), retelling the narratives (that already contain and describe the violence of racial hierarchy), and ultimately enacting that violence, become the various modes of "performance" of whiteness, or of membership. (Today, the police are increasingly becoming the designated actors for these performances of white identity.)

White-identified people cannot escape the effect of this structure. Identification of oneself as "white" brings with it the entire structure of racializing definitions, objectifications, and derogations (and now, of the many restratifications maintained or produced by police violence). It is the place where white liberalism and white supremacy are in conjunction. While the white supremacist accentuates exclusion, as a form of appropriation, white liberalism accentuates inclusion or absorption as a form of reified alterity. To the extent that both identify themselves as white, they both reduce a designated "other" to a meaning for themselves, and thus to a nonpersonhood. Furthermore, liberalism's attempt to deal with the effects of racial oppression continues the designated "other's" objectification while leaving the structure of whiteness that objectifies intact. The often-attempted separation of whiteness from white supremacy is a false one. To the extent one has not contested the language, narrativity, and identification of whiteness, one will have inscribed one's own identity in what has already formed the core and mortar of white supremacy.[14] One might include labor-union solidarity in this; though it may momentarily overcome racial antagonism, by remaining unaware of how white hegemony has conditioned class structures it inscribes white solidarity into its every economic and cultural act, rendering its class solidarity more rhetorical than real.

Ironically, it is precisely because whiteness is a language that racism, though its existence silences whole groups of people, has been able to coexist with the Bill of Rights, with the right of free speech—and even seek protection for itself within that right. For the racist, free speech extends only to the users of language; it does not extend to those who are a language. This may be the starkest form of the incommensurability noted at the beginning of this essay.

It might be added that the notion of abandoning "white-skin privilege" is unintelligible. The privilege granted to whiteness must have already been constructed as whiteness. The notion of abandoning privilege reduces privilege to a thing one can pick up or put down, add or subtract from whiteness, rather than as inherent in a structure of social relations. A complex cultural structure is not dispensed with so easily. With racism, one confronts a circle. The meaning of whiteness is already supremacy, the meaning of supremacy is already privilege, and the meaning of privilege is already whiteness. The insularity of this circularity expresses its extreme resistance to argument or experience. At whichever point one addresses racism, there is a preceding point for it to fall back upon.

One implication of this discussion might be that one cannot identify oneself as white and be antiracist at the same time. Yet a white identity cannot simply be discarded. First of all, it will be continually reimposed by the social institutions that preserve and reconstitute it. And second, a white-identified person could not reidentify with some other "group" or "ethnos" without being co-optive or opportunist. The primary political question for undoing white hegemonics and supremacism is how to transform society and culture insofar as it is white. The problematic of antiracism for whites becomes how to invent a deracializing identity for themselves for which "whiteness" would in turn be an otherness, without opportuning on others for whom whiteness is already other, and without leaving the institutions and discourses of whiteness intact or uncontested. However it is done, a structure of opposition to white supremacy that dehegemonizes one's thinking altogether must be found.

THE COLONIAL HISTORY OF WHITENESS

If whiteness and race are social constructs, how did they happen? What complex operation of economic, juridical, and social processes brought them into existence? And if there was a time, not so long ago, before the existence of whiteness, of race or white supremacy, is that process discernible?

History is a problem with respect to the politics of race, even after it is recognized that Europeans, in their guise as whites, constructed race, racial relations, and racism. If whites constructed race as hierarchical, then a racism had to already exist to stratify it. If white racism constructed race, on what racial ground did it construct whiteness? If the "white" is one of the races produced by a general process of racialization, how was it produced as unmarked? Even in the context of colonialism, if the process of racialization was driven by the construction of dominance, from whence arose the notion of race that drove dominance to construct itself as white? One of racism's mystifications is that mere chromatic difference was sufficient, through rejection of the strange and fear of the different. But it is racism that makes chromatic difference strange and fearful, as one of its central meanings.

If these ambiguities are usually decided ideologically, it implies that they make a difference. In the Marxist view, the necessities of class domination impel the racialization of labor (as slave vs. free, marginal vs. central) to divide and control. But to see racism as contingent upon class relations and dynamics reduces it to a political strategy without accounting for race as a structure of social relations with its own development and dynamic. Winthrop Jordan, on the other hand, in his still-influential historical studies, assumes that racism, and therefore the concept of race, accompanied the colonists to the Americas, as a social valuation if not political institution, and built slavery as its expression, in effect accepting a chromatic notion of race.[15] Theodore Allen, in response to both, argues that racialization conditioned the structure of class itself in early capitalist development. But even a cursory look at the Virginia colony reveals that the process was much more complex than any of that.

The story begins before the first Africans were imported as plantation labor in 1619. The Virginia colony was at first unable to cope with the land and its unfamiliar ecology, which it proclaimed for itself to be wilderness, and faced rampant starvation. Many English sought to escape to live with the surrounding indigenous society (a number of different Algonquin peoples) who understood the land and suffered no hardships there.[16] For the Virginia colony's elite, however, escape threatened the social fabric. Under the first governor (Thomas Smith), it was considered desertion, and punished severely. Recaptured escapees were publicly tortured, often to death.[17] This imposition of an absolute allegiance to English origins, to Christian membership against the so-called heathen, was the primary response to internal crisis. It rationalized itself through a demonization of the Algonquin, whose nature, personality, and intention were renarrativized as hypocritical and warlike, even in their most banal acts of friendship.[18] Accompanying this demonization were prohibitions of intermarriage with the indigenous. That is, the demand for allegiance was structured through both a prenarrativization of the "other's" personality or character and an enforced social separation.

The cultivation of tobacco rapidly became the main export commodity for the colony. Tobacco was a drug whose English market was assured, making it a ready and profitable cash crop. As a mass-produced commodity, tobacco not only became the colony's chief source of wealth, but it also served as currency for commodity exchange, wages, and the calculation of human value. Like the Spanish, the English colonized North America for profit. The colonial function was not alternative social community, but the development of productive processes. The English did so along a different axis of brutality, however. Rather than military conquest and occupation, the colony was established as a corporate entity (the Virginia Company), for which the English were employees. Even after the Virginia Company dissolved in 1624, its style of rule was sustained by the Colonial Council, which exercised controls on production, land use, and disposition of labor.

From the beginning, the company and the colony brought together the paradigms of membership, renarrativization, exclusion of the indigenous through restrictions on interaction, and an institutionalization of human activity. It was a structure into which the content of racialization could later be fit. As Pierre Bourdieu says, "the function of the act of institution ("which signifies to someone what his identity is") [is] to discourage permanently any attempt to cross the line, to transgress, desert, or quit."[19]

The problem of tobacco cultivation was labor. The Algonquin mostly refused servitude and escaped. At first, English labor was used; white indentured servants accounted for half the arrivals to the colony in 1619,[20] and constituted the main mode of plantation labor until 1650. English indenturees, however, whether volunteer, prison labor, or kidnap victims from the streets of English cities, came with written contracts establishing length of service, a release date, and sometimes a grant of land upon release. But the term of servitude was long, and many English indenturees escaped, blending into the colonial society developing broadly around them.

Escape was more difficult for imported Africans, who did not blend in. However, few were imported before 1650, at which time there were three hundred.

Though originally no legal distinction was made between African and English servants,[21] the Africans were not put under written contract. Without a contract, an
African's time of servitude was left to the whim of the landowner. Though some
were released after serving a period comparable to European laborers, more and
more had their time extended, some indefinitely. This practice reflected the
gradual consolidation of local markets in Africans. As extensions of their arrival as
cargo, these markets further commodified the Africans, transforming them gradually from laborers into wealth, that is, livestock. This process first reflected itself
juridically in the 1640s in the form of differential punishments for runaways;
Africans were sentenced to servitude for life, while runaway English were only
given extended time.

Politically, the question of African status (as slave or indentured, wealth or
labor) remained a contested notion until 1662, when perpetual servitude was legislated. Before then, different landowners adopted different stances. The Virginia
government groped toward codification of landholder practice, and control of
plantation labor, to regulate and protect landed wealth. No steps were taken to
provide Africans with the right to a contract; but until 1662, those Africans that
were freed were given recognition equal to the English. No steps were taken to
provide education for African children, though it was guaranteed to English children. But education was not prohibited to Africans, and those that did go to school
attended integrated schools.[22] In many cases, English indenturees made common
cause with Africans in escaping. To the extent that distinctions were made on
either a social or juridical level, they were not yet racialized. And slavery was not
yet the general rule. What came to be known as slavery was only in partial practice by 1640, generally recognized as a social practice throughout the colony by
1660, and finally codified into law in 1682 and 1705.[23]

Sixteen sixty-two marks a turning point with the passage of the first antimiscegenation law ("miscegenation" is a problematic term here because it generally
refers to mixed-race marriage, but is being used to refer to a time before the English, indigenous, or Africans had been racialized). Mixed marriage had been previously punished on religious grounds. Around 1640, the ability of servant labor
to marry was codified as part of a more general attempt to control the workforce.
Marriages between English and African servant labor were given special legislated
conditions, with prohibitions and punishments, whose tenor was to reduce both
partners to greater servitude. But in 1662, various statutes dealt with miscegenation as such. Strict fines were levied simply for sexual relations between "Negroes"
and "Christians," and mixed marriage was prohibited. The fact of such enactment
suggests that mixed marriage had become too prevalent for the colonial elite, and
that anti-African feeling was far from the rule among the laboring population.[24]

At the same time, in a bizarre statute, children were given the servitude status of the mother rather than the father. Again, the Colonial Council was juridically protecting the planter's economic interests. Through this unusual reversal of patriarchal tradition, a social distinction was created between English women and African women with respect to personal relations, marriages, and motherhood (regardless of the father). African mothers were placed in the position of breeding stock, while English women were placed in a situation in which the elite could more widely reserve the patriarchal right to control their sexuality, in light of the concomitant provision of perpetual servitude for Africans and their descendants. Women and womanly being were thus deployed to conceptualize a new level of English-African distinction in general. It was the first step in a process that would eventually transform a juridical distinction into a biological one.

But the fact that the elite adopted these juridical tactics at that time confirm that plantation slavery was not established full-blown at one stroke in Virginia. Rather, it underwent gradual construction and definition at the hands of the economic pragmatics of a corporate profit-oriented plantation society which did not begin with "race" as its foundation. "Negro slavery" as a term first appeared in the statutes in the 1660s; it marked a moment in a journey toward "racial" hierarchy, rather than being grounded on it.

The stages of racialization can be traced in the successive binaries by which the English distinguished themselves from Africans. The first distinction (as read in the Council proceedings) was a religious one, between "heathens" and "Christians," conjoined to the English distantiation of the indigenous. However, to characterize Africans in such religious terms implied that, for African labor, baptism would be a step toward eventual freedom. When this possibility threatened the planters' wealth, that avenue was closed by statute (in 1644 and 1667).[25] After 1650, as the African population grew and more converted to Christianity, the predominant binary shifted to that between "Negro" and "English," or alternately, "Negro" and "Christian." Both signified a more reified separation and denial of membership in the colony for Africans. After 1667, the term "Christian," when used in distinction to "Negro," increasingly connoted "non-Negro." That is, it occurs in those rhetorical roles that later would be filled by the word "white."

But the English were not generally referred to as whites, and biological characteristics did not yet enter the discussion. Color was used descriptively. In letters and literary texts of the preceding one hundred years, there were individual Europeans who sometimes referred to themselves or others as white. But the use of the term "white" only became institutional, perhaps conceptually based on such literary sources, but marking a *social* designation, at the end of the seventeenth century. In the sense that race must be understood relationally, the term "black" or

"Negro" (as the anglicized Spanish word for black) would itself become a racial-izing term only when it was used to racialize the English as white. The first juridical reference to "white" people only occurs in 1691, in an antimiscegenation statute, eighty-five years after the founding of the colony.[26] In other words, only gradually, over the course of a century, did the English coalesce around the notion of being "white." The legislation of gender was the machinery of that social coalescence for which the African was the marker, labor the terrain, and biologization the effect.

Some historians (e.g. Ballagh) argue that racialization directly substituted itself for the religious differential; but that view ignores, first, the conceptual evo-lution racialization required; second, the role of commodification and its juridical regulation; and third, the legislation of sexuality. That is, it is only out of the com-plex evolution and political regulation of labor, ownership, colony membership, markets, and sexuality within a profit-oriented corporate structure, which imposed on Africans what successively became commodity status, noncitizenship, and slavery, that the concept of race evolved. On the one hand, slavery evolved as socially racialized through the juridical regulation of property relations, which gradually codified contested attitudes within the landowning elite. And on the other, color and sexuality became socially renarrativized through legislation that color-coded labor and regulated sexuality. Both occurred within the commercial and social relations between English men, as extensions of a market structure in which Africans were renarrativized as commodities or wealth.

If the deployment of women in this process was grounded in the general com-modification of Africans, its effects went beyond that. To the female role of pro-ducing succeeding generations was added the female potential for producing further wealth. Under the partial abandonment of patriarchal tradition, all women found themselves juridically and socially placed somewhere on a spectrum between being the machinery of descendant heirs and breeding stock. English women were given the ability to aspire to a certain purity of being through a purity of social and sexual comportment. It was a purity originally determined and conceptualized by juridical enactments. And through the economization of women, it constituted part of the way women, as juridical objects, marked the interweaving of the biological into the socioeconomic separation between English and Africans. The modern concept of race, on this account, marks the culmination of this complex historical process which slowly transformed the socioeconomic differential between English and Negro into the racialized differential between white and black.

Bacon's rebellion in 1676 marked a critical moment in this process.[27] The rebellion erupted from a geopolitical class contradiction in the agricultural struc-ture of the colony. The main avenue to wealth, the acquisition of more land, was curtailed by Crown restrictions on land claims beyond the colony's boundary.

Newly arrived farmers or newly freed English indenturees were granted westerly or peripheral land by the colony's governing elite to serve as a buffer between the colony's center and the Algonquin. That is, they were marginalized politically, agriculturally, and territorially. Nathaniel Bacon, himself a large landholder, organized the outlying farmers to war against the Algonquin (that is, open new lands through military adventure), and at the same time turned them against the colonial elite for insufficiently defending the farmers against Algonquin counter-attacks. His campaign had three components: (1) a struggle of (outlying) county farmers against the central elite for greater county representation; (2) a struggle of small county farmers against the county elites for greater representation; and (3) a chauvinist campaign against the indigenous as the real enemy. Bacon's Rebellion reveals all the characteristics of subsequent populisms, such as Tom Watson's People's Party of the 1890s, or the anti-Chinese movement on the Pacific coast in the nineteenth century; that is, a conjunction of democratic pretensions (a rhetorical class struggle against the rich) with an extremely chauvinist but opportunistically machinated campaign against a nonwhite group (the Algonquin, in Bacon's case).

When Bacon's movement was defeated, many Africans were found in his ranks. Not only was such common cause significant, but these Africans were under arms, and welcomed as such by the English rebels, despite long-standing colonial prohibitions against this (since 1648).[28] It testified to the contested nature of social attitudes toward African status, and suggests that animosity toward the Africans was partially class-based, and top-down, having social importance mainly for the elite (i.e., it did not predate the colony, as in Winthrop Jordan's account).

According to Zinn, the rebellion convinced the colonial elite to take measures foreclosing concerted action against itself. Laws against the special danger of "Negro insurrection" appear in the slave codes of 1682,[29] in language that echoes John Smith's diatribes against the Algonquin. Further acts were passed strengthening policies of antimiscegenation and differential punishments. Still, the construction of social hostilities was not an easy task. The process of general social division took until 1705 to consolidate. Even the House of Burgesses, in 1680, referring to remnants of Bacon's army that still roamed at large in the woods, and to whom the pardon offered rebels who would return and surrender was to be extended, speaks of the holdouts only as "people," without differentiating between "English" and "Negro," though there must have been both since slaves were the most hesitant to return.

Ultimately, the juridical by itself was insufficient for the process of racialization. Two other factors bear mention in this respect. The first is that certain economic changes occurred in the 1680s. During that decade, the supply of African slaves increased, due to greater traffic and an easing of competition from Caribbean sugar plantations. In addition, the price of tobacco rose on the English market, rendering small Virginia farmers more viable. Overall, after 1650, the importation of European indentured servants diminished, and the weight of the labor force shifted from white to black. While white labor moved into farming, the center of gravity of labor rebellion shifted from labor in general to slave labor in particular. The effect was a general reconstruction of the labor system of the colony as a whole. The elite ideological warning, in 1682, against "Negro rebellion" not only reconceptualized the labor situation, but constituted a call to social solidarity against this internal "outside" danger. In general, it marked a shift in English self-conception through a transformed economic stratification from a corporate structure to a culture of solidarity, from allegiance to England to cohesion against a threat of slave rebellion, albeit a threat produced by the slave system itself.

The second factor was a social reflection of the juridical. When indentured servants were said to be sold, it was because their contracts were sold, and they accompanied the purchased contracts. But Africans were not held under written contract.[30] The body itself marked the African's servitude, and substituted itself for the juridical instrument, signifying both the labor contract and its absence. The bodily sign for the contract's absence was codified to mean permanent servitude; as such, it then marked the African slave, without title or "papers," as essentially outside or beyond the law. Beyond legislative enactment, the absence of juridical standing rendered the African's color iconic for social otherness and exclusion. That is, a mode of de facto and de jure criminalization resided at the very core and origin of racialization.

The capstone to these transformations was conscription of poor white farmers and laborers to the task of enforcing the slave codes. Their job was to be shock troops, patrols, and commandos under elite direction, guarding against runaways and suppressing any appearance of personal autonomy by slaves. Negligence in this duty was punishable. In the context of their disfranchisement, this limited citizen franchise was given to represent the poor white's share in colonial sociopolitics—policing rather than making policy. Elite control was exercised through granting the power to control within the newly consolidated slave relation (like a comprador bourgeoisie in twentieth century Latin America). And planter solidarity took the form of white solidarity. In this way, economic competition between white agricultural strata was prevented from becoming a class distinction by engendering a system in which the fundamental class antagonism was between planters and slaves. In effect, the power of paranoia, first constituted at the beginning through the renarrativization of the Algonquin, kept powerless whites from running away and hard at work by giving them a role, if not rule. And in the confluence of all these processes, the concept of race emerged and produced a white nationality out of an English colony.

In sum, the development of whiteness has never been divorced from the operations of the state. Under its influence, the settler mentality went through two shifts, in the first of which the Africans were transformed from enslaved persons to marketable goods (from commodified labor to reified commodity), and in the second, transformed from real estate to social nemesis. These would be the terms in which white supremacy, the concept of race, and the southern class structure were brought into existence together. In other words, white supremacy was not invented to simply "divide and rule," but to reorganize the structure of labor, to be the production of a class structure itself. Whiteness evolved not as part of a structuring of race relations, but a social relation that created racialized identities and races. The relation of whiteness and domination is not one of historical precedence, but of form and content. In Bourdieu's sense, whiteness is an institution, and an institutionalization of comportment, rather than an ideology or identity consciousness, and it is in this institutional sense that we must understand white identity—differentiating it from other racialized identities that emerge in response and resistence to white domination itself.

To recapitulate, the process of racialization was constructed through corporate allegiance, a pursuit of wealth through a conscription of labor, and a juridical re-narrativization of Africans. In its need for labor, the colony produced color as an icon first for labor identity, then for social identity, and finally as white solidarity, allegiance, and a language of whiteness. As racializing, whiteness is a social relation, but not in itself a race; as a social dependency relation on others, it racializes itself, and becomes a race. As a race, whiteness is a gender relation that depends upon the purity and impurity of women. As a gender relation, it must wholly overnarrativize itself and sexualize the other in order to forget the history of racialization that has produced it as such.

The identity relation of whiteness highlights a motif characteristic of all populism, from Bacon's Rebellion, through Tom Watson's People's Party, to Gingrich and the populism of right-wing movements today, namely, the necessity for two enemies: a class enemy ("the rich", or big government), and a racial enemy. For Bacon, the "other" was the Algonquin; for Watson, it was first the North, then African Americans;[31] for Gingrich, it is the racialized welfare paradigm, a signifier again for African Americans. In each case, the other is dehumanized, rendered faceless, alien, and treacherous, to which the proclaimed "class enemy" (government) is accused of surrendering, or of "betraying the nation." That is, "class" struggle in the United States is informed by the perception that the "class enemy" is an enemy through betrayal.[32] And the innermost goal of populism is to end the betrayal and reestablish white solidarity. It is not that a rabid chauvinist campaign is the essential condition for whites to confront the elite, or make common cause.

Rather, it is that populist whites fight their class enemy with a mode of class collaboration as their goal.[33] Populism has always been a confluence of citizenship and mastery that has substituted white solidarity and a strengthening of the racialized white bond for class solidarity. That is, the populist movements manifest a relation of racialized class and classicized race for which neither class nor race discourses can give a complete description.

Some Implications

In the colonies, if whiteness emerged from enforced membership to a plantation socius focused on wealth but which pretended marginalized whites were not non-participants, it was a pretense clothed in violence. All wealth implies violence toward those from whom it is extracted; whiteness was the way elite violence in the United States was transferred to those it dominated. Expressed in actual or verbal violence, whiteness constitutes an estheticization of politics for poor whites in the sense that Walter Benjamin associated the term with fascism: that is, as a means of political expression for people that both continues and hides their sociopolitical powerlessness.[34] This is not an idle analogy. Throughout U.S. history, one encounters state operations whose ideology is racialist, whose "ruling party" is whiteness itself, and which "party" has governed through a social acceptance of generalized local violence. And the "policing" power given poor whites renders them analogous, as a group, to the SA, the private army of Nazi-party storm troopers that facilitated Hitler's rise to power in Germany.

Fascism is not only capitalist tyranny, but a gratuitous terror used to constitute control for its own sake, sometimes even over capital.[35] What it always requires is the establishment of a boundary between a coherent inside group (nation or race), and an outside held in subjection through organized excessiveness, violence and dehumanization. If, inside that boundary, a modicum of democratic structure is possible, it only continues the facade covering the raw power by which the "other" is dominated. For the boundary marking the estheticization of U.S. politics, color has been the mark, and white identity has been the language. What constituted itself quickly in Germany, however, was built gradually in the North American colonies. If its political dynamic has been blurred, it is perhaps because over time its "storm troopers" have had less to do on a daily basis. The rise of white militias and Aryan Nation groups suggests that this situation may be changing.

Returning to the present, the ability of the Right to mobilize populist grass-roots energy for programs of inequality and injustice springs not from its speaking to what white people want, but to who they are. Tapping the wellsprings of whiteness, it has gained the initiative over the left not only through a resurgence of fears of rebellion, or betrayal of the "white nation," but also through the left thinking that one can be nonracist and still identify oneself as white. Sara Diamond, in calling for a renewed grassroots effort by the left on the issues the Right has been dominating, ignores the idea that what gives the Right its hegemony is precisely what hamstrings the white left. In making too strict a conceptual distinction between the Right and the so-called mainstream, she blinds herself to the structure that allows the hegemonic to appear nonhegemonic. To contest the Right within this structure is to accept its language, and to lose oneself in it.

The left's entanglement in this morass is evident. Though the left opposes the state (to varying degrees) as the enemy of equality and justice, it has traditionally gone to the state to rectify racial abuse and discrimination. In thus recognizing the state as guarantor of democracy, it participates in reducing the condition of the dispossessed to one of ideological contestation. To oppose racism from within the racializing function of the state is to accede to that racializing function, to betray oneself to it.

One implication of all this is that the left cannot return unquestioningly to traditional modes of movement organizing. If the Right can appropriate these modes, then their coherence for the Right, the mark of the white, must open those modes to question. Though the Right presents a threat to all the left upholds and understands as the political, it is also a signifier for what the political is in the United States, requiring greater circumspection concerning its organizational means (the media, etc.). What the left requires, if it wishes to develop movements of opposition to oppression and capitalist domination, is a strategy to unravel the cultural framework, to invent a corrosive alternative to the white identity that is woven into it, not only at the level of social structure, but at that of cultural meaning.

NOTES

1. The paper, delivered March 13, 1996, in UC–Berkeley, was entitled "Martin Luther King and the Reinvention of Christian Leadership in the U.S."

2. Sara Diamond, *Roads to Dominion* (New York: Guilford Press, 1995), pp. 261–70.

3. I give the "left" a lower case designation, while capitalizing references to the Right, to suggest that it is more involved in process, less institutional than the Right, which seeks to reaffirm, reconstruct, and return to former institutionalized structures and practices. Part of the point of this paper is that the Right does not question the fundamental institutions of the United States, while the left does in seeking to transcend and transgress the dehumanized and antidemocratic institutions that have been bequeathed by U.S. history.

4. See, for example, the following: Theodore Allen, *The Invention of the White Race* (New York: Verso, 1994); David Roediger, *Towards the Abolition of Whiteness* (New York: Verso, 1994); Ruth Frankenberg, *White Women, Race Matters: The Social Construction of Whiteness* (Minneapolis: University of Minnesota Press, 1994); Michael Rogin, *Blackface, White Noise* (Berkeley: University of California Press, 1996).

5. Naomi Zack, *Race and Mixed Race* (Phildelphia: Temple University Press, 1993).

6. Ashley Montagu, *The Concept of Race* (New York: Collier Books, 1969).

7. Albert Memmi, *Le Racisme* (Paris: Gallimard, 1982), p. 159. See also Tuen Van Dijk, *Communicating Racism* (Newbury Park: Sage Pub., 1987).

8. Memmi, *Le Racisme*, p. 45.

9. Ibid., p. 111.

10. Toni Morrison, *Playing in the Dark* (Cambridge: Harvard University Press, 1992), p. 17; Simone de Beauvoir, *The Second Sex*, trans. H. M. Parshley (New York: Bantam, 1970).

11. Ian Lopez, "White by Law," in *Critical Race Theory*, ed. Richard Delgado (Philadelphia: Temple Univ. Press, 1995), p. 547. Ironically, Lopez advances this notion of the double negative in a critique of the apparent ongoing need for a juridical definition of race, even in the twentieth century.

12. Michelle Fine, "Witnessing Whiteness," in *Off White: Readings on Race, Power, and Society*, ed. Michelle Fine, Linda Powell, Lois Weis, and L. Mun Wong (New York: Routledge, 1997), p. 58.

13. Ibid., p. 58.

14. It is precisely "good standing" that European immigrants bought by embracing racism and "melting in." For a critique of the melting-pot idea, see Nathan Glazer, *Beyond the Melting Pot* (Cambridge: MIT Press, 1963); also Allen, *Invention of the White Race.*

15. Winthrop Jordan, *White Over Black: American Attitudes Toward the Negro, 1550–1812* (New York: Norton, 1977).

16. Howard Zinn, *A People's History of the United States* (New York: Harper and Row, 1980), p. 24.

17. Ibid., p. 24.

18. It is worth noting that John Smith was one of the prime inventors of these narratives of demonization and allegiance. Throughout the colonial period, a succession of charters with different kings all contained clauses demanding allegiance, and defining the conditions of its administration. Cf. William W. Hening, ed., *Statutes at Large: A Collection of All the Laws of Virginia* (Richmond, Va. 1809), vol. 1, p. 105; vol. 2, pp. 94, 485.

19. Pierre Bourdieu, *Language and Symbolic Power* (Cambridge: Howard Press, 1991), p. 336. Quoted in Fine (*Off White*, p. 58).

20. Joseph Boskin, *Into Slavery: Racial decision in the Virginia Colony* (Washington, D.C.: University Press of America, 1979), p. 14.

21. Ibid., p. 38.

22. Ibid., p. 24.

23. James Curtis Ballagh, *A History of Slavery in Virginia* (Baltimore: Johns Hopkins Press, 1902), chap. 2.

24. Many commentators on the colonial period interpret the anti-miscegenation laws as symptomatic of early "antipathy" toward Africans, and argue that racism produced enslavement of Africans (cf. Boskin and Vaughan [notes 20 and 30]). But they tend to ignore a small detail in the record. In 1630, a white man named Hugh Davis was reported in Virginia Council proceedings to have been whipped for having sexual relations with a "negro" (Hening, *Statutes at Large*, vol. 1, p. 146). However, no prohibitory laws were passed at the time, suggesting an absence of pressure to do so, or an absence of widespread "antipathy." But the Virginia council records state that Davis was whipped "before an assembly of Negroes and others" for the offense of "lying with a negro." Why prioritize the "Negro" contingent of the audience? Would this satisfy a widespread antipathy toward Negroes by white colonists, given that Davis was white? Or was the punishment administered to Davis to make a point to the African population of the colony? And what might that be?

A second historical detail raises similar questions. Africans were not brought into the colony in large numbers until after 1650. The first rebellion in the colony against the governing Council occurred in 1663, a year after the antimiscegenation law and other slave codes were passed. Could the passage of the slave codes, which accorded with the interests of the plantation owners, have participated in instigating the rebellion by the poorer colonists and servants? In other words, was there a class dimension to the antipathy that certain historians have assumed was universal?

25. Boskin, *Into Slavery*, p. 45.

26. Hening, *Statutes at Large*, vol. 3, p. 86.

27. The nature of Bacon's rebellion has been widely debated among historians. Much has been written about it, including novels and diatribes, as well as careful research. The account I give is a rough composite of interpretations from Washburn and Zinn. Cf. Wilcomb Washburn, *The Governor and the Rebel* (Chapel Hill: University of North Carolina Press, 1957). Two accounts from the period by Ann Cotton and Thomas Burwell (pro and contra) are printed in Peter Force, ed. *Tracts and Other Papers* (Washington, 1836).

28. Hening, *Statutes at Large*, vol. 1, p. 39.

29. Ibid., vol. 2, p. 492.

30. Alden T. Vaughan, "Blacks in Virginia, the first Decade," in *Roots of American Racism* (Oxford: Oxford Univ. Press, 1995).

31. See C. Vann Woodward's fascinating account of Watson in *Tom Watson, Agrarian Rebel* (New York: Oxford Univ. Press, 1970).

32. Even Jack London falls prey to this. In his novel *The Iron Heel*, the main charge his ideologue levies against capitalism is that it has "mismanaged;" that is, it has betrayed a trust.

33. Cf. Alexander Saxton, *The Indispensible Enemy: Labor and the Anti-Chinese Movement in California* (Berkeley: University of California Press, 1995).

34. Walter Benjamin, "The Work of Art in the Age of Mechanical Reproduction," in *Illuminations*, trans. Harry Zohn (New York: Schoken Books, 1969).

35. Alfred Sohn-Rachel, *The Economy and Class Structures of German Fascism*, trans. Martin Rethel (London: Free Association, 1987).

4

"The Chinese Woman": A Female Object from Two Feminist Perspectives

Xiaorong Li

eminist scholars and commentators on women's changing social and political status in the People's Republic of China have often produced conflicting reports and felt much frustration as well. Who are "Chinese women," the
subject matter of their discourse? How are they to characterize Chinese women
when generalizing about their conditions? What have the Chinese women aspired
to achieve as they marched for sexual equality under the Communist leadership?
Or, more generally, when assessing women's conditions in historically unfamiliar
and culturally foreign contexts, what should be the appropriate criteria for objective assessment? How much does generalization from one's own theoretical perspective and political agenda detract from objectivity?

Though feminists have approached women's issues in contemporary China
from a variety of angles, I will focus in this paper on two feminist perspectives in
North American and European feminist discourse which have had significant
impact on the studies and analyses of women in the People's Republic since the
1970s. One is what I will call leftist-Marxist feminism, which was most active in
the 1970s.[1] Those who take this approach are essentially committed to a historical
analysis of women in particular historical contexts. The other may be called a universalist-cosmopolitan-liberal approach, which has only been active in the study
of Chinese women since the 1980s. This approach implicitly refers to female roles
in current Western societies as the backdrop for analyzing women's condition in
China or, more generally, in the "Third World." Those who take this latter

approach tend to work from the premise that the "Chinese woman" has a gender agenda similar to those of other "Third World women." I will argue that an ahistorical, singular, sometimes monolithic, and political construction of "Chinese woman" is operative in this approach. These two approaches will be further defined later since for now, I assume, most readers are familiar enough with them to follow the discussion.

For the sake of clarity, I should say in advance that my inquiry will not analyze the theoretical problems pertaining to these two approaches, but rather the issues concerning their application and impact on the study of women in China. Pure theories sometimes have unintended consequences in practice. But political and ideological affiliations often influence theorists' perspectives, agendas, and interpretations of specific realities. This is the kind of issue that concerns me most here.

THE MARXIST FEMINIST APPROACH

Leftist-Marxist feminism's interest in contemporary Chinese women dates back to the cold war era of the 1970s. Socialist reforms in the former Soviet Union, Eastern Europe, and China seemed then to Western Marxist feminists to promise an assured path for women's liberation from capitalist/patriarchal oppression.[2] According to Marxist feminism, sexual oppression is essentially a part of proletarian class struggle against capitalist exploitation, and such a struggle will ultimately be transcended in a classless society. Nonetheless, class conflict, not sexual conflict, is the primary dynamic in social progress. Women can only achieve liberation and equality with men in a classless communist society, and socialism (as presumably practiced in the People's Republic of China) is a preparation period during which the question of sexual inequality can be, for the first time in history, confronted and tackled. Western Marxist feminists have been impressed by the mass public participation of women in China, by the fact that since the Chinese Communist government came to power, it has legislated equal political and social rights, equal opportunities, and legal protection for women.[3] Their enthusiasm is not entirely unjustified. In the past forty-five years, the Chinese Communist Party has mobilized numerous political campaigns to eradicate inequalities between men and women, which attracted millions of women to participate in public life.

However, these Marxist feminists would today have difficulty confronting the fact that gender inequality has persisted under the Communist regime: Women continue to trail far behind men in leadership positions, in the professions, and in school enrollment; and women as a group have become much more vulnerable than men to unleashed social violence due to recent relaxation of government control. Nineteen-seventies-style Marxist-socialist feminists would be troubled by the lack of enthusiasm among Chinese intellectuals and feminists today with the Maoist-socialist formula for women's liberation, especially in the post–Cultural Revolution era. There is now even an acute sense among many feminists in China that Marxism is no longer relevant to their cause, though not all Chinese feminists have given up on Marxist rhetoric.

This sense of irrelevancy has to do with a basic thesis of Marxist feminism— the priority of class struggle, as discussed above, or the priority of a materialist analysis, which stresses economic empowerment as the dominant precondition of women's liberation. According to this thesis, gender analysis should be subordinated to an analysis of socioeconomic conditions.[4] This thesis has enabled Marxist feminism of the 1970s–1980s to have a broader perspective linking women's unequal status to basic social and economic structures, a perspective which is often lacking in other schools of gender analysis. From such a perspective, the problems facing women in China can not be solved and gender inequality in Chinese society can not be abolished without making systematic social and economic changes. The Marxist-feminist perspective is thus able to explain that, for example, trafficking in women and the sale of women into marriage, prostitution, or forced labor had their roots in the social changes brought about by capitalist marketization. Inequality between men and women would be a superficial explanation for the causes of such crimes. Capitalist commodification of "human cargo" as well as deregulation of the labor market would be seen as part of the problem. For the Marxist feminist, when the proletarian class comes to power, it will end capitalist exploitation and thus eliminate the conditions of gender oppression; if the proletarian dictatorship is under threat, then, the struggle for gender equality should become secondary. This reasoning has led to the conclusion that women's struggle for liberation should therefore be in harmony with, and instrumental to, the priorities of the proletarian class struggle. Though this approach has some explanatory strength in exploring the structural (or social and economic) causes of women's subjugation in society, the priority of class struggle thesis, I think, has nevertheless disabled Marxist feminism to such an extent that it is unable to deal adequately with the reality that the proletarian leadership itself in former and current socialist states has often been patriarchal and sexist.

Chinese women's experiences under the Communist regime should provide one of the best illustrations. In China, "women's liberation" has been part and parcel of the Communist Party's mass political campaign to eliminate enemy classes and solicit mass support. The Party embraced the Marxist view that the relationship between the sexes is a function of class relationships. This party ideology has defined the roles of women in the "socialist revolution" and "socialist construction." Since the Long March, the Party vowed to "liberate" women from the home. But the explicit purposes have been, respectively, for women to assist the party in struggling against feudal-bourgeoisie ruling classes and imperialists, and later, after the Party took power, to assist it in constructing the socialist state, in increasing productivity (as during the Great Leap Forward), and in rallying support for Mao in the ruthless power struggle during the Great Cultural Revolution and more recently for the population control campaign. This politically defined role for women left the patriarchal structure largely intact because women were instructed or dictated by the Party not only to become men's equal, but also how to be men's equal. They were to behave like men, even dress like men, and to work in job-positions originally designed for men with wives taking care of children at home. They were to rid themselves of any femininity and remake themselves in the image of the dominate male or male-defined role model. To be equal human beings has been for women to become male.

These experiences have raised interesting and challenging questions regarding the nature of the communist "liberation of women:" Can a patriarchal leadership genuinely designate women a social and political status that is the equivalent to that of men? One may argue that it is possible to achieve gender equality under such a paternalistic arrangement, and that in socialist China, women may to some extent have gained more venues and means to voice their concerns and criticisms about social injustice. But one may also argue that, if women are not allowed to take the initiatives to set their own agenda, articulate their own conception of the "good," and define their roles in society, genuine sexual equality is impossible. The Chinese government's instrumentalist handling of "women's liberation" to serve various Party priorities demonstrates how women should first fight to break away from the status of passive recipients accepting charity handed to them by a "benevolent" patriarch. When the Party's political priority demands otherwise, the Party has always been ready to sacrifice women's well-being. The recent rise of social violence against women and female children in China's drive for economic efficiency demonstrates the instrumentalist approach's harmful impact on the well-being of women. If women's place in society and their social roles continue to be designed and defined for them by a patriarchal government, their subjugation will continue and their "liberation" will be subjected to the whims of their "liberators."[5] Thus, when Margery Wolf argues that Chinese communism "postponed" women's "revolution" for sexual equality, she may have come close to the realization that, in a sense, the party politics based on prioritizing class struggle may never be able to carry out a real women's revolution.[6] The Marxist view that basic changes of production mode and women's participation in the labor force will end sex inequality fails to take into consideration the dominance of Party patriarchs in this process. As some scholars have argued, the Chinese experience shows that "a commitment to female equality cannot be simply the outcome of economic development but that it can and must shape the patterns and processes of development itself."[7] Women should empower themselves so as to have the ability to identify and enforce their own interest.[8]

This is not to deny that Marxist-feminist analysis has certainly provided insights into traditional "women's work" by building on Engels's insight that the family is the root of female oppression and by looking into the human reproduction process and the role of the family in providing the means of subsistence,[9] particularly in the study of China.[10] But, this analysis also has its blind spots. One of them, I argue, is created by excessively relying on class relation analysis and subordinating analysis of sexual relations.

A more general concern about the Marxist approach has to do with suspicion toward relying on any kind of ideological, utopian, comprehensive, political revolutions to change social, economic, and political institutions responsible for women's subjugation. Such revolutions often require women's support and the revolutionary agendas tend to justify suspending the women's agenda, particularly when these agendas clash. Examples include the ways in which women were treated in the Islamic revolution in Iran, in recent Afghanistan after the Islamic rebels took power, and in Nazi Germany during World War II. As Hanna Papanek argues, gender subordination was practiced for the need of political movements and ideological purposes in Nazi Germany, the former Soviet Union, and Islamic Iran.[11] The eradication of perceived social and political injustice through fundamental social changes in these cases required putting off or sacrificing women's agendas. But indeed, for how long should women (and why always women) have to wait for their turn for social justice? The time lag between men's and women's "liberation" needs justification. Can we stop certain discriminatory and violent practices against women right away, or at least start doing so, short of revolutionizing overall social political structures and before perfect and ideal societies are actualized (if it is ever possible to actualize them) according to various well-designed blueprints?

With the fall of communism in the former Soviet Union and Eastern Europe and the rapid development of the women's rights movement globally, it has become tempting (and sometimes seems only fitting) to approach issues concerning women in the People's Republic of China from what I have called the universalist-cosmopolitan-liberal perspective, in order to avoid the pitfalls of Marxist feminism and to respond to a need to theorize new developments in women's movements. But this approach has unfortunately had its own pitfalls. In the next section, I will try to explain how and why these pitfalls have occurred.

THE UNIVERSALIST-FEMINIST APPROACH

The universalist-feminist approach, adopted primarily by activists monitoring women's rights in developing countries and by scholars studying Third World women and development, has only been active more recently in the study and analysis of women's condition in China. Since the early 1980s, women's subjugation in Communist China has become widely acknowledged as China opened its doors and as the subjugation worsened during the introduction of market economics to the country. Those who favor this approach have serious concerns about the prevalence of domestic violence against women, the disappearance of female infants, and the low rates of female school attendance in China. This approach identifies the causes of Chinese women's subjugation as traditional sexist and patriarchal domination and women's economic dependency in society. It thus tends to treat women's conditions in China in the same way as in other developing countries. This generalization, however, shows little sensitivity to, and makes it difficult to explain, the fact that Chinese women's presence in public life is much more prominent than in neighboring South and Southeast Asian societies such as India, Bangladesh, and Japan. Those who accept this generalization would seem to be reluctant, for example, to recognize that government legislation for the protection of women, though often flawed and largely unenforced or unenforceable, could at least serve to provide Chinese women with limited means of empowerment and give Chinese feminists an instrument for critiquing government policies and legal practices.[12] For example, Chinese feminists could refer to the legislation in their critique of such policies and practices as discrimination against females in the family-planning campaign, in education, employment, and opportunities for leadership positions.

The universalist feminists' female subject—the "Chinese woman," not unlike the Marxist feminists' "woman under Chinese communism"—is based not so much on knowledge about the particular subject but on their own theoretical perspectives and political ideologies. Their analysis thus tends to lose sight of the specific problems concerning women in China, discounting the particular political, economic and social sources of oppression. The universalist analysis tends to construct the lives of women in China with an ahistorical homogeneity. For example, in an anthology about marriage and household inequality in China, one author refers to the practice in the People's Republic with a description that seems to apply timelessly to Chinese women of any dynasty: "In the People's Republic, . . . families have often been loath to endow a daughter or daughter-in-law with property or skills because of the possibility, near certainty in the case of a daughter, that these resources will be alienated from the family itself."[13] The lack of historical context here is evident in that the collective ownership in the rural "People's Commune" system, which was abandoned since the rural reform in the late 1970s, left very little in terms of private property in the family for children of either sex to inherit; and agricultural and hand-craft skills were mostly passed to children in collective production activities since the collectives managed the land and private hand-crafts enterprises were mostly banned. The situation since the rural reform, which allows semiprivatization of land and private production and trade of hand-crafts, has also been different from Watson and Ebrey's description. Young women from rural areas have flooded cities, making cash income from household jobs and sweatshops. Daughters of rural parents thus not only learn skills on the job but also have gained some economic independence. In many cases, they send home their savings to help their families in the villages.

When I say that the universalist approach assumes a homogeneous notion of "Chinese women," it is the above type of example that I have in mind. Such a notion categorizes "Chinese women" as being generally undereducated, poor, traditional, family-oriented, obedient, and powerless. This construction of "Chinese women" is often projected from the observer or narrator's own theoretical orientation or political agenda. When this agenda clashes with women's agendas against specific oppressive forces in Chinese society, the universalists sometimes downplay the severity of such oppression and the importance of the specific agenda. Resistance to forced abortion and sterilization in China's family-planning campaigns, for instance, does not fit the political agenda of some universalist feminists, particularly those who are active in the fight for abortion rights in Western countries and in the campaign for "women in international development." Lowering birth rates in Third World countries is a primary objective of international development. The domestic necessity of liberal feminists to support abortion rights in the United States and some European countries is perceived as in tension with criticisms of forced abortion. This tension was at play in the debates over the language of the Platform for Action at preparatory meetings leading to the Fourth World Conference on Women in Beijing. While some religious groups and Chinese human rights organizations lobbied to emphasize women's right not to be forced to have abortions, some Western feminists preferred to emphasize women's right to economic empowerment in development, while family planning was seen as a way to women's economic self-reliance. Meanwhile, Western human rights groups, such as Human Rights Watch/Asia and Amnesty International, have been reluctant to expand their investigations into the realm of reproductive rights, though Amnesty has recently come around with a thin report on violence against women in China's family-planning campaigns.[14] There is a fear by these groups that if they engage in such investigations, they would be unwillingly associated with right-wing antiabortion groups in Western countries, which may seem to compromise their principles and weaken their liberal democratic political alliance.

The problem with mixing "Chinese women" in the general pot of "Third World women" lies also in the gross simplification in categorizing "the Chinese women" by a single description; that is, victims of gender discrimination. When measured by their capacity to access social and political opportunity and re-sources, "Chinese women," as "Third World women" in other countries, are not a homogenous group. Not all women in China, particularly under communism, are socially oppressed, unequally treated, violently discriminated against, and stigma-tized by their traditional gender roles.[15] In a similar way, Chandra Mahanty has argued that there are no homogenous "Third World women." There are "rural Chinese women," "urban professional women," or "intellectual (elite) women" and "women with political power and privileges."[16] No doubt, the undifferentiated description of all Chinese women as victims of gender discrimination provides some insight. But it contributes little to an understanding of the hierarchy among Chinese females of various social strata, power positions and privileges, life-plans, needs, and political demands. Some are accomplices in the oppression of other women, though they might themselves be victims of other forms of discrimina-tion. One example of this hierarchy among women is the often opposing attitudes of urban, elite women and rural women toward the government's family planning policy and practices. Urban privileged women tend to advocate the policy and some even think it necessary to use compulsory measures to implement it. They accept that China's modernity is delayed by its large population and they blame the slow progress of lowering birth rates on rural women's backwardness and feudal traditional disposition. However, they are insensitive to rural women's social pressures and economic vulnerability. In comparison to rural women, urban professional women in general have much better opportunities in education and career choices. For them, the "one child" policy is not so much of a threat to their basic social economic security. Their basic means of living is relatively indepen-dent of the number and sex of their children. Rural women are the main target of communal pressure, psychological humiliation, and legal punishments because they are often under tremendous pressure from the extended family and their community to have "illegitimate children" and thus violate the policy. They con-sequently have to suffer the punishment for defying government policy. Rural resistance to the birth control measures has incurred harsh treatment of mostly rural women.[17] Some urban professional and intellectual women may have in fact been active in propagating, sometimes defending, and enforcing, the birth control policy in rural areas. As Anagnost has argued, Chinese intellectuals and urban population in general regard raising the quality of Chinese people by reducing population quantity as the key to achieve Chinese modernity.[18] The "cultural self-examination" (*wenhua fansi*) among intellectuals in the 1980s, in agreement with the government, laid blame for China's backwardness on a deficiency in the "quality" of the population. This analysis helps to explain why urban professional and intellectual women have a role to play in China's population campaign that has subjugated (mostly) rural women.

The generalization about "the Chinese woman" thus is not only vulnerable to an epistemological critique, but also has to some extent compromised the feminist political agenda to end female subjugation in China. I do not mean to suggest that there is no important concern over discrimination against all females in China no matter what their ethnicity, cultural identities, and social classes. But in doing country or local studies of women, it is important to "localize differences in female subject."[19] This is not only because the female subject in China and elsewhere defies any simple ideological characterization and refuses to be readily categorized to fit any particular political agendas. It is also because such a simplification hinders the understanding of specific problems facing women in different contexts.

CONCLUSION

Neither the Marxist nor the universalist-feminist approach is thus adequate for understanding women's conditions in China. Neither can sufficiently explain the causes of continuing subjugation and inequality under communism or under today's regime. A more appropriate approach should address questions of women's interest in specific, changing contexts, asking: How do different governmental policies on economic production and social organization deal with and affect the needs and interests of women in various sectors of society? What are the particular advantages and costs of particular policies for the affected female population? How do the experiences of women in different social/political strata vary? How do these policies affect the structure of traditional male dominance and patriarchy? A new approach should above all seek clear and complete knowledge instead of filtering facts and patterns through particular perspectives or ideological objectives.

And finally, critiques and analyses based on specific knowledge of women in context should not fall into relativism. The criticisms of specific government policies affecting women's well-being in particular countries can still be based on internationally accepted principles such as the UN convention against gender-specific violence and discrimination. The principle—gender-specific violence and discrimination constitute social injustice—need not be compromised, but the sources and causes of violence and discrimination vary from country to country, from one group of women to another, and this fact should be acknowledged and theorized by feminists.

NOTES

1. See Zillah R. Eisenstein, ed., *Capitalist Patriarchy and the Case for Socialist Feminism* (New York: Monthly Review Press, 1979); Judith Stacy, "When Patriarchy Kowtows: The Significance of the Chinese Family Revolution for Feminist Theory," *Feminist Studies* 2, no. 3 (1975); Marilyn B. Young, ed., *Women in China: Michigan Papers in Chinese Studies*, no. 15 (Ann Arbor: Center for Chinese Studies, The University of Michigan, 1973); Janet Weitzner Salaff and Judith Merkle, "Women and Revolution: The Lesson of the Soviet Union and China," *Berkeley Journal of Sociology* 15 (1970) reprinted in Young, *Women in China*.

2. Young, *Women in China*.

3. Stacy, "When Patriarchy Kowtows."

4. Alison Jaggar, *Feminist Politics and Human Nature* (Sussex: Rowan & Allanheld Publishers, the Harvester Press, 1983).

5. For more discussion about the Chinese Communist Party's instrumentalist policies on women, see Xiaorong Li, "Gender Inequality in China and Cultural Relativism," in *Women, Culture and Development*, ed. Martha Nussbaum and Jonathan Glover (Oxford: Clarendon Press, 1995).

6. Margery Wolf, *Revolution Postponed: Women in Contemporary China* (Stanford: Stanford University Press, 1985).

7. Phyllis Andors, *The Unfinished Liberation of Chinese Women: 1949–1980* (Bloomingdale: Indiana University Press, 1983), p. 171.

8. Salaff and Merkle, "Women and Revolution."

9. See Eisenstein, *Capitalist Patriarchy*; Nancy Chodorow, "Mothering, Male Dominance and Capitalism," in *Capitalist Patriarchy*; Eli Zaretsky, "Socialist Politics and the Family," *Socialist Revolution* 19 (Jan.–Mar. 1974); Wally Secombe, "The Housewife and Her Labor Under Capitalism," *New Left Review* 83 (Jan.–Feb. 1973).

10. Andors, *The Unfinished Liberation*.

11. Hanna Papanek, "The Ideal Woman and the Ideal Society," in *Identity Politics and Women: Cultural Reassertions and Feminisms in International Perspective*, ed. Valentine M. Moghadam (Boulder: Westview Press, 1994).

12. Jonathan K. Ocko, "Women, Property, and Law in People's Republic of China," in *Marriage and Inequality in Chinese Society*, ed. Rubie S. Watson and Patricia Buckley Ebrey (Berkeley: University of California Press, 1991).

13. Watson and Ebrey, *Marriage and Inequality in Chinese Society*, p. 351.

14. See Amnesty International, *Women in China: Imprisoned and Abused for Dissent* (1995).

15. Chun Lin, "Toward a Chinese Feminism," *Dissent* 42, no. 4 (fall 1995).

16. Chandra Talpade Mahanty, "Under Western Eyes: Feminist Scholarship and Colonial Discourse," in *Third World Women and The Politics of Feminism,* ed. Chandra Talpade Mahanty, Ann Russo, and Lourdes Torres (Bloomington and Indianapolis: Indiana University Press, 1991).

17. For more discussion on violence and discrimination against women in China's family planning campaign, see Xiarong Li, "License To Coerce," *Yale Journal of Law and Feminism* 8, no. 1 (1996).

18. Ann Anagnost, "A Surfeit of Bodies: Population and the Rationality of the State in Post-Mao China," in *Conceiving the New World Order,* ed. Raye D. Ginsburg and Rayna Rapp (Berkeley: University of California Press, 1995).

19. Mingyan Lai, "Female but Not Women: Gender in Chinese Socialist Texts," in *Forming and Reforming Identity,* ed. Carol Siegel and Ann Kibbey (New York: New York University Press, 1995).

PART II
Past, Present, and Future
of Class Analysis

5

Recognizing Capital: Some Barriers to Public Discourse about Capital

Patrick Murray and Jeanne Schuler

Though a certain Ph.D. in philosophy who never got a job in the field wrote a long, unfinished work on the subject over a century ago, the determining social form under which the globe increasingly groans remains poorly understood. We still have a long way to go in recognizing capital.

We want to examine some of the reasons for that as well as some of its consequences. Our essay divides into three parts. First we consider what capital is and why it is difficult to recognize. Second, we examine some consequences of the failure to conceptualize capital for thinking about the politics of identity. In this part we will first respond to a recent article by Nancy Fraser, "From Redistribution to Recognition: Dilemmas of Justice in a 'Post-Socialist' Age," and then do some thinking of our own on capital and the politics of identity. Third, we survey some conceptual and political barriers and openings to a better recognition of capital.

RECOGNIZING CAPITAL: WHAT MAKES IT HARD

What is capital?

Capital is a peculiar and stunning social form of wealth and the production of wealth. It is inherently dynamic and global. Capital is not use values, not money, not commodities, not means of production, as many common sense or social scientific notions would have it. Capital is not "wealth," that is, it is not merely wealth capable of being employed in the production of new wealth. Rather, capital is *a specific social form of* wealth and the production of wealth that is organized around a definite, if bizarre, purpose, namely, the endless accumulation of surplus value. Capital involves a class system of expropriation in which wage-laborers are free to contract with those who own the wherewithal to produce (the capitalists), since workers are legally free and "free" of alternative means of support. What capitalists expropriate from wage laborers is not surplus "wealth" but surplus *value*, that is, wealth in a determinate social form, in the *value form*. Value is the basis for the equivalencies asserted when commodities are exchanged. Value is the residue of the blind, coercive, abstract, and impersonal social form of labor under capitalism. Value itself cannot appear—what would congealed "socially necessary abstract labor" look like?—value can appear only as something other than itself, namely, money. Money is not a mere "technical support" to the production of "wealth"; no, capital necessarily expresses itself and takes its own measure in money.

To identify capital with commodities or with money is wrongly to reduce an internally more complex value form (capital) to value forms proper to simple commodity circulation. But to identify capital simply with means and materials of production is utterly to fail to recognize capital for what it is: not a thing, and not a historical constant, but an uncanny and astoundingly powerful (asocial) social form of wealth turned into an "automatic subject" lording it over the globe. As Marx put it, "[c]apital, as self-valorizing value, does not just comprise class relations, a definite social character that depends on the existence of labor as wage-labor. It is a movement, a circulatory process through different stages, which itself in turn includes three different forms of the circulatory process. Hence it can only be grasped as a movement, and not as a static thing."[1] The circulation of capital involves not simply a flow of materials but ongoing metamorphoses, an endless *flow of forms* from money capital to productive capital, to commodity capital, and back to money capital—which explains why capital cannot simply be identified with money, means of production, or commodities.

To sum up, capital is not "wealth." "Wealth" is not inherently dynamic and global; capital is. "Wealth" need not be measured in money; capital must. "Wealth" is not bound by class antagonism; capital is. "Wealth" does not force the generalization of commodity circulation, including the commodification of land and labor power; capital does. "Wealth" does not set a determinate collective good; capital does, endless moneymaking. "Wealth" is not bound up with liberalism's formal recognition of the dignity of each (bargaining) person; capital is. "Wealth" lacks any determining social form and is therefore merely an abstraction, nothing actual; capital is the actuality of coercive rule by abstractions.

What makes capital hard to recognize?

The concept of capital involves great subtlety and complexity—and we just scratched the surface. We need only contrast it with the common, ahistorical notion of capital as "wealth-producing wealth," that is, use values of undetermined social form that can be used to produce new use values, in order to identify one high and unavoidable hurdle to recognizing capital. Thinking about capital is intellectually very demanding.

Capital is a particular social *form*, and not only is it difficult to attend to forms, forms and formal causality have been whipping boys of modern and postmodern thought. Our intellectual climate is generally hostile to forms, social or otherwise. Modern and postmodern antiessentialism close off the conceptual space for recognizing capital and tracking its pervasive influence throughout culture and the world. Form speaks to the peculiar necessity exerted by something. What makes something what it is cuts deeper than an interpreting framework and with more specificity than an amorphous underlying power. To speak of forms is not to deny that forms can come and go; neither is it to assert that any one form determines the way events actually occur. But form best describes the insistence at work throughout advanced capitalist society: the insistencies of the value forms (commodity, money, wages, capital) are real enough. Giving up on form makes us less able to get hold of the forces at work in the world. Ironically, just as capitalism's grip intensifies dramatically, the conceptual resources to talk about this penetration are being cast off as out of date. That's not accidental, for, Marx argues, this modern resurgence of anti-Aristotelian thought is itself bound up with capitalism's rise to hegemonic status. But to show that would require another paper.[2]

Classical and neoclassical economics—and much of what goes under the name of socialist or even Marxist "economics"—fail miserably at conceptualizing capital. They fail to recognize it as a particular social form of wealth and the production of wealth. Martha Campbell reminds us of the chasm that separates Marx's critique of political economy from classical and neoclassical economics when she writes: "There are no counterparts to Marx's concepts in either classical or utility theory."[3] Marx's *critique of* political economy—Marx was no "economist"—rests on a profoundly different conceptualization of "the economy" from those commonplace in the dismal science. The difference lies in Marx's insistence that human wealth, needs, labor, and productive interchange with nonhuman nature, always have a determining social form, and that these social forms matter all the way down. "All production is appropriation of nature on the part of an individual within and through a specific form of society," writes Marx in the *Grundrisse*.[4] Capital is such a social form. In short, almost all of modern economic and social science, including socialist and Marxist contributions, conspire to make capital unrecognizable.[5]

This sorry situation is no simple testament to the ill will or blockheadedness of modern economic and social science. We shouldn't jump to the conclusion that Smith, Ricardo, Boehm-Bawerk, Jevons, Weber, and Parsons were all on the take. For capital conceals itself; capitalism writes its social form, the value form, all over itself—in invisible ink! This takes us into the socioepistemological dimension of Marx's theory of value as social form. For unlike Ricardo's naturalistic or, better, asocial approach to value, *Marx's theory of value just is his theory of the social form of labor and wealth under capitalism.* Marx identified the omission of any analysis of the value *form*, as opposed to the *magnitude* of value, as a cardinal sin of classical political economy—a judgment that extends to neoclassical economics, whose forerunner, Samuel Bailey, Marx carefully evaluated. What Marx's analysis of the value form revealed, however, is that value—that is, the social form of labor and wealth in capitalism—cannot appear itself but only as something other, as a thing, as money.[6] The oddities of the value form, then, set up a situation more baffling than that presented by a ventriloquist. For while the ventriloquist appears not to be speaking, just as the capitalist production process appears not to have a social form, at least what is "thrown" by a ventriloquist is recognizable as a voice. But who would identify what is "thrown" by value, a bare thing, money, as a social form? This creates the illusion that the capitalist economy is "the economy" pure and simple, "the economy" finally "disembedded" from "noneconomic" encumbrances and thereby a proper object of study for the science of "economics."[7] But this notion of an actual economic order free of any determining social form, the idea that there can be an actually existing "economy in general," is really only "the illusion of the economic." It is truly the "illusion of the epoch."

Clearly, capitalists and their minions are in no hurry to see capital recognized for what it is. Given the power they wield in capitalist societies, this constitutes a pervasive obstruction to our recognizing capital. Thus, the elusiveness of capital results jointly from conceptual complexity, capital's self-concealing character, and political reluctance to bring the subject out of hiding.

RECOGNIZING CAPITAL AND THE "POLITICS OF IDENTITY"

What are the consequences of failing to recognize capital for the politics of identity? We begin with Nancy Fraser's article and then turn to several observations of our own regarding capital and identity politics.

Critique of Fraser on redistribution and recognition

In an article published by the *New Left Review* in 1995, Nancy Fraser observes: "The 'struggle for recognition' is fast becoming the paradigmatic form of political conflict in the late twentieth century. Demands for 'recognition of difference' fuel struggles of groups mobilized under the banners of nationality, ethnicity, 'race,' gender, and sexuality."[8] Fraser worries about ascendent "identity politics" being disconnected from a much-needed politics of "redistribution." "My larger aim is to connect two political problematics that are currently dissociated from one another."[9] We share Fraser's aim of conceptualizing a nonreductive politics of redistribution *and* recognition, but we question her way of framing the issue.[10]

We reconceive Fraser's project as one that investigates the relationship between *capital* (rather than redistribution) and *the politics of recognition*. That leads naturally to the question: What is Fraser's concept of capital? Answering that question leads us to make three judgments: (a) Fraser's notion of "redistribution" belongs to a "left-Ricardian" approach to capital rather than a Marxian one; (b) Fraser's view of capital and the politics of recognition is too "demarcationist," too external—even though her purpose is to join the forces fighting for recognition and for redistribution, and even though she repeatedly insists on how the two are "intertwined," the framework of Fraser's analysis remains dualistic; and (c) the shortcomings of a conception of capital which neglects the basic question of the social form of wealth and wealth-producing activities, *explain* why she's stuck with an external relation between redistribution and recognition. Fraser's demarcationist account keeps from view many powerful conceptual connections between capital and identity. Capital's power, the causality of capitalist social forms, is altogether left out of the "left-Ricardian" picture of inequitably divided "wealth." Unlike capital, "wealth" is a dull concept. It won't do much work.

(a) Fraser associates "redistribution" with redressing "material inequality" and with "a socialist imaginary centered on terms such as 'interest,' 'exploitation,' and 'redistribution.'"[11] But this "imaginary" may be termed a "left-Ricardian" one, for it identifies capital with the systematic expropriation by capitalists of surplus wealth created by wage-laborers. Like Ricardian thought in general, what this leftist version neglects to theorize are questions such as: What is the social form of this inequitably divided wealth? and What is the specific social form of the labor that produces it? By not theorizing these and related questions, Fraser slips into the "illusion of the economic"; that is, that wealth and the creation of wealth can exist without determining social forms, and by the same token she forecloses any investigation of the powers of capitalist social forms. Here is the heart of our counterproposal: We suggest reframing the project of reconceptualizing "redistribution" and "recognition" and building it out from the Marxian theory of capital in place of the left Ricardian horizon of redistributing "wealth."

(b) Despite her efforts to the contrary, Fraser's conceptualization of capital and recognition is demarcationist, that is, it conceives of the two as independent spheres. Fraser emphasizes that the distinction between redistribution and recognition is an analytical one, and she repeatedly notes the *inter*connectedness of the two. It's the *inner*connectedness that slips through these terms of engagement. When she writes, "[i]n the real world, of course, culture and political economy are always imbricated with one another, and virtually every struggle against injustice, when properly understood, implies demands for both redistribution and recognition,"[12] we need to inquire further: exactly how are "culture" and "economy" being conceptualized? The term "imbricated" refers to an overlapping, as with tiles or shingles. But tiles and shingles can stand alone; "culture" and "economy" cannot. Fraser's concepts suggest a multilayered interaction of independently constituted, free-standing spheres. That's the flypaper "illusion of the economic" again. No actual economic order can be adequately conceptualized in abstraction from cultural factors, notably, from ways of recognition. In particular, the form of abstract recognition involved in wage labor, like wage labor itself, *belongs to* what makes capital, capital. It's not a cultural *accompaniment*.

So, despite the talk of "a constitutive, irreducible political-economic dimension" to culture, the picture remains demarcationist. Moreover, the text confirms this:

> Thus, far from occupying two airtight separate spheres, economic injustice and cultural injustice are usually interimbricated so as to reinforce one another dialectically. Cultural norms that are unfairly biased against some are institutionalized in the state and the economy; meanwhile, economic disadvantage impedes equal participation in the making of culture, in public spheres and in everyday life. The result is often a vicious circle of cultural and economic subordination.[13]

Fraser is surely right that sexual, racial, religious, and other biases get institutionalized in the state and the economy,[14] but this institutionalization of prejudice remains a fundamentally external relationship.

Fraser writes:

> Gender, for example, has political-economic dimensions. It is a basic structuring principle of the political economy. On the one hand, gender structures the fundamental division between paid "productive" labor and unpaid "reproductive" and domestic labor, assigning women primary responsibility. On the other hand, gender also structures the division within paid labor between higher-paid, male-

dominated, manufacturing and professional occupations and lower-paid, female-dominated "pink-collar" and domestic-service occupations.[15]

But what counts as "a basic structuring principle of the political economy"? While affirming that male supremacy is institutionalized in the "really existing" capitalist economies, we contend that it is not a "basic structuring principle" of capitalism that domestic work be done by women; neither is it a principle of capitalism that the paid labor force be structured to advantage men at the expense of women. We distinguish between what are truly structural principles of a capitalist economy—what is essential to capitalism—and what are not. The distinction between paid, "productive" labor and unpaid domestic labor is essential, since wage laborers must be free persons—not capitalistically produced commodities—reared in a domestic sphere at least formally independent of capital. But the further specification that domestic labor be unequally divided, with women shouldering the greater portion of it, while deeply entrenched, is not an essential feature of capitalism.

Why should the distinction between what is essential to capitalism and what is not matter? Isn't it a squabble over words or, worse, special pleading for a Marxist hobbyhorse? Making the distinction is important because the conditions for reproducing the structural principles essential to a capitalist economy differ from the conditions for reentrenching patriarchy (or racism or homophobia).[16] Do we have any good reason to believe that it would spell the end of capitalism if domestic labor were equally shared out between men and women or if women were not superexploited and marginalized? Institutionalized discrimination against targeted groups in the economy and politics is painfully real, but such discrimination does not belong to the conceptualization of what a capitalist economy *is*. What needs distinguishing is the difference between how *what a particular economic order essentially is* affects recognition, and recognition's being affected by *how a particular economic order happens to behave* in a specific time and place. What indications there are suggest that Fraser has the second thought in mind, not the first.

Relatedly, the way Fraser uses the term "dialectical" suggests that she understands it to mean a back and forth interplay between two entities each capable of standing alone, what might better be termed "synergy," not the exposition of the actual inseparability of two putatively independent entities, which we take to be the proper use of the term "dialectical." In this connection we note that Fraser identifies Hegel as the paradigmatic philosopher of recognition and the intellectual ancestor of two prominent philosophers of recognition, Charles Taylor and Axel Honneth. By contrast, we would argue that Hegel (like Marx) is better thought of as conceptualizing the inextricability of modes of recognition from definite economic orders.

Fraser worries that pursuit of political and economic equality requires putting one's group identity "out of business." This dilemma appears to be based on a non sequitur: Redress of political and economic injustices does not require identity groups to disclaim their distinctiveness. Here Fraser seems to slip back to the position Bruno Bauer took on the Jewish question: To become true Prussian citizens the Jews would have to give up their Jewishness and Christians would have to quit being Christians. To this Marx countered: Nothing of the sort is required; on the contrary, modern liberalism explicitly protects religious and other freedoms of association. Capitalism has other ways of dissolving group identities, for example, gradually eroding thicker understandings of particularity with the watery goodwill of consumer society. Maintaining a strong identity requires too much deliberate effort once basic civil rights or economic security seem possible.

(c) Fraser's demarcationist conceptualization of recognition and economy as tightly overlapping one another stems from the fundamental shortcoming of the "redistributionist" or "left-Ricardian" imaginary, namely, its failure to ask: *What, exactly, is it that is being inequitably distributed?* To answer, "wealth," is to ignore the insistent follow-up question: Wealth determined by what social form? To know *what wealth is* requires identifying its determinate social form, for definite forms of recognition *belong to* rather than *accompany*—no matter how closely—any given form of wealth and wealth creation, and these forms matter.

On capital and the politics of identity and recognition

If we replace a "left-Ricardian" concept of capital with a Marxian one, how does that influence our approach to the politics of identity? Why should it matter? One short answer: Capital is rich in conceptual determinations, while "wealth" is poor. The strategy of demarcation goes hand in hand with a static, flat notion of capital that requires all resistance to capital to come from somewhere outside the "economic" realm. Demarcation establishes external oppositions meant to generate limits or brakes on the domination of a runaway "economic" logic. By contrast, a more dialectical and dynamic notion of capital as the flow of forms which aren't restricted to the "economic" sector refashions the meaning of resistance. Resistance now begins internal to the value form—prior to distribution—in the tensions between exchange value and use value. The interplay between use value and exchange value occurs in a force field with resistance occurring internal to the forms, for example, in the friction exerted by nonhuman nature, space, time, desires, needs, or household life to the spiralling requirements of the value form. It is bad capitalist ideology to conceive of nature as infinitely malleable—passively drafted by the roving capitalist imagination to serve capital's purposes—nor does resistance occur for the most part "outside" the pressure field, for example, in the realms of culture or politics.[17] The genuinely oppositional force of some kinds of identity politics goes through the value forms, rather than attempting the increasingly futile task of locating a vantage point from without.

How does a more exacting concept of capital shed light on the politics of identity? To this basic question, we offer the following observations.

(a) Identity politics involves a reflective stance toward one's identity; no longer tacit and submerged, the politics of recognition makes identity thematic: "Black is Beautiful," "Sisterhood is Powerful," "Gay Pride." Though reflection may be provoked in various ways, capitalism fosters a reflective society like nothing else. Why? For several reasons. To mention two, capitalism has its own table of values, one which inevitably conflicts with customary codes and parochial ways of forming identity. The intrusion of the new table of values compels reflection on the customary ones. Plato's *Republic*, set in Athens' commercial port, the Piraeus, may be read as taking stock of this sort of upheaval. Secondly, capitalism is expansive; world trade is its destiny. Such commerce brings people of very different customs, religions, and practices into face-to-face relation with one another. This, too, spurs reflection as trading partners begin to recognize their identities *as identities*, particular and different from those of others.

(b) The egalitarianism implicit in the wage-labor form, with its built-in respect for the bargaining person, lays a strong foundation for liberal political ideals, including those of equal treatment, tolerance, and human rights generally. Often, identity politics functions on this liberal plane, where value forms shape its agenda and give it force.

(c) The egalitarianism implicit in money and the wage-labor form is a double-edged sword, however. While it promotes tolerance, it can also be a powerful force for social homogenization. Soren Kierkegaard wrote of traditional cultures being consumed in the "hopeless forest fire of abstraction" whipped up by the spread of markets and modernization.[18] Georg Simmel called money "the frightful leveler."[19] And in the *Communist Manifesto*, Marx and Engels wrote of the impact of capitalism on traditional identities: "All that is solid melts into air; all that is holy is profaned."[20] As a human habitat destroyer, capital is a huge force for assimilation. With an irony that much disturbed John Stuart Mill in *On Liberty*, the commercial forces that open up new horizons of tolerance are also conducive to an ominous conformism. Beware the body snatchers!

The "leveling" power of capital acts both on the plane of generalized commodity circulation (money and commodities, buyers and sellers) and on the level of capital.[21] In commodity circulation we are identified as freely contracting persons responding to our own needs. The scrawny identity of the individual that matters for simple commodity circulation is pretty much Michael Sandel's "unencumbered self."[22] At the capital level, the demands that capital accumulation places on the time and mobility of wage laborers work as powerful forces to destabilize and break up strong identity-forming practices and institutions. As Marx put it in the *Grundrisse*, "[i]f money is not the community, it destroys the community."[23]

(d) "Identity politics" (domestically and internationally) can arise as a *reaction* to the shallow, amnesiac, "white-bread" identities ground out by commercial life. What Dorothee Soelle calls a "rebellion against banality" can spur forms of identity politics varying in their authenticity or artificiality.[24]

(e) Identity politics in some postmodern forms seems to mimic the apparent powers of capital freely to dissolve and recreate any content. The utopian vision of identity "quick change" acts where identities are swiftly constructed and deconstructed resembles a capitalist fantasy more than human liberation.

(f) Ever clever about making a buck, and no stranger to profitably coping with the mess it makes, capital gets involved in the booming "identity industries" in several ways:

- Capital instrumentalizes existing identities—or, at least, popular images of them—to sell products, for example, when an "old-world" Italian grandma hypes mass-produced spaghetti sauce. More slowly emerges the pitch to marginalized groups, for example, young gay and lesbian audiences gradually being targeted by mainstream media.
- Capital uses identity to segment markets and fine-tune product design and marketing campaigns, Marlboro's reversal from being a woman's to a man's cigarette being a classic case. As "identity markers" become increasingly sophisticated, so do products and ads.
- As consumption goods are increasingly designed not just to serve a purpose but to "make a statement" or "show attitude," capital expands its business of constructing and deconstructing more or less complex identities up for sale. A real estate ad in our local newspaper for a swinging new "singles" complex proclaimed: "Rent a lifestyle." Increasingly, identity functions like a computer's "format painter," just drag Eddie Bauer or Wrangler across a recreational vehicle; Barbie across a lunchbox or umbrella; Harley Davidson across a tavern; Michael Jordan, well, you name it: We like Mike. Identity spreads and sells.
- Not only does capital instrumentalize identity, it turns multiculturalism and identity politics themselves to a profit. Think of Benneton's "United Colors" or its AIDS deathbed ad; Virginia "You've come a long way baby" Slims; homoerotic ads for clothing or perfume; and so on. And progressive corporations jostle for the public's attention and goodwill by visibly putting

themselves at the cutting edge of identity politics in the business world: providing child care, sponsoring diversity workshops, providing benefits for same-sex domestic partners, and so forth.

• Of course, searching for, maintaining, and enhancing one's identity opens up profitable opportunities for capital, ranging from genealogical services to all sorts of identity paraphernalia.

(g) Often, imputed social identities are meshed with capitalist social forms and class divisions. Moishe Postone argues that Nazi anti-Semitism was a variety of misplaced and misconceived anticapitalism in which "the Jew" was the scapegoat for the most hated capitalist roles: merchant, landlord, banker.[25]

Or consider gender identities. The association of the masculine with the moneymaker and the feminine with unpaid domestic work illustrates the problems with a "demarcationist" approach to capital and recognition. Male and female roles are defined in part by the going capitalist forms of labor and recognition.

Common stereotypes of targeted ethnic and racial groups collect around specifically capitalist forms: impoverished African Americans are unemployable, that is, make poor wage laborers, and African Americans generally lack the entrepreneurial skills for small business. Conversely, the stereotypes have it that Jews and "Asians" are rapacious small merchants.

To conclude this section: In capitalist societies the social forms that belong to the makeup of capital enter, in multiple ways, into the determination of group identities and into identity politics. The rich Marxian category of capital provides conceptual resources to sort out those ways, while the Ricardian notion of "wealth" draws a blank.

CONCEPTUAL AND POLITICAL BLOCKAGES AND OPENINGS TO RECOGNIZING CAPITAL

Getting beyond the conversation stopper: "It's the economy, stupid."

I can recognize and fight a cold without knowing about viruses. Similarly, many of capital's effects can be known and combatted without their being recognized as effects of capital. Nonetheless, it is the task of critical theory to articulate what capital is and to show the practical relevance of such knowledge. In recent elections, public discussion seems to break off after determining that "it's the economy, stupid." What more is there to say?[26] The work of critical theorists involves, on the one hand, identifying and removing conceptual and political

blockages to recognizing capital, and on the other, making the most of the opportunities to recognize capital that come our way. We begin by identifying a few
overlapping conceptual blockers.

Three common and crude views of capital that impede recognition of what
it really is are: (a) the "commerce and industry" picture, (b) "wealthism," and (c)
"consumer society." All three derive from what we earlier labeled "the illusion of
the economic."

(a) A natural way of looking at wealth in a capitalist society is to break it down
into a generalized circulation of wealth whose basic forms are money and commodities, buying and selling, accompanying a process of production that, devoid
of any determining social form, simply transforms material inputs to create new
wealth. This pictures a *capitalist* economy as a *commercial* and *industrial* one. The
trouble is that the picture excludes capital itself, for capital is not simply commodities, money, or the use values needed for production. It does not belong to the
nature of any of those to produce surplus value (profits, rents, interest), yet
bearing surplus value is capital's ruling passion.

(b) The common celebration of "industry" and "wealth" is an expression of
what may be called "wealth fetishism" or "wealthism," which takes the endless
spewing of products of an undisclosed social form to be the purpose of production.[27] By contrast, in book 1 of the *Politics,* Aristotle observed that true wealth is
limited: Nothing should count as wealth but what contributes to the attainment of
some identifiable human good, and any such good inescapably stands in relation
to the good of the *polis.*[28]

Though the wealth fetish is a by-product of the capitalist mode of production, the notion that what drives capitalism is the restless desire to accumulate
"wealth" is a falsehood stemming from the incapacity of common sense and various economic theories to recognize the actual social forms ruling capitalism. For
it is the uncanny impulsion to accumulate surplus value, not "wealth," that keeps
capital's heart pumping.

"Wealthism" paints a conveniently false picture of the reality of capitalism; it
gives capitalism a thin but tolerable tale to tell about itself: to speak with Lyotard and
Baudrillard, it provides a "metanarrative" of material progress that is only an "alibi."

(c) Representing capitalism as "consumer society" has its good and bad points.
On the negative side it tends to white out the class distinction between capitalists
and wage laborers, for at least two reasons: (1) Capitalists and wage laborers are
both consumers and as such enjoy roughly the same sorts of formal freedoms of
the marketplace. Identifying people simply as consumers erases the class divisions
essential to capitalism.[29] (2) Relatedly, talk of "consumer society" implicitly gives
the impression that the marketplace is populated only with "consumer goods," but

that overlooks the fact that "production goods" are constantly being purchased—just not by those in the class of wage laborers. But reproducing the class division between those who control "production goods" and those who must sell their labor power in order to be employed is an essential feature of capital.

How does ordinary language block or open up our recognizing capital? Consider the term "capital" itself. "Capital" is widely used simply to mean a resource of whatever sort. Labor power for sale as wage labor is "human capital," which is a deceptive half truth: Once it is purchased by a capitalist it becomes productive capital, but wages are not profits, so for the wage laborer her labor power does not function as capital. Writing in *America* magazine, the Jesuit sociologist John Coleman observes how religion's contributions to "civil society" can buck up "social capital."[30] If capital is to be recognized for what it is, either we must find a new term or these obfuscating usages need be challenged by critical theorists.

The terms "industry" and "product" are interesting examples of the power of capitalist social forms to determine linguistic usages. What allows us to speak of the entertainment "industry," the health care "industry," and even the insurance and banking "industries"? They are all moneymaking operations. This tells us that "industry" is tracking the social form, not the material features of the activities. Similarly, we now find "product" at every turn: Loan options at the bank are different "products," and a chaplain friend of ours informs us that at his for-profit hospital the distribution of Holy Communion is classified as his "product." In the notion of the Gross Domestic Product, we unthinkingly collapse "product" into goods and services in the commodity form.

Slurred usages like these are not immune from critical reflection, as the women's movement of the seventies demonstrated in the case of the word "work." The question "Do you work?" was politicized. There's a model for us.

Ordinary language does not simply streamline itself to the requirements of capital, often enough it offers handholds for critical observations or commentary on capital. The ordinary distinction between "commerce" and "commercialism" is one. The emergence of the term "consumer" to supersede "customer" is another. It marks a new level of capital's intrusiveness that can be conceptualized in Marxian theory in terms of the "real subsumption" of consumption under capital.[31] Our favorite example is the growing usage of "Mc" as the "prefix of commercialization." Thus, *USA Today* is "McPaper"; for-profit schools, "McEducation"; the television around which the family gathers, "McHearth"; and so on. These nonconforming usages provide openings to a more articulated recognition of capital and its powers, and they signal popular discontent with capital's effects.

NOTES

1. Karl Marx, *Capital: Volume 2*, ed. Friedrich Engels, trans. David Fernbach (Harmondsworth: Penguin Books, in association with *New Left Review*, 1978), p. 185.

2. Here is a sketch of the argument. In modern philosophy, forms, essences, natures come to be thought of as "fictions" (Bacon) because they are believed to be the products solely of "the workmanship of the understanding," as Locke put it. For it is assumed that this "workmanship" is the pure activity of the mind—projecting cognitive "value-added" onto the "materials" provided by sensation. The products of this (purely subjective) "work" of the knower, then, are not "real essences" but "purely subjective" impositions, fictions: made up, not found out.

Marx explains how the capitalist mode of production summons this notion of "purely subjective" "value-added." In capitalism, products have the peculiarly inscrutable social form of value, which, since it is congealed socially necessary abstract labor (a "ghostly objectivity"), can appear only as something other than itself, namely, money. Going into a production process, the needed means and materials have a price; consequent to the production process, the products are sold, leaving the impression that the difference in the two monetary sums measures the "value added" by (pure) labor. In this way everyday forms of life under capitalism lend an air of plausibility to what Marx regards as a couple of bad abstractions: pure thought and pure labor—and thereby some respectability for the modern attack on Aristotelian (real) essences.

3. Martha Campbell, "Marx's Concept of Economic Relations and the Method of *Capital*," in *Marx's Method in "Capital*," ed. Fred Moseley (Amherst, N. Y. : Humanity Books, 1993), p. 152.

4. Karl Marx, *Grundrisse*, trans. Martin Nicolaus (Harmondsworth: Penguin Books, in association with *New Left Review*, 1973), p. 87.

5. In this connection see Simon Clarke, *Marx, Marginalism and Modern Sociology* (Basingstoke, England: Macmillan, 1982).

6. On this point see Patrick Murray's "The Necessity of Money: How Hegel Helped Marx Surpass Ricardo's Theory of Value," in *Marx's Method in "Capital."*

7. For a critique of Karl Polanyi along these lines, see pp. 5–7 of the "General Introduction" to *Reflections on Commercial Life: An Anthology of Classic Texts from Plato to the Present*, ed. Patrick Murray (New York: Routledge, 1997).

8. Nancy Fraser, "From Redistribution to Recognition? Dilemmas of Justice in a 'Post-Socialist' Age," *New Left Review* 212 (July 1, 1995): 68. Reprinted in Nancy Fraser, *Justice Interruptus: Critical Reflections on the "Postsocialist" Condition* (New York: Routledge, 1997).

9. Ibid., p. 69.

10. A valuable, earlier investigation into how the politics of redistribution and recognition match up may be found in Milton Fisk, "Feminism, Socialism, and Historical Materialism," *Praxis International* 2, no. 2 (July 1982): 117–40.

11. Fraser, "From Redistribution to Recognition?" pp. 68–69.

12. Ibid., p. 70.

13. Ibid., pp. 72–73.

14. An excellent recent study of just that sort of institutionalization of racism leading to a vicious circle is Melvin L. Oliver and Thomas M. Shapiro, *Black Wealth/White wealth: A New Perspective on Racial iIequality* (New York: Routledge, 1995).

15. Fraser, "From Redistribution to Recognition?" p. 78.

16. In a plenary talk she gave at the "Rethinking Marxism" conference held at the University of Massachusetts at Amherst in November of 1996, Judith Butler argued that Fraser wrongly classifies homophobia as a struggle for recognition. Butler argued that homophobia is, in Fraser's terminology, "bivalent," like racism and patriarchy, because capitalism institutionalizes homophobia to maintain the private, "domestic sphere," where the working class must be constantly reproduced. This makes a good point against Fraser, but it is not clear that homophobia is a necessary principle of a capitalist economy any more than is racism or patriarchy. On the contrary, the abstractness and impersonality of capitalist social forms work—not without contradictions—against such prejudices.

17. As Marx observed in the *Grundrisse*: "Use value in itself does not have the boundlessness of value as such" (p. 405).

18. Soren Kierkegaard, *Two Ages*, ed. and trans. Howard V. Hong and Edna H. Hong, (Princeton: Princeton University Press, 1978), p. 107.

19. Georg Simmel, "The Metropolis and Mental Life," trans. Edward A. Shils, in *Georg Simmel: On Individuality and Social Forms*, ed. David Levine (Chicago: University of Chicago Press, 1971), p. 330. Appeared originally in *Social Sciences III Selections and Selected Readings*, vol. 2, 14th ed. (University of Chicago, 1948).

20. Karl Marx and Frederick Engels, *Manifesto of the Communist Party*, in *Karl Marx, Frederick Engels: Collected Works, Volume 6: Marx and Engels: 1845–1848* (New York: International Publishers, 1976), p. 487.

21. These are nicely sorted out in David Harvey, "Money, Time, Space, and the City," in *The Urban Experience* (Baltimore: Johns Hopkins University Press, 1989), pp. 165–99.

22. See Michael Sandel, *Liberalism and the Limits of Justice* (Cambridge: Cambridge Univesity Press, 1982).

23. Marx, *Gundrisse*, p. 224.

24. See Dorothee Soelle, "Rebellion Against Banality," in *The Strength of the Weak* (Westminister: John Knox, 1984).

25. See Moishe Postone, "Anti-Semitism and National Socialism," in *Germans and Jews Since the Holocaust*, ed. Anson Rabinbach and Jack Zipes (New York: Holmes and Meier, 1986).

26. Michael Sandel narrates a history of the watering down of the civic humanist elements of U.S. public discourse regarding political economic matters in *Democracy's Discontent: America in Search of a Public Philosophy* (Cambridge: Harvard University Press, 1996).

27. On this score it is worth noticing that, where Adam Smith called his masterwork *The Wealth of Nations*, Marx named his *Capital*.

28. Aristotle, *The Politics*, ed. Stephen Everson (Cambridge and New York: Cambridge University Press, 1988).

29. Marx points this out in the *Grundrisse*: "What precisely distinguishes capital from

the master-servant relation is that the *worker* confronts [the capitalist] as consumer and possessor of exchange values, and that in the form of the *possessor of money*, in the form of money he becomes a simple center of circulation—one of its infinitely many centers, in which his specificity as worker is extinguished" (pp. 420–21).

30. John A. Coleman, "Under the Cross and the Flag," *America* (11 May 1996), p. 8.

31. Here we are widening the employment of the distinction between formal and real subsumption under capital set forth in Marx's manuscript *Results of the Immediate Production Process*, in *Capital: Volume 1*, trans. Ben Fowkes (New York: Vintage Books, 1977).

6

The Systematic Place of Technological Rents in *Capital* III

Tony Smith

The term "technological rents" refers to surplus profits won by individual units of capital as a result of monopolies on innovations.[1] This term is not used by Marx himself in *Capital*, although the concept clearly plays a significant role in his writings.[2] In the standard interpretation of volume 3 the notion of technological rents refers to a part of the process whereby prices of production are formed as centers of gravity around which market prices revolve. I shall argue in contrast that this category defines a distinct stage in the dialectic of industrial capital; the dominant tendencies regarding profits and prices that hold on the level of prices of production are "transformed" with the move to technological rents.

TECHNOLOGICAL RENTS AND THE DIALECTIC OF INDUSTRIAL CAPITAL

It is widely recognized that the three volumes of Marx's *Capital* unfold on a variety of theoretical levels. The theory moves from relatively simple and abstract economic categories to determinations that are progressively more complex and concrete, with each category defining a social form with its own structural tendencies.[3] The overarching architectonic of this systematic progression is a move from "capital in general" to "many capitals."[4] The two major topics on the level of capital in general are the accumulation and the reproduction of the total social capital. The main conclusion of volume 1 is that any difference between the aggregate of money capital initially invested and the total money capital subsequently realized can be adequately explained solely on the assumption that surplus labor is performed in production, surplus labor appropriated by capital in the form of surplus value. Volume 2 first explores how the accumulation of total social capital increases with a faster turnover time, and then turns to the disaggregation of the total social capital into two divisions—producing means of production and means of consumption, respectively—and the conditions that must be met if exchanges between these divisions are to proceed smoothly.

Throughout both volumes Marx referred to representative individual units of capital in order to illustrate points regarding the total social capital. In Marx's phrase, an individual unit of capital is considered as "an aliquot part" of the total social capital.[5]

In the beginning of volume 3 the transition from the level of capital in general to the level of many capitals is continued. The category "cost prices" disaggregates the total social capital into a multiplicity of different sectors. On this level of the theory Marx introduced two features of capitalism from which he had previously abstracted. First, different sectors typically have different value compositions of capital, that is, different ratios between the amount of money capital invested in the purchase of means of production ("constant capital") and the amount invested in the purchase of labor power ("variable capital"). Second, different sectors typically have different turnover times as well.

Throughout this discussion Marx continued to refer to individual units of capital. These references should be taken in the same way as references to individual units of capital in volumes 1 and 2: an individual unit of capital is taken simply as "an aliquot part" of a particular sector. Marx writes:

> For this whole investigation, when we speak of the composition or the turnover of capital in a specific branch of production, it should be clear enough that we always mean the normal, average situation for capital invested in this branch of production, and refer always to the average of the total capital in the sphere in question, not to chance differences between individual capitals invested there.[6]

What structural tendencies hold on this theoretical level? If commodities exchanged at cost prices plus the surplus value produced in the given sector $(C+V+S)$, different industries would have wildly divergent rates of profit, everything else being equal. Consider, for example, two sectors with an equal amount of total investment and the same rate of exploitation. If one of the sectors had a significantly higher value composition than the other, its rate of profit would be significantly lower.[7] An analogous point holds for two sectors with equal levels of capital investment and exploitation but different rates of turnover.[8]

At this point Marx moved to a more concrete and complex theoretical level by introducing two new factors, capital mobility and competition among capitals. Once these two notions have been introduced, the systematic tendency for rates of profit to diverge based solely on different compositions of capital or different turnover times no longer holds.[9] Capital investment now tends to flow away from sectors with lower rates of profit and towards sectors where profit rates are higher. Competitive pressures tend to decrease in the former industries and increase in the latter, which in turn generates a tendency for rates of profit to increase in the former and decrease in the latter. On this more concrete and complex level of analysis, there is thus a dominant tendency for rates of profit to equalize across sectors; any remaining unequal profit rates are explained by barriers to capital mobility.[10] Commodities produced by industrial capitals now tend to sell at prices of production $P=(C+V)(1+R)$, with R defined as the rate of profit tending to hold equally across sectors.[11] These prices of production are conceived as centers of gravity around which market prices revolve, depending on temporary contingencies of supply and demand.

Capitalist competition here has to do with the allocation of capital to various sectors in response to price signals, taking the composition of capital in different sectors as a given—which for all practical purposes is equivalent to holding technical factors constant.[12] This sort of competition results in a redistribution of surplus value from some sectors to others, granting all units of capital a share in the appropriation of surplus value in proportion to their size.[13] All units of capital remain standing at the end of the reallocation process that were present initially. For this reason we may term this form of competition "weak competition."

In volume 3, Marx next went on to discuss the drive by individual capitals to win surplus profits through innovations. With the introduction of this notion of "technological rents," the dialectic of industrial capital is concluded, that is, the transition from the level of capital in general to that of many units of (industrial) capital is completed. With the category "cost prices" and the initial formulation of "prices of production," capital in general is disaggregated to a variety of different sectors, distinguished first by different average compositions of capital and turnover times, and then by differences in the amount (and direction) of surplus value redistributed. For the dialectic of industrial capital to be completed, the total social capital must be disaggregated all the way down to individual units of capital.

Most Marxists explicitly acknowledge the importance of technological rents. This notion allows us to make a distinction between the "weak competition" mentioned above and "strong competition." "Strong competition" is a war unto death, a war in which size is no guarantee of survival, let alone a guarantee of a proportional share of surplus value. In strong competition technologies are crucial weapons in the war of all against all, technologies that can change the value composition in sectors. "Victory" is defined as winning surplus profits while forcing devaluation upon one's opponents.[14] One of the great theoretical strengths of the Marxian position lies in the ability to explain the technological dynamism of capitalism. This is in sharp contrast to standard neoclassical theories, which treat technological change as an exogenous matter. The drive to appropriate surplus profits through introducing innovations is crucial to Marx's explanation of this technological dynamism, and so most commentators grant this concept a privileged place in Marxian theory.

Yet there is a sense in which "technological rents" is typically treated as a subordinate category in *Capital*. On this view, the dynamic of technological rents provides a fuller picture of how prices of production are formed, but does not transform the dominant tendencies defined by the category "prices of production." The story of capital mobility and capital competition underlying the tendencies for rates of profit to equalize and for prices of production to be formed is simply fleshed out, not essentially revised and modified. In this sense, "technological rents" does not itself define a distinct theoretical stage in the reconstruction of the capitalist mode of production in thought. It is a subordinate category falling on the theoretical level defined by "prices of production."

There is considerable textual evidence that this standard account is true to what Marx himself thought.[15] Nonetheless, I believe that it is better to conceive "technological rents" as a category defining a distinct theoretical level, one that sublates the level defined by "prices of production," just as the category "prices of production" goes beyond "cost prices." In order to make this claim plausible, it would have to be shown that a new set of dominant tendencies regarding profits and prices arise once technological rents have been introduced into the theory, tendencies that transform those holding on the more abstract level of prices of production. Can this be shown?

TECHNOLOGICAL RENTS, PROFITS, AND PRICES

Closer consideration of the drive to appropriate technological rents by individual units of capital leads to two further notions, *technological trajectories* and *technological systems*. Although Marx mentioned these notions at various points in *Capital*, I believe that they have their proper systematic place here. They have an absolutely crucial role to play in comprehending both the dynamic of technological rents and the connection of that dynamic to the further transformation of profits and prices.

Dosi, a leading contemporary Schumpeterian, has introduced a concept of "technological trajectories" or "paradigms" that has proven quite influential in contemporary accounts of technological change. According to this view, technologies "develop along relatively ordered paths shaped by the technical properties, the problem-solving heuristics, and the cumulative expertise embodied in *technological paradigms*."[16] This concept is already explicit in Marx. In the following passage from volume 1, the process whereby "the form of a machine becomes settled" refers to this notion:

> It is only after a considerable development of the science of mechanics, and an accumulation of practical experience, that the form of a machine becomes settled entirely in accordance with mechanical principles, and emancipated from the traditional form of the tool from which it has emerged.[17]

The sequence of innovations in machinery introduced by various units of industrial capital thus has a basic pattern ("trajectory"). This pattern is a function of material (use-value) considerations, including both the principles discovered in the course of scientific labor and the practical experience of workers at the point of production.

A second notion, "technological systems," refers to the way that certain technical advances may be employed to improve productivity levels in a number of sectors. The extent to which this is the case also has to do with material (use-value) considerations. The significance of this phenomenon was fully grasped by Marx. He wrote:

> [T]he development of the productive power of labour in *one* branch of production, e.g. of iron, coal, machines, construction, etc., which may in turn be partly connected with advances in the area of intellectual production, i.e. the natural sciences and their application, appears as the condition for a reduction in the value and hence of the costs of means of production in *other* branches of industry, e.g. textiles or agriculture. This is evident enough, for the commodity that emerges from one branch of industry as a product enters another branch as means of production. Its cheapness or otherwise depends on the productivity of labour in the branch of production from which it emerges as a product, and is at the same time a condition not only for the cheapening of the commodities into the production of which it enters as means of production, but also for the reduction in value of the constant capital whose element it now becomes, and therefore for an increase in the rate of profit.[18]

Insofar as the category "technological rents" is considered solely as a stage in the dialectic of the value form, there is no reason to assume that the drive to appropriate this form of surplus profits operates differently in different sectors of the economy. But the notions "technological trajectories" and "technological systems" show that use-value matters must be taken into account; the drive to win technological rents generates material differences among sectors.[19] For one thing, in certain industries "science . . . and an accumulation of practical experience" uncover a much wider range of technological possibilities than in others. For another, innovations arising in certain sectors may have profound positive consequences for units of capital dispersed throughout the economy, consequences innovations elsewhere lack, however successful they may be on their own terms. In other words, *the technological frontier does not expand at the same rate in all industries at all times*.[20] The use-value considerations clearly possess a value dimension as well:

> If the productivity of labour has increased in the place where these instruments of labour are constructed (and it does develop continually, owing to the uninterrupted advance of science and technology), the old machines, tools, apparatus, etc. will be replaced by more efficient and (considering their increased efficiency), cheaper ones. . . . Like the increased exploitation of natural wealth resulting from the simple act of increasing the pressure under which labour-power has to operate, *science and technology give capital a power of expansion which is independent of the given magnitude of the capital actually functioning.* They react at the same time on that part of the original capital which has entered the stage of renewal.[21]

This implies that different industries have different "warranted rates of growth" due to their material differences.[22] And this in turn implies that units of capital operating in sectors with a greater horizon of scientific-technological possibilities and a greater potential to improve productivity in numerous industries will tend to accumulate capital at a faster rate than other units of capital over an extended period of time.

We are now finally ready to return to the thesis that the category "technological rents" introduces new tendencies regarding profits and prices, tendencies that transform those derived on the level of "prices of production." The dominant tendencies on the level of "prices of production" were for rates of profit to equalize and for prices of production to serve as centers of gravity for market prices. But with the move to the level of technological rents, where notions such as "technological trajectories," "technological systems," and "warranted rates of growth" have their proper systematic place, rates of profit do not tend to equalize and prices of production $[P=(C+V)(1+R)]$ are not the centers of gravity for market prices.

On the abstract level of prices of production, the flow of capital into higher profit areas tended to equalize profit rates; unequal profit rates reflected barriers to capital mobility. On the level of technological rents, in contrast, capital investment unlocks the growth potential in certain industries, a growth potential that is not identical across sectors.[23] And so the mobility of capital investment now necessarily tends to lead to uneven rates of growth in the economy, reflected in different rates of profit across sectors.[24] This is a *transformation*, not a modification, of the general tendency holding on the previous level.

If the dominant tendencies regarding profits are transformed with the move to technological rents, this has implications for the theory of prices as well. Once we drop the assumption that warranted growth rates and profit rates are identical in all sectors, we must also drop the assumption that market prices revolve around prices of production $P=(C+V)(1+R)$. On the most concrete stage of the dialectic of industrial capital, market prices instead revolve around a different center of gravity, which Walker terms "prices of expanded reproduction." While prices of production involve a redistribution of surplus value towards those units of capital operating in sectors with a higher than average organic composition of capital (or longer than average turnover time), prices of expanded reproduction redistribute surplus value to units of capital with an above average rate of warranted growth and an above average profit rate. For any sector i, the formula for prices of expanded reproduction will be $Pi=(Ci+Vi)(1+Ri)$; as profit rates differ so, too, do these prices. As far as I can see, Walker's reasoning here is compelling:

> I suggest the term *prices of expanded reproduction* to capture the dynamic element. That is, centres of gravity are now set by long run conditions of uneven growth in different industries, which are determined by the real terms of production, but in a way that includes change. Unit costs (and behind them, labor time) are still the foundation for price formation, but in a way that combines both levels in the present and change over time. Surplus value is still generated from labor and reallocated among industries, not just in terms of *already invested* capital and its composition, but in terms of *future* build up of production in faster- and slower-growing industries. Because of the latter, prices of reproduction are a *third approximation* to market prices.[25]

Industries with higher growth trajectories thus have higher prices (relative to unit costs), not so much because of their present organic composition, but because they are able to generate funds for future expansion. Weak competition, which tends to lower prices (relative to unit costs) in higher profit sectors, does not dominate here. In the most technologically dynamic sectors, unit costs may fall quite rapidly, so prices can remain high relative to unit costs and yet still be falling in absolute terms. Prices may not even fall at all if the new products produced in these sectors are so attractive to buyers that the units of capital in question operate in the inelastic portion of demand curves.[26] This is generally the case for innovations that play a crucial role in technology systems, that is, innovations that have a significant impact on productivity throughout the economy. Also, the most dynamic industries in capitalism are often more concerned with creating new markets than with meeting preexisting market demands. Price competition is secondary to new use-value considerations in such cases.

This concludes the argument for assigning the category "technological rents" a distinct place in the systematic reconstruction of the capitalist mode of production. The following graph presents in summary form the reconstruction of the beginning of *Capital* volume 3 that is being defended here:

Stage	Abstracted From	Dominant Tendencies
cost prices $P=C+V+S$	technical change; capital mobility across sectors; individual differences within sectors; material differences among sectors	profit rates differ across sectors due to differences in composition/turnover time
prices of production (1) $P=(C+V)(1+R)$	technical change; individual differences within sectors; material differences among sectors	weak competition generates profit equalization tendency
prices of production (2) / technological rents (1) $P=(C+V)(1+R)$	material differences among sectors	strong competition compatible with medium- to long-term tendencies for profit equalization & prices of production as centers of gravity for market prices
technological rents (2) $Pi=(Ci+Vi)(1+Ri)$	(————)[27]	unequal profit rates; prices of expanded reproduction replace production prices as centers of gravity

It is worth emphasizing that the distinction between an abstract level of theoretical analysis in which rates of profit tend to equalize and a more concrete level in which they do not clarifies matters that often remain quite confused in the literature. Consider the disparate arguments in defense of the equal rates of profit assumption presented by Foley:

> Economic theorists generally agree on the relevance of models of economies in which profit rates have actually achieved equality across sectors. These models are motivated on a variety of grounds. First, if the adjustment process is rapid, actual economies would exhibit profit rates in different sectors that are very nearly equal to one another, and the model of exact equality might be a good approximation. Second, even if actual economies are subject to large shocks and have important barriers to the mobility of capital, the study of models in which profit rates are equalized is a good logical test of the consistency of the economic theory being developed. Third, if a theory can successfully deal with the situation in which profit rates are equalized, then there is a good chance that it can deal with failures of competition if it is appropriately modified to take into account the specific limits on competition that are important in the real economy. ... [Finally,] because we want to begin to study an ensemble of capitals, it is natural to start with the assumption that they are all alike in this basic determination, that is, that they all have the same profit rate. This is the first step toward a complete analysis in which we would introduce those particular features that differentiate capitals from one another and lead to differences in their potential rates of self-expansion, features such as the unevenness of technical change, monopoly, and legislative barriers to competition.[28]

These four arguments cannot be held simultaneously without falling into incoherence. If the first consideration is valid, the remaining three must at once be dismissed as false. If the fourth argument is accepted, the study of models in which profit rates are equalized does *not* provide "a good logical test of the economic theory being developed," but at most only a test of a relatively simple and abstract stage in the theory. And if the fourth point is correct, there is no "situation" in which profit rates are equalized, but only a theoretical stage in which those features of situations which generate a systematic tendency for unequal profit rates are abstracted from. In my view only the fourth point—which Foley correctly terms "Hegelian"—is compelling.[29]

One final issue must be raised before concluding this section. Why did Marx himself fail to see that the category "technological rents" counts as a distinct stage in the dialectic of industrial capital? It is certainly not because Marx failed to recognize that different sectors have different warranted rates of growth, and thus different rates of profit:

> Since the development of labour productivity is far from uniform in the various branches of industry and, besides being uneven in degree, often takes place in opposite directions, it so happens that the mass of average profit [= surplus value] is necessarily very far below the level one would expect simply from the development of productivity in the most advanced branches. . . . [T]he development of productivity in different branches of industry does not just proceed in very different proportions, but often also in opposite directions. . . .[30]

Marx, however, seems to have assumed that the different warranted rates of growth in different sectors are short-to-medium-term phenomena, and so do not force us to modify the medium-to-long-term tendencies holding on the level of prices of production:

> Something that must also be considered here, however, is the cycle of fat and lean years that follow one another in a given branch of industry over a particular period of time, and the fluctuations in profit that these involve. This uninterrupted emigration and immigration of capitals that takes place between various spheres of production produces rising and falling movements in the profit rate which more or less balance one another out and thus tend to reduce the profit rate everywhere to the same common and general level.[31]

But differences in warranted growth rates in different sectors are a function of differences in technological trajectories and differences in the impact of innovations on the economy as a whole, and these are *not* necessarily short-to-medium-term phenomena. As Mandel notes, the most dynamic sectors of the economy generally enjoy advantages in these two areas that last throughout a "long wave" of capitalist development.[32] Once we move to the most concrete and complex stage in the dialectic of industrial capital, we cannot continue to abstract from such phenomena.

TECHNOLOGICAL RENTS AND CLASS STRUGGLE

Theoretical and political issues are intertwined in all Marxian categories. In this concluding section, I would like to shift focus from the theory of technological rents to some implications of this category for revolutionary class politics.

On the level of the category "cost prices," there is a necessary tendency for a form of capital fetishism to arise. On this level it appears that profit is at least partially a function of investment in constant capital, and thus not solely generated by the exploitation of the wage labor purchased with variable capital. For example,

> [T]he economical use of constant capital still appears to the capitalist as a requirement completely alien to the worker and absolutely independent of him, a requirement which does not concern the worker in the least ... [T]his economy in the use of means of production, this method of attaining a certain result with the least possible expense, appears as a power inherent in capital and a method specific to and characteristic of the capitalist mode of production.[33]

With the category "prices of production" this capital fetishism is exacerbated. On this level of analysis, profits tend to be proportional to the size of the capital invested, and so the connection of profits to the exploitation of wage labor is even more opaque. With the subsequent move to "technological rents," capital fetishism attains its highest development prior to the move to non-industrial forms of capital. Capital investment, motivated by the desire to appropriate surplus profits, now unlocks the growth potential latent in various industries. And so it appears that capital investment in and of itself creates economic growth. This appearance, which is inevitably generated by the workings of the capitalist system, has a profound practical consequence: the formation of class consciousness is tremendously hampered.

This is, however, hardly the entire story. The drive for technological rents unleashes a search for technological innovations, and the process of technical innovation is vastly more complicated than the formulation of abstract blueprints alone. These blueprints must be embodied in technical artifacts and put into operation in concrete settings. In the sphere of production this demands a learning process on the part of the work force. Sometimes formal training is required; at the least an informal process of "learning by doing" must occur. Either way, a certain degree of initiative on the part of the work force must be present for the learning process to be successful. Regarding innovations that result in economies of scale in the employment of constant capital, for example, Marx referred to the absolutely crucial role of learning by doing:

> [A]ll these economies, arising from the concentration of means of production and their employment on a massive scale, presuppose as an essential condition the concentration of the workers in one place, and their cooperation, i.e. the social combination of labour. They thus arise as much from the social character of labour as surplus-value does from the surplus labour of each individual worker taken in isolation. *Even the constant improvements that are possible and necessary arise solely from the social experiences and observations that are made possible and promoted by the large-scale production of the combined collective worker.*[34]

The same point, Marx insisted, also holds for the use of more efficient machinery[35]; for the reconversion of waste into new elements of production[36]; and so on.

As technological rents have come to play an ever more central role in con-temporary capitalism,[37] there has been a belated discovery in the business press that laborers are human beings with intelligence and creativity. A central theme of much recent literature in the business press is the rise of "knowledge workers," "empowered" to participate in the production and distribution process by sharing their insights. Ordinary line workers and office workers are uniquely situated to suggest incremental improvements in production and distribution, and there is evidence that such incremental improvements have a great impact on produc-tivity.[38] They are also in a unique position to evaluate product designs in terms of ease of manufacturability. Units of capital that tap into the creativity and insights of the labor force are more likely to discover and successfully implement innova-tions resulting in surplus profits; units of capital that treat the work force simply as a cost to be minimized will find themselves vulnerable to devaluation.[39]

Talk of the "high-performance workplace" is hollow in many, many ways.[40] Nonetheless, this talk does suggest the following point: *on the level of technological rents there is within capital itself a drive to undermine capital fetishism.* However, many neoclassical economists teach that labor is merely a "factor" of production, an object to be purchased; units of capital seeking to appropriate technological rents must implicitly acknowledge that the working class is a collective *subject.* We may conclude that the intensification of the drive to win technological rents will result in two contradictory effects: the importance of "knowledge workers" for capital will be acknowledged more and more explicitly, while the constraints capital places on knowledge workers will become more and more obvious as well. This contradiction can be expected to form an ever-greater component of the lived experience of more and more sectors of the work force. This contradiction cre-ates a space in which plausible arguments regarding socialism may once again be made to large sectors of the working class.

Other tendencies at work on this level also create a space for the emergence of class consciousness. Consider the way the drive to appropriate technological rents leads capital to seek to subsume science to the capital form.[41] This is a con-tradictory process in a number of respects. Capital requires scientific research, yet familiar free rider problems lead individual units of capital to underinvest in research. And so there is a systematic tendency to socialize the costs of research and development. There is an objective contradiction between this socialization and the privatization of the fruits of R&D through technological rents. This con-tradiction is part of the lived experience of social agents, and can in principle lead them to call into question the surface-level appearances of capitalism.

Another part of this lived experience is the way certain sorts of inquires are subjected to hyperintensive research while there is a systematic tendency to neglect areas of research that do not involve the commodity and capital forms, such as the medium-to-long-term environmental consequences of capitalist development, the long-term physical and psychological effects of laboring in capitalist production processes, the physical and psychological effects of consumption, and so on. In this sense the dynamic of technological rents provides a material foundation for an alliance between the labor movement and other social movements, such as the consumer movement, the environmental movement, and so on.[42] Here, too, is an opening for arguments for socialism.

NOTES

1. Innovation is not the only source of surplus profits. Units of capital enjoying exceptionally favorable locational advantages can also lower costs below the social average. Gifts of nature enjoyed by one firm and not by others allow surplus profits as well. These factors cannot be easily imitated, and so they do not play a role in Marx's theory of industrial capital, although they are central to his account of differential rent. See Karl Marx, *Capital,* volume 3 (New York: Penguin Books, 1981).

2. To my knowledge, the term was first introduced by Ernest Mandel in his masterwork, *Late Capitalism* (London: New Left Books, 1975).

3. See Chris Arthur, "Hegel's *Logic* and Marx's *Capital,*" in *Made in America: Regaining the Productive Edge,* ed. M. M. Dertouzos, R. Lester, and R. Solow, (Cambridge: MIT Press, 1991); Geert Reuten and Michael Williams, *Value-Form and the State* (London: Routledge, 1989); Tony Smith, *The Logic of Marx's Capital* (Albany: State University of New York Press, 1990), and *Dialectical Social Theory and Its Critics* (Albany: State University of New York Press, 1993).

4. Fred Moseley, "Capital in General and Marx's Logical Method: A Response to Heinrich's Critique," *Capital and Class* 56 (1995).

5. Note that if the beginning stages of *Capital* deal with capital in the aggregate, the discussion of technological rents in chapter 12 of volume 1—which deals with individual units of capital—must be an anticipation of a category that has its proper place much later in the theory.

6. Marx, *Capital,* volume 3, p. 243.

7. This presupposes, of course, Marx's claim that the ultimate source of profits is the exploitation of wage labor purchased with variable capital.

8. Marx, *Capital,* volume 3, p. 250.

9. It is worth noting that capital mobility and intercapital competition do not depend simply on industrial capital; labor power mobility, a reserve army, and the credit system are necessary preconditions. See John Weeks, *Capital and Exploitation* (Princeton: Princeton University Press, 1981) and Marx, *Capital,* volume 3, pp. 566, 742.

10. "If there are barriers to the free mobility of capital, obviously the process of

equalization cannot work. Thus if some capitals have advantages due to the scale of production or to access to some technology that can be kept secret from potential competitors or to protection from legislation, the tendency of capital mobility to equalize profit rates may be frustrated, even for a very long time. These possibilities do not contradict the tendency for the profit rate to be equalized because they represent qualifications of the general tendency." (Duncan K. Foley, *Understanding Capital* [Cambridge: Harvard University Press, 1986], p. 93)

11. This R is to be taken as the rate of profit fixed on the level of aggregate social capital explored in volume 1, that is, $S/(C+V)$ with S, C, and V defined with reference to the total social capital (Fred Moseley, "Marx's Logical Method and the "Transformation Problem," in *Marx's Method in* Capital: *A Reexamination* [Amherst, N. Y.: Humanity Books, 1993]). According to this formula, units of capital in sectors with a higher than average organic composition of capital will tend to have prices of production that exceed $C+V+S$, while those in sectors with a lower than average organic composition of capital will tend to have prices of production below the sum of the cost price and the produced surplus value.

12. In part 1 of volume 3, Marx introduces the notion of cost prices under the following assumption: "[I]n this Part we also proceed from the assumption that commodities are produced under normal social conditions and are sold at their values. We therefore assume in each individual case that the productivity of labour remains constant. In actual fact, the value composition of the capital applied in a particular branch of industry, i.e. a specific ration between variable and constant capital, expresses in each case a definite level of labour productivity." (Marx, *Capital*, volume 3, p. 143) In the initial derivation of prices of production all of these assumptions are retained, except the one regarding sale at values. Foley writes: "Marx's concept of the price of production shows how profit rates in a capitalist system of production can be equalized when all the capitalists have access to the same techniques of production." (Foley, *Understanding Capital*, p. 106) Of course in principle the same value composition is compatible with quite different technical compositions. But there is no systematic reason why different technical compositions would tend to have the same value composition. And so the simplifying assumption that a stable value composition reflects a stable technical composition appears warranted, as long as the value of money is held constant.

13. Marx, *Capital*, volume 3, p. 258.

14. Ibid., pp. 361–63.

15. "The capitalist who employs improved but not yet universally used methods of production sells below the market price, but above his individual price of production; his profit rate thus rises, until competition cancels this out." (Marx, *Capital*, volume 3, p. 338). The notion of "canceling out" invoked here captures the sense in which "technological rents" is seen as a subordinate category.

16. Giovanni Dosi and L. Orsenigo, "Coordination and Transformation: An Overview of Structures, Behaviors, and Changes in Evolutionary Environments," in *Technical Change and Economic Theory* (London: Pinter, 1988), p. 16.

17. Karl Marx, *Capital*, volume 1 (New York: Penguin Books, 1976), p. 505.

18. Marx, *Capital,* volume 3, p. 174; see also pp. 175, 177, 179, 266.

19. Throughout *Capital* examination of the value form is intertwined with use-value concerns, for example, "[i]n so far as constant capital is involved in production, all that matters is its use-value, not its exchange-value. The amount of labour that the flax in a spinning mill can absorb depends not on its value, but on its quantity, once the level of labour productivity, i.e. the level of technical development, is given. In the same way, the assistance that a machine gives to three workers, say, depends not on its value but rather on its use-value as a machine." (Marx, *Capital,* volume 3, p. 173) On the general topic of the significance of use-value in Marxian theory see Roman Rosdolsky, *The Making of Marx's 'Capital'* (London: Pluto Press, 1977), chap. 3.

20. The classic contemporary example is provided by the computer sector. Two decades ago Gorden Moore, a founder of the computer chip industry, correctly predicted that computing power would quadruple every thirty months. As a result of this steep trajectory, information technology has diffused rapidly throughout the economy (see Don Tapscott, *The Digital Economy* [New York: McGraw-Hill, 1995]). The trajectory of technological development in the shoe industry has obviously been quite different, as were the consequences of innovation in that industry for the economy as a whole.

21. Marx, *Capital,* volume 1, p. pp. 753–54; emphasis added.

22. Richard Walker, "The Dynamics of Value, Price and Profit," *Capital and Class* 35 (1988): 169–72.

23. Marx, *Capital,* volume 3, p. 166.

24. This point is missed by Weeks: "Competition tends to equalize returns by industry and also to generate unequal returns within industries. . . . The tendency for the rate of profit to equalize hides a fiercely competitive struggle within industries between the strong and the weak." (*Capital and Exploitation,* p. 172) Reflection on technological trajectories and technological systems suggests that there are strong and weak *sectors,* and not just strong and weak individual units of capital within sectors, as Weeks supposes.

25. Walker, "Dynamics of Value, Price and Profit," p. 167.

26. Ibid., p. 172.

27. Of course all stages in the dialectic of industrial capital abstract from the determinations of nonindustrial capital. Abstraction also continues to be made from many concrete features of capitalist competition, such as the actual social agents who have participated in intercapital competition, the specific historical and regional circumstances in which they have found themselves, the concrete strategies and tactics they adopted in those specific circumstances, and so on. All of these sorts of themes remain to be considered, and would have their appropriate place in the promised work on competition left unwritten at Marx's death. (Marx, *Capital,* volume 3, p. 205)

28. Foley, *Understanding Capital,* p. 94.

29. Foley also fails to note that three factors mentioned in the fourth argument fall on different levels of abstraction. The first, the unevenness of technical change, falls on the level of technological rents. Monopoly and legislative barriers have their proper systematic place at later stages of the theory.

30. Marx, *Capital*, volume 3, pp. 368–69.

31. Ibid., p. 310.

32. Mandel, *Late Capitalism*, pp. 130 ff.

33. Marx, *Capital*, volume 3, pp. 177–78.

34. Ibid., p. 172; emphasis added.

35. "Finally, however, it is only the experience of the combined worker that discovers and demonstrates how inventions already made can most simply be developed, how to overcome the practical frictions that arise in putting the theory into practice—its application to the production process, and so on." (Marx, *Capital*, volume 3, pp. 198–99)

36. "This branch of savings . . . is the result of social labour on a large scale. It is the resulting massive scale of these waste products that makes them into new objects of trade and therefore new elements of production." (Marx, *Capital*, volume 3, pp. 172–73)

37. "At a higher level of development of social productivity, therefore, all existing capital, instead of appearing as the result of a long process of capital accumulation, appears as the result of a relatively short reproduction period." (Marx, *Capital*, volume 1, p. 525) It is the faster rate of innovation—brought about by an ever-more-central role of technological rents—that shortens reproduction periods. See also Mandel, *Late Capitalism*, chap. 8.

38. Dertouzos, Lester, and Solow, *Made in America*.

39. Martin Kenney and R. Florida, *Beyond Mass Production: The Japanese System and Its Transfer to the U.S.* (Oxford: Oxford University Press, 1993).

40. See Tony Smith, "Flexible Production and the Capital/Wage Labour Relation in Manufacturing," *Capital and Class* 53 (1994), and *Lean Production: A Capitalist Utopia?* (Amsterdam: The International Institute for Research and Education, 1994).

41. Marx clearly grasped the tendency for production to become more science-intensive under the capital form: "The principle of machine production, namely the division of the production process into its constituent phases, and the solution of the problems arising from this by the application of mechanics, chemistry and the whole range of the natural sciences, now plays the determining role everywhere." (Marx, *Capital*, volume 1, 590)

42. Tony Smith, "The Case Against Free Market Environmentalism," *The Journal of Environmental and Agricultural Ethics* 8 (1995).

7

What's "Left" of Our Spirituality?[1]

John Brentlinger

I

As a Marxist philosophy professor, I have understood atheism and a critique of religion to be integral parts of the tradition of Marxism. As an activist, I have identified in various ways with left-wing political groups that have adopted the antireligious tradition of Marxism. We have viewed religion as an outmoded component of precapitalist traditions that would die away when, to use the phrases of the early Marx, "the heartless world" and "its soulless conditions" are replaced by socialism. The consequence has been that I, along with other Marxian socialists, have reproduced in our practice the same indifference to spirituality and the sacred that is characteristic of the capitalistic exploitation of human life and natural resources we have hoped to transform. And the socialist experiments of the twentieth century have often reproduced the "heartless world" and "soulless conditions" of capitalism in different forms.

I now believe that spirituality and the sacred cannot and should not die away, and that they can be reinterpreted compatibly with a scientific outlook—what Marx and Engels called "the materialist conception of reality." And I think that socialists should respect and encourage a positive core in religious spirituality and its acknowledgement of the sacred; the deep, ultimate value it places on life and community, among ourselves and with nature. We should recognize that not only has capitalism depleted the ozone layer and the rain forests, it has also depleted

133

our spirituality by undermining established forms of community, of tradition, and of contact with nature, all historical foundations of spirituality. Socialists need to reconstitute and nurture our capacity to feel deeply bonded with all beings on this earth who have/are/will be taking part in the historical struggle for life and liberation within the same creative, evolutionary process. In short, we need to renew and nurture our spirituality.

This much is easy and vague enough to be relatively noncontroversial. Where difficulties enter is when we try to be more specific about forms of spirituality and political practice that incorporate spiritual qualities. I want to approach these difficulties by referring to my own background.

Like many leftists in this country, I grew up belonging to a religous tradition—in my case, Christian, southern Baptist. The experiences and ideas that led to my becoming a socialist and a Marxist involved criticizing and rejecting that tradition, partly because of its conservatism and moral hypocrisy—its sexual repressiveness, its cultural and racial intolerance—and partly because of its unscientific acceptance of myth and miracles. As a result, my belief in socialism, and a new form of community defined by its committment to economic and political justice, further increased the alienation I already felt living in capitalist society— I became alienated from the members of my family, my friends, and the community I grew up in, as an irreligious atheist.

I was not aware of the irony of my situation. I had rejected the practices which had given a modicum of communal and historical identity and validity to my life, in order to bring about a community in the future about which I had only the most abstract conception. What is especially ironic about this is how oblivious I was to the fact that this rejected religious tradition had nurtured in me the values of justice and brotherly/sisterly love which had brought me to socialism.

The paths I have taken since have all had this ambivalent, largely unconscious relationship with the spiritual values of my religious tradition. I have never revised my early estimate of the institutional and scientific failings of that tradition. And with various degrees of success and failure I have tried to overcome my alienation through my work as a teacher, through friendships and relationships, and by taking part in progressive actions, groups, and organizations. These connections have been essential to my continuing commitment and sanity, and I value them enormously. The relationships I have formed while doing political work have often had the depth and sustaining value that can be provided by religous communities. Yet the political communities with which I have identified continue to remain not only marginal, but separate and alienated from the larger society.

Can anyone with integrity and political awareness be other than separate and alienated in a society based on exploitation and greed? During most of my career as an atheist Marxian socialist I would have said, "No: We must live in capitalist society like strangers in a strange land." Now I still want to say yes, and for exactly the same reasons—but in good dialectical fashion I want to add a "no," to say "yes and no." We can achieve political and spiritual growth in an alienating society—not simply as individuals, nor in apolitical new-age groups, but by uniting with all people who contribute in various ways to the revolutionary transformation of society.

I want to refer to two experiences which have influenced me to think differently—and to note that these experiences have further convinced me of the Marxist insight that it is experience much more than reflection that causes changes in our thinking.

The first experience is with a community of poor people in Puerto Rico, which I first visited in 1982. This community of "landrescuers" had taken over sixty-five acres of goverment-owned land; built houses, gardens, a clinic, a pre-school, and an ecumencical church; and organized in struggle against the government's efforts to evict them. Over the fourteen years since 1982, I have maintained contact with this community through periodic visits, alongside two devoted community builders, Ruel Bernard and Dorothy Bukantz. I worked with the photographer Mel Rosenthal to create an exhibit of photographs and text, and a book, to publicize and document their struggle. In capsule form, and in a way relevant to the present discussion, I would say that what this experience has taught me is that in the midst of the most intensely colonized nation in the world, many ordinary people are struggling to meet their immediate needs, and to gain independence of the system, and that these struggles are revolutionary in content—revolutionary, I would insist, even though, and even partly because, they lack political affiliation as a group, other than simply the identity of poor people struggling for survival.

I stress that their struggle actually depends, in part, on a lack of political affiliation, because—as they often said—a connection to one or another group would divide and divert them. They have been united, while being very diverse in religion, political identity, ideology, and so forth, because of a common need. Many of them have a sophisticated social and historical self-awareness, and this has been especially true of their leaders; yet their strength and effectiveness lay in their willingness to unite with whoever sincerely wished to struggle with them for their survival.

They defined themselves not in orthodox political language, but simply as poor Puerto Ricans, and the main aspiration they expressed was to have a bit of land, to restore their relationship to the country they knew to be theirs, and to live in a supportive community. They enacted these values from the beginning of their community—in its organization and in their relationships; for instance, they built a house for an elderly couple who had left the housing projects because of being robbed repeatedly. They worked together to build roads and put in utilities, and helped each other with all sorts of needs—food, building materials, labor, transportation. They cultivated their gardens with remarkable love and attention, praising the land effusively for its richness and potential. They hoped to begin a movement to rescue Puerto Rico from industrial degradation. Their faith, though perhaps naive, was powerfully moving. For instance, after they had received final notice of eviction, the day before the government police and shock troops moved in and drove them out with tear gas and bulldozed everything away, I saw a family clearing a section of thick grass, and planting rows of little tomato plants.

For me to unite with them meant that I had to meet them on their terms. And the words I found myself having to use to describe their relationships to each other, to their community, and to nature, were words that came from my religous tradition: words like "spirit," "caring," "creativity," "love," "courage," "sacrifice," "faith," and "endurance."[2]

A second experience of formative importance to me was gained from a series of visits to Nicaragua during and after the Sandinista period, in which I spent altogether almost two years in that country. In Nicaragua, as most of us know, religion actually provided revolutionary ideology to many of the activists, and religious language and sentiment were intimately fused with Marxism and practices of social transformation and anti-imperialist struggle. This was not only a matter of ideology; religious people were an important presence in the revolution, and revolutionary practice often had a deeply spiritual quality.[3]

Sandinista policies and practices provide examples that help to render our concept of spirituality more specific and concrete. For brevity's sake I'll list some of the most important examples:[4]

- Rootedness in national history; especially, of course, the struggle led by Sandino
- Connection with human struggles for liberation worldwide, reaching back in time even to those written about in the Old and New Testaments
- A moral commitment to selflessness, self-criticism, sacrifice, love, and forgiveness
- A great stress on culture, not instrumentally, as propaganda for the revolution, but as an opening for the people to express themselves
- Historically new and greater openness to various kinds of participation—by women, religious people, non-Sandinistas who supported the goals of national self-determination, whether from the church, the bourgeoisie, or political parties that opposed socialism (The police chief of Managua was

a woman. Four ministries were headed by priests.)
- An autonomy policy responding to the diverse needs of the indigenous nationalities
- A variety of new, very progressive environmental programs
- Stress on rituals and events that enacted joy in struggle and community bondedness
- Priority to basic needs: food, health, education, housing, work, land—and thus especially to the problems of the poor

Those who are familiar with people's movements, in this country or else-where, will see that many of these examples are not unique to Nicaragua—my focus on Nicaragua is because of my own experience there. Those familiar with Nicaragua's history will be thinking how limited was the fulfillment of these poli-cies. Yet I believe Nicaragua was relatively outstanding in many of these areas, and would have been more so, except for the repression imposed by the U.S. govern-ment—the economic blockade and the Contra war.

How do these examples show a growth of spirituality in politics? Because, I suggest, they increased interconnectedness among people—they were policies of inclusion. Through caring and responsibility and democratic faith, they trans-gressed old barriers and separations.

Humans create spiritual life and relationships when they connect with each other with love and respect, in the process of building or rebuilding community. The quality of openness is pervasive in these examples—opening old barriers of class, sex, ethnicity, race, religion, and political ideology. Yet openness is an expression of handedness or connection. Spirituality exists when a connection is acknowledged and realized between people or between people and nature; and spirit is expressed when connection is acknowledged across old boundries of exclusion. I have been helped here by Joel Kovel's book *History and Spirit.* He defines spirit as "what happens to us when the boundries of the self give way." He writes:

> [H]istory entails an unending dialectic of splitting and the overcoming of split-ting. These splits are created in domination and overcome in liberation. . . . '[S]pirit' occurs in the motion of the dialectic, as splitting is overcome. . . . Spirit is not opposed to matter, or the flesh; rather it is revealed, indeed created, in the freeing of matter and the flesh. . . . And spirit is not a by-product, or an indicator, of this overcoming, it is the lived process itself. This liberation is a spiritual pro-ject, and spirituality is emancipators.[5]

Kovel's perspective suggests that the concepts of spirit, spirituality, and the sacred, are capable of definition in this-worldly terms. And that a religious attitude and consciousness is likewise definable without reference either to other-worldliness or a belief in a transcendent being.[6]

What is it to be religious? In my conception, it isn't to belong to an institution, profess its doctrines, and practice its rituals. The great religious figures from history were not part of institutions, and they differed much in belief or doctrine: people such as Muhammad, Moses, Jesus, the Buddha, Gandhi, Martin Luther King Jr., Emma Goldman, Fidel Castro, Che Guevara, and Carlos Fonseca; all have a religious spirit as I think of it because they are bonded reverently to the world. They share a deep, unbreakable connectedness that implies love and a sense of responsibility toward other people and nature. This connectedness unites all who struggle for justice and new forms of community, with no matter what ideology, from every historical period or society. It can exist without worship or any particular belief system, and many who do worship or believe in traditional religions lack this quality. Yet it is alive in many of the religious communities around us, in communities of struggle such as Villa Sin Miedo, and revolutionary movements like the Sandinistas. It is not conspicuously present in most leftist political organizations, or the political practice of most leftists.

This concept of the religious is not in conflict with Marxism—on the contrary, it adds depth to Marxism. And it adds depth to Marxism's conception of religion. It encourages Marxists to see that religion, insofar as it embodies love *and* commitment to justice for all, is a liberation movement. It allows political leftists to see the relationship between what we describe as our political commitment toward the world and our religious traditions. And it provides the basis of emotional and practical connectedness with communities of faith and people more generally who lack political identity with the left but who share the values of community.

II

The preceding discussion is part of a broader tendency on the Left to reassess traditional Left politics and its coldness toward spirituality and religion. I mentioned earlier that differences arise among leftists who acknowledge the importance of a spiritual dimension in political practice. Before offering my own proposals, I want to discuss two examples of this reassessment by important writers on the Left. My concern is to clarify the practical implications of the concepts of spirituality and religion I have outlined above.

In a special issue of *Monthly Review* in 1984, Cornel West observes that for the most part the cultures of capitalist societies seriously fail "to give existential moorings and emotional assurance to their inhabitants," and that "religious impulses are one of the few resources for a moral and political commitment beyond the self in the capitalist culture of consumption."[7] He points out that the resurgence of religious movements worldwide have expressed popular opposition to western imperialist penetration of non-Western cultures, and, though often reactionary (as in Iran), they have empowered anti-imperialist, anticapitalist movements throughout the world, especially in Latin America (of which the Nicaraguan case is a star example). West concludes that Marxists should view actual religious practices as instances of the popular creation of ". . . contexts and communities wherein meaning and value can be found to sustain people through the traumas of life." He adds that such communities ". . . represent an ethical challenge to Marxism."[8]

In a later, more autobiographical discussion, West explains that his primary ethical identification has been with the Christian religion, and adds that *because* he is a Christian he is not a Marxist. He sees irreconcilable differences between the two ideologies. Again, he expresses his view that a basic lack in Marxism lies in an incapacity to provide what he calls "existential wisdom," the forms of life that generate meaning and sanity and enable us to ward off ". . . disempowering reponses to despair, dread, disappointment, and death."[9] He does find this existential wisdom in the narratives and rituals of Christianity. And he points out quite correctly that Marxism cannot serve as a religion. "If it is cast as a religion," he says, "it is a shallow secular ideology of social change that fails to speak to us about the ultimate facts of human existence."[10]

By contrast, he says, there are good reasons for accepting Christian claims, reasons that are persuasive to some while being nonsense to others. We are required to choose traditions, he says in a paraphrase of Marx, under conditions not of our own choosing. And for many, the claims of Christianity are both rationally acceptable and existentially enabling. "To chose a tradition," he writes, "is more than to be convinced by a set of arguments; it is also to decide to live alongside the slippery edge of life's abyss with the support of the dynamic stories, symbols, interpretations, and insights bequeathed by communities that came before."[11]

West's perspective raises valuable points and questions concerning spirituality and the Left. If the life-orientation provided by traditional religious communities is importantly supportive for leftists such as West, then the usual critical distance Marxists maintain between themselves and communities of faith seems doubly inappropriate. Inappropriate for themselves, and inappropriate to appreciate the positive values these communities provide their members. However, I question

West's view that it is necessary to accept a certain set of Christian beliefs on a theoretical level, and thus presumably to reject the naturalistic philosophy of Marxism, in order to identify with and claim for oneself the "existential wisdom" of the Christian tradition. Can't Marxists learn from this tradition—for example, the commandments of Moses or the exemplary life of Jesus—as profoundly and devotedly as any self-professing Christian?

I have other questions. West writes that in choosing to live on the basis of a tradition, one endorses "its claims" as "rationally acceptable." He then adds that these claims will be "persuasive to some, nonsense to others." My first question is, how can we decide which claims define the tradition we wish to adopt? A historical religious tradition comprises many conflicting currents and a wide spectrum of "claims," none of which can be proven to be "the real" Christianity, Judaisism, Buddhism, and so forth. This suggests that major religious traditions such as Christianity are not held together by beliefs at all—though beliefs are obviously very important, and religious institutions often canonize beliefs into a set of doctrines that seem to make them all-important—but by the historical relationships and rituals practiced by successive generations of its members. Identification with a tradition is usually based more on family and community ties than doctrinal unity. There may be greater similarity of belief among members of different religious traditions than between different sects within the same tradition.

The solution—which I believe intellectuals on the Left need to ponder deeply—is to reject the assumption that practical and communal uniting with others must be based on a set of shared beliefs, a common theory. The splits and divisions in the Left over sectarian issues of theory have shown how crippling an intellectualist approach is to the problem of unity. It is equally crippling to the need for unity among those committed in various practical ways to justice and a world of brotherly-sisterly love. Unity should not be treated as an absolute, but as a process that occurs when people join together because of specfic values, to work toward specific goals. People who unite to struggle for one issue (unionization, economic rights, abolition of the death penalty, etc.), may be in opposition over other issues. Even people who share a common theoretical point of view (feminists, Marxists, etc.) often disagree over both theoretical and practical issues. Leftists (and nonleftists as well, of course) have tended to see unity as a rigid and universalistic relationship of "us" vs. "them" rather than as relative and fluctuating, as a fixed condition rather than an ultimate goal. In contrast, we need a practice that is infused with openness, respect, and modesty; we need to search for unity with others, and nurture it, on the basis of life values and practical concerns rather than prioritizing theoretical frameworks which define others as "beyond the pale."

West's view that religious belief is necessary for facing the struggles of life has a second problem, the extreme relativism implicit in his suggestion that what is rational to some may be nonsense to others. Surely Jews, Christians, Muslims, Buddhists, Hindus, and so forth, may disagree about many things and still share standards of rational acceptability; they can agree, for instance, that the earth travels around the sun, or that Marxism has the best theory of history that we know, and still maintain their different religious identities.

Religious belief and scientific standards of rationality evolve historically alongside, and in connection with, each other. Yet, though they interact in dialogical tension, rational knowledge and religious belief come from different sources, answer to different needs, and cannot be forced into a single "scientific religion"— such as Catholicism or Christian fundamentalism profess to be—without dogmatism and repression. There is a revealing analogy here with the political sphere. Religious institutions and political parties need to be kept separate from, yet interact with, the overarching laws and institutions of the state, for analogous reasons: so that the various groups with which we identify and in which we are different can peacefully and fruitfully coexist and interact.

I conclude that West's approach is faulty in several respects. First, he is wrong to see a contradiction between Marxism and the spiritual appropriation of the traditional ethics and "existential wisdom" of Christianity (and of other major religious traditions). This mistake arises from another one: He assumes that one can only identify with a religious tradition if one endorses "its [theoretical] claims." Finally—and this issue leads into the next section—West looks only to traditional religions as sources of spiritual nourishment and meaning. He does not critique or advocate changes in the (un)spiritual politics of Left groups themselves. He ignores the possibility that in the struggles of modern life, new communities may arise that are both spiritually rich and politically progressive.

III

Michael Lerner's idea of the "Politics of Meaning" seems to avoid all three of the problems I have attributed—fairly or unfairly—to Cornel West. Lerner is very concerned, like West, with the spiritual crisis of modern capitalist society, and also like West, feels that the traditional Left has failed to deal with this crisis even in its midst. His book *The Politics of Meaning* offers a critique of the present situation, and gives a detailed rationale and program—and this is how his approach differs most strikingly from West's—for what he hopes will become a conscious political movement, in which a "politics of caring" will replace the "politics of selfishness" current in our national life.[12]

There is much that is important and true in Lerner's critique of existing society and its politics—of the Right, center, and Left—and much that is admirable in the alternative programs he proposes. His ideas on education (especially religious education), the family, economics, compassion, and many other topics—ideas that clearly have evolved through years of reading, and discussion with, and contributions from, other progressive thinkers—show a mature, creative intelligence and a great will for change. Yet I also felt disappointment, such as I have often felt when reading utopian plans formulated by intellectuals—"Ah, of course, if things were only that way, and they could be, if . . . enough people would become enlightened and get together and do it."

Why did I have that reaction, and what, if anything, is its basis? The crucial chapter in Lerner's book is entitled "How do we get there?" In answer, Lerner sets as the first task, regional and national summit meetings of concerned "ordinary citizens" in which people discuss their work and lives from a perspective of the politics of meaning. A second step is for networks of meaning-oriented professionals, intellectuals, journalists, and so forth to unite with each other to critique existing social relationships and practices and to create ideas for new ways of work and recreation. A third is the creation of ethical impact evaluations on national and local policies and laws, in government and business (created, in their spare time, by these "meaning-oriented professionals"?); other steps are the formation of a network of consciousness-raising groups, growth of the nonprofit sector of public life, national service work, labor strategies that would stress family support networks, a family day, occupational stress reduction, full employment, a thirty-hour work week, and other immediately achievable progressive goals.

These practical proposals dropped me to the ground with a thump. What "ordinary citizens" are going to come to the conferences he proposes (and has organized)? Who will have read his book, or *Tikkun* magazine? I have lived my adult life in a community with a very high percentage of the sort of people Lerner seems to be placing his hopes on: There are enough highly conscious, educated, professional, meaning-dissatisfied liberals in my community to qualify as an "enclave," like university-dominated sections of Berkeley, Austin, Minneapolis, Cambridge, and so forth. Yet I cannot place my hopes on these people, either to bring about social change on their own, or to create groups that will draw in people of other sorts. They neither compel the attention of most business-oriented people, who are solidly committed to the status quo; nor the more numerous members of the population who earn much less and work much harder to survive, among whom we find most Latinos, Blacks, and Asians; nor the poor. The reason is simple and probably too obvious to dwell on. Professional people are highly privileged, and in 98 percent of the cases will only work for social change, if at all, within the precincts of their "very important" lives. These lives are busy, self-absorbed, and disqualify people for understanding and communicating with the majority of people in our society.

Lerner circumscribes his constituency in the first sentence of his book: "Most Americans hunger for meaning and purpose in life."[13] In fact, everyone in America may share that hunger, but those who recognize themselves in that statement, who find that statement prioritizing the problem in their life, are a privileged minority. Most Americans are facing problems not of lack of purpose, but of lack of power—the means to achieve purposes about which they are already highly articulate: education for themselves and their children; a home of their own; a safe community; a secure and sufficient income. Many, perhaps, have time and energy to devote to consciousness-raising groups, but how could they be convinced of their ultimate value when they are being promulagated by people who do not share their language, their basic condition of powerlessness?

Michael Lerner is a "reformed leftist," but the reform doesn't reach to an old habit. Like the party-oriented Left of the past, Lerner's approach is to work from "the center" outward, the center being the institutions, such as *Tikkun* and the Institute for Labor and Mental Health, that he founded and heads. It is the assumption that people will flock together, drawn as if magnetically by his rationally coherent and progressively innovative program, that lends Lerner's work its utopian unreality; and this is an assumption that many Left parties in this country have made and continue to make.

What is wrong is the model of change: it remains centrist and hierarchical. It will not attract the vast majority, because it does not empower them.

Lerner explicitly bases his model of change on the women's movement, which, like every social movement, is pluralistic and uncentered. Yet he exaggerates the progress that women have been able to make, and fails to note very fundamental differences between "the injustices suffered by women" and "the problem of meaning." According to Lerner, the women's movement has made vast and unprecedented changes in the character of male-female relationships and in women's economic status.

True, there has been progress for women in the last twenty-five years. For example, women's wages, about 58 percent of what men made in 1970, have been reported recently to be 70 percent of what men make (such reports need to be analyzed and confirmed, however. Is any of this increase due to falling wages of most men, for instance?). Yet male support for feminist goals has decreased markedly since the 1970s, as violence against women has increased. And the treatment of women in the media has actually declined in the last decade and a half when measured by feminist values.[14]

The progress of the women's movement has had the bulwark of law behind it. Women have been denied their equal rights as required by law. The real progress has been toward receiving more equal status, with men, in their job, in court, and to a much lesser extent, in the home, through use of the law. The proof of this is in the treatment of women in the media, where free expression has the law behind it; there women suffer more violence, more objectification, more sexual exploitation, than ever. Lerner's analogy would apply only if the absence of caring, spiritual relationships in our society were illegal; unfortunately, but not fortuitously, the force of the state stands behind the rights of property owners, who have with few exceptions been consistently unwilling to subordinate the value-return of their investments to concerns of human welfare—even the long-range welfare of themselves and their families; even though, in the past they have been surrounded as much or more than now by meaning-concerned critics, able to explain to them the destructive folly of their ways.

Also, Lerner's description of the women's movement is very uncritical. In fact, the movement has been plagued by inequalities and conflicts owing to class and race: the problem of middle-class white women universalizing needs and solutions in their own terms; the failure of privileged women to bridge the differences of class and race and imperialist privilege and genuinely unite with poor and oppressed women. Imagine how successful the women's movement of the second wave would now be if it had lacked legal recourse, and depended on the ability of white, privileged women to persuade other women, and men, to struggle to change the way women are treated in the workplace. The distances and differences due to class, race, and imperialist privilege—the subject of much discussion and practical work in the women's movement, and some progress—are minimized or ignored in *The Politics of Meaning*.

This lack is extremely important, and seems entirely to accord with Lerner's "center-outward" political vision. An exemplary case is his discussion of capitalism. He is "agnostic," he says, on whether capitalism is compatible with a renewal of spirituality and meaning—the future behavior of capitalists will have to decide the issue. He goes on to say that ". . . the socialist/capitalist debate is a red herring issue today. . . . The key is not to ask, 'Who owns?' 'but . . . 'To what extent does the economy produce spiritually, ethically, and ecologically sensitive human beings who are capable of sustaining loving and caring relationships, and who feel themselves actualized and fulfilled in the world of work?'"[15]

Take the Nicaraguan case, where capitalists have had their way and where, since the defeat of the Sandinistas, per capita consumption of calories is 80 percent of the daily requirement, 70 percent of the population live in poverty, and 45 percent live in extreme poverty. Hundreds stand in line daily hoping to get work at the *Zona Franca*, a "free zone" for capitalist sweatshops, where wages are 60 cents an hour; work is boring, repetitive, and dangerous; benefits are nil; and union organizing is illegal. Certainly that is better than being unemployed, as are 60 percent of the adult population, or than scouring the Managua dump for garbage, where hundreds of families find their food. And education? It is now basically private, because school fees are imposed on all students, and over half of school-age children, whose parents can't afford the fees, are on the streets. I'll spare the reader more details, but it needs emphasizing that this situation is typical for most of the world's population, and that for most blacks and Latinos in the United States, conditions are little better.

Lerner's perspective blatantly obfuscates the present reality and direction of capitalism in the world today and the manner of functioning of capitalism as an economic system (as if individual, meaning-concerned capitalists were free to radically change their behavior and still survive in the board-rooms or the marketplace!). I have to express a suspicion that Lerner is bending his theory out of shape for expediency's sake—in order not to alienate the privileged people toward whom his program is primarily directed. Again, the problem is a center-outward, elitist program. One of the saddest aspects of older left-wing parties and governments (not to imply that they are unique in this—far from it!), has been a willingness to ignore unpleasant and difficult realities in order to avoid the risk of losing popular support. The need to sacrifice theoretical clarity and honesty for pragmatic purposes always arises when the conception of change is center-outward, and is a clear symptom of a basic separation of leaders from the people. I believe that the program of *The Politics of Meaning* partakes of the same elitism that characterized the old left parties.

IV

It is easy to criticize. What can I suggest instead, as strategy for the Left to regain spiritual depth in its midst and enlarge its relationships with others?

Many have said that the Left needs to incorporate a spiritual dimension into its work. How can actual change come about? I believe that the spiritual quality that has been taken from our lives can only be restored by changes in our lives: by actual work, practice, lived relationships and commitments, in which we cross the distances of class, race, ethnicity, religion, and imperialist privilege that keep us from coming together as people and as part of nature. Unless we renew and maintain our relationships with those whose lives we profess to care about, we will continue to be marginal.

The more recent movements for social change in this country, such as the civil rights movement, the antiwar movement, the welfare rights movement, the gay and lesbian movements, the women's movement for equal rights, the abortion rights movement, the women's health movement, the movement against sexual harrass-ment, abuse, and rape; all, with the possible exceptions of the environmentalist movement and the Central America solidarity movements, have derived their strength directly from the efforts of people who were suffering, who had imme-diate and pressing need for change, and who for that reason have been willing to sacrifice and work for change. None of these movements arose from, or were guided by, some ideological center led by professionals (though professionals have contributed their skills in various ways). Also, it should be noted that a strikingly large number of activists in these movements either belonged to, or received much support from, faith communities. There is a lesson here, and in the further fact that these movements were largely tail-ended by Left organizations in ways that have lended credence to charges of opportunism.

Perhaps the marginal position occupied by the left in our society has mostly resulted from cold-war anticommunist repression and the pervasive power and cynicism of capitalist culture. We are marginal as a result of the powerful forces that marginalize us. Yet such an explanation does not suffice. History delivers us powerful defeats, but does not tell us how to respond to them.

The liberation priests in Latin America say that their work is founded on an option for the poor, who they define as those who die too soon, those of whom the system denies the conditions needed for life. This option expresses a spiritual con-nection, a sense of bondedness, a recognition of the inalienable dignity and value of all people, and a radical refusal to accept the inhumane status quo. It is a spiri-tual option, and one I believe that we political radicals must also follow and live by.

I suggest that if we leftists want examples of how to cross the barriers of alien-ation in this strange land, we can be greatly helped by uniting with the religously identified progressives in our midst, the people who set up soup kitchens and cots for the homeless, who unite to support the southern congregations whose churches have been burned, who house undocumented refugees, who go to Washington to protest the growing impoverishment of women and children. People who, though busy tending the needs of themselves and their families, reach out to others in practical ways; who are open to the analyses and insights of intellectuals when rel-evant to them; and whose efforts, alongside those of many, many others, can fuse to form the molecular structure of a revolutionary people's movement.

Ultimately such a movement will—because it must—take political power away from the power elite who presently run our country and economic power from the large owners of capital, and create a new version of democratic socialism.

That it will do so, is, of course, a matter of faith, but a faith that is placed where it ought to be, in the hearts and souls of the people.

NOTES

1. An earlier version of this essay was read at the Radical Philosophy Association Conference, Purdue University, November, 1996. I am grateful to the editors for the opportunity to rework the essay for this publication, to Bat-Ami Bar On for her careful, perceptive comments and suggestions, and to Sandra Mandel for suggestions, encouragment, and this essay's title.

2. I should add that I am now more aware than I was formerly how these words have also been used quite appropriately in describing the struggles of many Marxist revolutionaries in modern times.

3. I am speaking relatively and qualifiedly: This is not the place for an overview or evaluation of the Sandinistas, and I am well aware of the faults and limitations that led to the present moral shambles of the Sandinista movement, more devastating even than its political collapse.

4. For detailed study of these aspects of the Sandinista movement, see Donald C. Hodge's books, *The Intellectual Foundations of the Nicaraguan Revolution* (Austin: University of Texas Press, 1986); and *Sandino's Communism* (Austin: University of Texas Press, 1992); also my book, *The Best of What We Are: Reflections on the Nicaraguan Revolution* (Amherst: University of Massachusetts Press, 1995).

5. Joel Kovel, *History and Spirit* (New York: Beacon Press, 1991), p. 7.

6. I have argued this in more detail in *The Best of What We Are*, chap. 11.

7. Cornel West, "Religion and the Left: An Introduction," *Monthly Review* (July–Aug. 1984): 10–16.

8. Ibid., p. 16.

9. Cornel West, *The Ethical Dimensions of Marxist Thought* (New York: Monthly Review Press, 1991), p. xxviii.

10. Ibid., p. xxvii.

11. Ibid., p. xxix.

12. See Michael Lerner, *The Politics of Meaning* (Reading, Mass.: Adison-Wesley, 1996).

13. Ibid., p. 1.

14. See Susan Faludi, *Backlash: The Undeclared War Against Women* (New York: Anchor Books, 1992).

15. Lerner, *Politics of Meaning*, p. 234.

8

Reflections on a Dialectical Ecology

Joel Kovel

Let me state, in a somewhat telescopic manner, some theses upon which the main argument rests:

First, that civilization is in an unprecedented ecological crisis pertaining to the human metabolism with nature. The scale of this crisis, involving as it does virtually every ecosystem in a quite unpredictable set of interrelations, is sufficient to call into question the continued existence of humanity in recognizable form.

Second, that although there are many mediations entering into the crisis, there is one efficient cause driving it on as a whole; and that is the capital system.[1] This is a large claim, which can be defended at two levels: first, that tracing any particular element of the ecological crisis to its cause tends to bring us to the doorstep of some branch or other of the capital system; and second, that study of the system as a whole discloses certain structural features, especially the drive toward uncontrollable growth, that are ecodestructive on a planetary scale insofar as capital is the hegemonic system of global production—a state of affairs that unhappily cannot be denied. To this must be added capital's command over ideological production which can enable it to control consciousness, including that of the ecological crisis itself. That capital escapes critique and censure, much less overturn, for its demonstrable role in the ecological crisis is one of the greatest propaganda feats in history—and, considering the stakes, the most ominous.

Third, that the ecodestructive effects of capital combine with its structural

148

effects on labor—massive immiseration and unemployment, widening of class differences, destruction of community—as well as upon the political process, with the corruption of democracy, the breakup of the welfare state, and the inculcation of racism and fascism.

Fourth, that these developments occur in the midst of, and are to some degree the inevitable outcome of, the failure of socialism to constitute itself as a viable alternative to capital's rule. Thus the deadly idea that there is no alternative to capitalism now prevails. The accelerating pace of crisis is in part a function of the uncontestation of the rule of capitalism, even by such fatally compromised standards as had been represented by the USSR.

It follows that the old adage, socialism or barbarism, must be now reinterpreted to include ecocatastrophe as a main feature of barbarism. It also follows that socialism—by which we mean that form of society and mode of production which supercedes the regime of capital—needs to be conceptualized and practiced in such a way that consciously overcomes the ecological crisis. Thus the mode of production which supercedes the capitalist will have to be fundamentally ecological, promoting a harmony between humanity and nature based upon an ethos of reciprocity and mutuality.

And it also follows that the only feasible form of society which can stave off ecocatastrophe is one beyond capital. The word for such a society is *socialism*, which must be interpreted in the sense given above, as an ecological socialism. I am aware of how strong a claim this is, and how out of touch with the vast majority of opinion that prevails across the spectrum, from conservative to liberal environmentalism to various radical ecologies, including the so-called deep ecology. The harsh fact of the matter, however, is that any attempt at a fundamental resolution of the ecological crisis which acts within the premises of capitalism is as viable as a house built on the sands of the beach exposed at low tide. To plan for fundamental ecological change without an anticapitalist frame of reference is to ignore the tremendous power capital has to penetrate and colonize all forms of social relations. Only a profound misconception of the nature of capital—such as unhappily prevails thanks to the above-mentioned ideological victory—would be so obtuse regarding capital's radically antiecological power, and so neglectful of the structures in place whose drive is to dedifferentiate nature for purposes of conversion into the commodity form.

I am not being apocalyptic here: There need be no end of the world, nor is there supernatural intervention, in the scenario now developing. The situation, however, by any rational reckoning, does constitute a civilizational crisis of the first magnitude. It is of a scale able to dwarf the imagination and intellect, so that serious and informed people, even radicals, are brought up numb before its prospect, and fail to draw and act upon the obvious conclusion to the syllogism: Capital is destroying the natural ground of its own social order, and essentially of any worthwhile society; therefore, those who wish to live in a worthwhile world have to overcome capital and build a society beyond its terms, that is, an ecological socialism. This is a really remarkable and deadly fact, worthy of the utmost attention but rarely pondered. It is as though we were living in a community being victimized by a serial killer, and could readily establish the identity of said killer—and yet passively stood by and did nothing.

The above reasoning does not negate the importance of incremental and intermediate reforms and environmental interventions—these are, after all, the available steps we find in the real world. Nor am I denying the fact that such steps need also to be taken in light of powerful gendered and racial configurations to the ecological crisis—configurations that cannot be explored within the limits of this contribution. I am claiming, rather, that it matters greatly whether these steps are taken along a path consciously oriented toward a socialist telos, in which production is self-determined by the associated producers. Indeed, in a time of proletarian enfeeblement such as the present, it can be argued that the collective revolutionary subject of socialist revolution now has to incorporate the voice that speaks for nature as well as labor.

But in the service of what? Here we encounter a dreadful dilemma which plays into the abovementioned passivity. For even though it has never been more urgent, the notion of a "socialist telos" is more doubtful today than at any other moment in the last 150 years. And as for incorporating the voice of nature, the blunt fact is that the principle of ecological balance sits uneasily with existing conceptions of socialism. I am not speaking only of the atrocious record of the USSR, which, as is well known, was even more concentratedly ecodestructive than capitalism, but of even those efforts as have been referred to in the title of a recent anthology as the "greening of Marxism."[2] Let me speak to this from personal experience. I have spent a good deal of time in the last few years addressing this issue to various audiences, many members of which have been more or less sophisticated adherents of one branch or another of ecological politics. I have learned a lot from the experience of these audiences. But I have also learned of the large gulf which looms between certain configurations of ecological politics. Let me schematize two such positions, bearing in mind that a degree of abstraction and hence reduction is necessary to appreciate certain points. Thus we have:

- a "green," or primarily ecocentric position, in which humanity and nature are placed upon the same ethical level and primary attention is given in terms of "saving the earth," or the creatures upon it; and

- a "red," or primarily anthrocentric position, in which humanity is placed foremost and primary attention is given in terms of overcoming oppression and poverty.

The experience I have had is that greens and reds do not share worldviews. Of course, very few admit this; and it is quite easy to get a green to share the assumption that we need to attend to labor; or that economic imperialism is an important factor in ecodestruction; or that overpopulation will only yield if people are given control over their lives. Similarly, it is quite easy to get a red to share the assumption that nature no less than humanity must be spared the depredations of capital. However, my experience has been that the zone of shared assumptions is really quite limited and in fact can be used to obscure a quite fundamental gulf between the two positions. This gulf is defined in its depth by the lack of a common existential passion, in that each side does not really feel the distress and the emphasis of the other; and in its breadth by uncomprehension of either the logos or the telos of the other.

Another way of saying this is that green and red each have to be reminded of the other. Thus they suffer from partial consciousness, or in other words, a failure of imagination. For each position one side of the whole is *present*, as an internalized structure of desire and logic, while the other is *absent*. Lacking subjective appropriation, it will not present itself spontaneously but has to be imported from external sources. Both the immediate feeling for the object of the other and the theoretical development of this feeling are absent. Lacking such, reds and greens fail to develop organic and integral ecological politics. The inner compass of greens is drawn neither to the suffering of labor nor, therefore, to the imperative of socialism; while the inner compass of reds is not drawn to the devastation of nature, nor does it comprehend the actual contours of an ecological society, in particular, the tremendous changes in social relations, technology and concrete relatedness to nature as would be implied by an ecological transformation.

Consciousness is a function of social being. Therefore gaps and absences in social relations mediate the failure of imagination observed above. To focus on one side for now, the average socialist of my acquaintance tends to be a highly urbanized individual, whose relation to nature is densely mediated by technological inputs. Such a way of living leads to insufficient rapport with the kinds of radical transformation in life world (or, as popularly but inadequately put, in "lifestyle") implied by the notion of an ecological society. Put bluntly, most socialists, indeed, most intellectuals, are simply too cut off from the concrete reality of nature to appreciate the ecological crisis as lived experience. It is true that we encounter only "second," that is, humanized nature, so that nature as we live it is always a kind of construction. But humanized nature does not exist as an undifferentiated mass. There are complex relations between humanized nature and nature as such, different ways of constructing nature and living in relation to it. Thus there are degrees of removal between second and first nature, which is to say, the concrete body ultimately destabilized in the ecological crisis. It is in this sense that we can speak of living too far removed from nature to develop an effective imagination of the ecological crisis. It goes without saying that these considerations hold also for that vastly larger body of people who have no particular social or ecological engagement, that enormous mass of the "practico-inert"[3] whose denial and passive manipulation by the ruling ideological apparatus comprise the most daunting obstacle to necessary change.

What role are we to give to dialectic in this complex and by no means promising situation? That depends, of course, on just what we mean by the term. However, insofar as we adopt the minimal definition that dialectic pertains to the motion of entities through their negations, we can see that it will take something of a dialectic to rescue the red and the green from their mutual isolation and polarization. Dialectic is the motion from absence to presence and back. It is also the motion from subject to object and back, hence from consciousness to being, and from the imaginary to the actual. Another way of putting this is that for humanity, dialectic appears as the unity-in-negation between imagination and the real summed up in the notion of "praxis." Thus the green position will have to negate its negation of labor, and the red position will have to negate its negation of nature, in both consciousness and being, and hence in praxis, if they are to mutually appropriate the other, and so build an ecological politics worthy of overcoming capital. From another angle, this implies that what is wrong, or lacking, in both red and green positions, is an sufficiently developed sense of dialectic.

The above reasoning commits us to a notion of dialectic which is more than merely methodological or epistemic. To say that x has to "negate" himself is to claim more than that x needs to change his thinking, or technique, or style (hence the inadequacy of the term "lifestyle"), but rather that x needs to concretely change his whole way of being in order to become more open to forms of negation. In this sense, dialectic constitutes an ontological as well as an epistemic claim; or, from another angle, it is to argue the functional unity of ontology and epistemology. Further, to make such a claim for dialectic is itself an important value judgment, with fundamental political implications. Since dialectic is a way of regarding being from the standpoint of becoming, to the extent one opts for a dialectical ontology, so, too, does one value a radical transformation of the given. In the history of Marxism, the dialectical "moments" correspond to peaks of revolutionary ardor, while the attentuation of dialectic corresponds to troughs of quiescence in the face of counterrevolutionary pressure, or to one strategy or another of accommodation to the given.

The ecological crisis unfolds during an intensely counterrevolutionary epoch. Thus the sense of dialectic is attenuated in current discourse, as a glance at the intellectual landscape will reveal. However, the clear implication that the current mode of production leads to catastrophe provides another opening for dialectic. Because the ecological crisis signifies that revolutionary overthrow of the existing order is a necessary condition for survival, it also becomes a source for the renewal of dialectic. This opening is itself a dialectic—a dialectic of dialectics, if you will, in which the absence of dialectic becomes a moment to be negated by its regenerated presence.

The source of this presence would seem to be along the lines of a "dialectics of nature," as an active principle in a green, or ecological fertilization of the dialectic of class struggle. At first this seems paradoxical, smacking of the "diamat" which haunted Soviet marxism and was associated with rampant destruction of the environment. The issue, however, is not to dismiss the dialectics of nature as dangerous nonsense, but to develop an ecologically adequate notion. A truly ecological dialectic preserves the free play of negation in nature as well as humanity. By this standard, the dialectics of nature was in fact quite undialectical in the Soviet worldview, and sank into mechanism under Stalinist hands. In the deformed Marxist dialectics of nature, the external, natural world is severed from human agency and reduced to instrumental substance. It is, if we may play with a metaphor, to take Marx's characterization in the *1844 Manuscripts* of nature as "man's inorganic body," and to highlight only the inorganicity of nature, reserving the wealth of organicity only for humanity. If, however, we differentiate humanity within nature instead of splitting it from nature, then we regard nature as our true body. We have now made possible an "ecologized" dialectics, and opened a path toward the theoretical synthesis of red and green. Some preliminary and sketchy reflections on the nature of this dialectic follow:

First, the notion of dialectic has suffered considerably, indeed becomes undialectical and indeed mechanical, when it is served up in a form which projects the human desire for command, control, or mastery of nature into nature itself; that is, imposes hierarchies and spurious regularities onto natural schemata. For in nature, dialectic is intrinsically irregular and does not imply equilibrium, or stasis, or some kind of "balance of nature." The ethos of reciprocity and mutuality which underlies an ecological worldview is justifiably an awesome process and gives no ground for sentimental idealization. As birth, death, and suffering are intrinsic to the real, so need they be incorporated in a dialectical ecology.

Second, insofar as the "inorganicity" of nature persists in this dialectic, it defines the boundary between such consciousness as exists in the nonhuman world (an issue we set aside for now[4]) and the species-specific consciousness of humanity. At this boundary the self-consciousness which is our species-destiny marks the specifically human dialectic, as the creature who is part of nature, yet negates and so transforms nature. The emergence of humanity is the appearance of this consciousness; history is the story of its further evolution.

Third, the line of argument followed here implies a kind of "dialecticology." Since the choice of dialectic also implies the possibility of not choosing dialectic, it follows that dialectic is no automatism, nor inherent in every real instance. It makes sense, therefore, to talk of states of "dialectical stasis," or of a "frozen dialectic"; or of imperfect, partial realizations of dialectic, dialectics that are subject to explosion, reversion, or other kinds of deformation.

Fourth, and to elaborate a point already made, such a dialectic entails a "feeling" for nature, which is to say, it requires abandoning the instrumental orientation that characterizes capitalist and traditional Marxist views. For there is an overarching quality to the dialectics of nature which is fundamentally absent in the order of capital. And that is an elusive notion suggested by the terms interpenetration, differentiation, and contact. In the dialectic that affirms life, negations (or absences) exist, as they must in the world. But they are also brought together, they make contact with each other, and they differentiate. Interpenetratingly they combine, absence becoming presence, as new life emerges.

By choosing ecological dialectic, one seeks a way to "go with" a movement of the real that fosters the care; that is, the sustenance and differentiation of life itself. One also opposes, therefore, whatever blocks that process. I hasten to add that there is no intent to be smug here, as though the dialectical approach were a prefigured party line fostering the care of life. It is rather the other way around: One opts for the care of life, and then reasons back from this through various theories/praxes inevitably stained with partiality and weakness, to grope towards a position which we then may call, alternatively, ecological or dialectical. In the process of this derivation, we engage in what may be called successive approximations of dialectic, without being deluded into thinking we are in possession of absolute truth (which would imply dialectical stasis), but affirming hope, justice, and the essential belief in the goodness of life.

It is in this manner that one arrives at the conclusion that the capital system is the superordinate antagonist of life, and therefore antiecological and antidialectical. The cancerous growth of capital's order of social reproduction is itself grounded in a deformation of dialectic. The hegemony of value, with its institution of abstract social labor, implies the de-differentiation of the world into exchangeable objects. The fetishization of commodities observed by Marx as the necessary concomitant of this process also describes the deformation of dialectic under capital, in which an emptied-out, indeed, hollow subject relates itself greedily to an abstracted and deadened object, thus setting into motion an increasingly destabilized and uncontrollably deformed dialectic in which negations become split from each other and fly apart as though in nuclear fission. This is the condition of capital's cancerous growth.

Capital's barrier of value fosters splitting by reducing entities to their abstract equivalent. Thus nothing is sacred, and true differentiation is lost. Objects are deterritorialized and become simulacra. In the virtual world of capital, negation passes into phantom. Dialectic is brushed aside, itself becoming a simulacrum in the frenzy of accumulation. Ecocatastrophic production is the sign of this process.

Though there can be no absolute knowledge or privileged epistemology, there is a method useful toward the synthesis of green and red politics. It may be summarized as the holding together of negations, encountering them in their concrete specificity and staying with them so that absence and presence enter upon dialectical development, and the life within them can grow. Waging class struggle or overcoming the alienation of labor would come under this category. So also, however, does gardening, the education of children, and making love. For revolution, however varied and limited it may be in its concrete aspects, necessarily embodies the moment of total transformation, and drives toward this goal so long as it seizes the imagination. As Marx wrote in *The Poverty of Philosophy*, people must change "from top to bottom the conditions of their industrial and political existence, and consequently their whole manner of being." In this way the synthesis of ecology and socialism will not be a reversion to biocentrism but the the flowering of what is specifically human into an embrace of nature. For "all history is nothing but a continuous transformation of human nature"—a transformation that now requires transforming the totality of our relationship to nature.[5]

NOTES

1. I am working within the distinction drawn by István Mészarós in his *Beyond Capital* (New York: Monthly Review, 1996), in which the capital system represents a social order grounded in expropriation of surplus labor. In this view, capitalism constitutes such an order in which labor is exploited according to the market, surplus value, etc., while Soviet communism, with its "command economy," represented the exploitation of labor through political means. Needless to say, this highly complex point cannot be developed here. Also, it goes without saying that unless specifically stated otherwise, for the purposes of this text, capital and capitalism can be treated under the same heading.

2. Ted Benton, ed., *The Greening of Marxism* (New York and London: Guilford, 1996).

3. J. P. Sartre, *Critique of Dialectical Reason*, trans. Alan Sheridan-Smith (London: NLB, 1976).

4. Except to say that it must exist and needs to be theorized. For if there were no consciousness at all in nature, then humanity could not be a part of nature, and the dialectic would be ruptured.

5. Karl Marx, *The Poverty of Philosophy* (New York: International Publishers, 1963), p. 107. Though the point obviously cannot be developed here, Marx, too, has to be transformed, since his own position was, when all is said and done, insufficiently ecological and hence insufficiently dialectical as well. Marx's greatness lies in opening his own theory to just this possibility. In this way, it remains perhaps the most signal approximation to dialectic yet achieved.

PART III
Community Identity, Violence, and the Neoliberal State

Chapter 9

Left Communitarianism and Liberal Selfhood

Thomas M. Jeannot

The communitarian critique of liberalism is potentially radical, but its radical implications have not been developed by its major proponents, possibly because the hermeneutical orientation of at least some of them—Alisdair MacIntyre, Charles Taylor, Robert Bellah and his colleagues—has situated their critical focus on the retrieval of lost traditions, and at first blush, an emphasis on tradition may seem inconsistent with radicalism. However, there are also Marxist and socialist traditions, they are communitarian in some sense of the term, and radicals who still take their bearings from Marx may be intent to retrieve and conserve them. Resources recoverable from the past might still give us guidance to the future. That is the project I propose here, as a Marxist, and also as an American with an eye on the radical potential of John Dewey's social criticism.

In the first section, I attempt a survey of the communitarian landscape. In the second, I outline an argument drawn from communitarian resources to suggest that the liberal conception of selfhood is consistent with postmodern themes, and therefore to agree with Slavoj Zizek's conclusion that "postmodern theory... simply designates *the form of subjectivity that corresponds to late capitalism*."[1] In the final section, I argue that because communitarianism has so far failed to be a radical critique of capitalism, it has not been sufficiently critical of liberal ideology, even though its critique of the liberal conception of the self sustains Zizek's conclusion.

CHARTING THE TERRAIN

In *Race Matters,* Cornel West ponders the difficult question "whether a genuine multiracial democracy can be created and sustained in an era of global economy and a moment of xenophobic frenzy."[2] Reflecting on the larger implications of the uprising in Los Angeles in April of 1992, he wonders what meaning *e pluribus unum* can have in a society riven by racism, sexism, and heterosexism, by mounting violence and paranoia, by fractured meanings and "the collapse of... spiritual communities," and by a renascent politics of hate.[3] "The Los Angeles upheaval was an expression of utter fragmentation by a powerless citizenry that includes not just the poor but all of us."[4] From a Marxist perspective, the most salient fact on which West seizes in joining the ranks of the communitarian critics of liberalism is that the "real weekly wages of all American workers since 1973 have declined nearly 20 percent, while at the same time wealth has been upwardly distributed."[5] Moreover, he reminds us that "as of 1989, 1 percent of the [U.S.] population owned 37 percent of the wealth and 10 percent owned 86 percent of the wealth."[6] The further question bears on how these data are to be understood, other than as more free-floating factoids on the landscape of liberal anxiety.

The sense that Americans are facing a crisis of community is broadly shared today, cutting across political and philosophical lines. West writes from the Left, but public articulations of the crisis range from Pat Buchanan to Jesse Jackson, from the Christian Coalition to the secular sanctuary of Harvard, and from Alisdair MacInytre to bell hooks. The communitarian critique converges on the common target of liberalism, where political liberalism in the United States is understood roughly the same way across the ideological spectrum, summarized by the title of an essay by Michael Sandel written in the early rounds of the liberalism/communitarianism debate: "The Procedural Republic and the Unencumbered Self."[7]

"Proceduralism" denotes a theory of polity and public life in which the purpose of government is to act as a neutral referee in the adjudication of conflicts that arise when competing private interests collide in public space. The "unencumbered self" is the "self" whose core is "liberty"—negative freedom, the absence of external constraints on the declinations of Epicurean atoms—enshrined in the classical tradition of liberalism by Mill among others, and carried forward to the end of the American century by John Rawls in *A Theory of Justice* (1971).

Rawls has been the lightning rod. *A Theory of Justice* precipitated the communitarian critique of liberalism in its current incarnation, beginning with Sandel's *Liberalism and the Limits of Justice* (1982). Since then, Alasdair MacIntyre, Robert

Bellah and his colleagues, Charles Taylor, Michael Walzer, E. J. Dionne, and many others have added their names to the list. On the political and cultural Right (represented by MacIntyre, for example), the character of the communitarian position as a *rejection* of liberalism has been more or less straightforward and unequivocal. On the Left, however, matters have not been quite as cut and dried: A profound ambiguity marks the final disposition of most communitarians toward the liberal tradition they criticize.

The general trend has been to conceive the communitarian project as a *reform* of liberalism from within, perhaps most clearly stated by Michael Walzer's distinction between a "liberalism 1" and a "liberalism 2."[8] "Liberalism 1" denotes what Sandel names the "procedural republic" and what Taylor names "procedural liberalism." In this account, the public sphere ought to be organized by the formal procedures of a putatively universal justice. On the other hand, "liberalism 2" is exemplified by Taylor's "politics of recognition," which could be conceived either as a contextual supplement to the formalism of "liberalism 1," or else as an alternative form.

In charting alternatives, Taylor, for example, upholds what he calls the "republican thesis" and a "civic humanist tradition," which he suggests may be more evident in Canada than in the United States.[9] Or, to take an example native to the United States, in *Habits of the Heart* (1985), Bellah and his colleagues propose a retrieval of the biblical religion and civic republicanism that Tocqueville admired; and in *The Good Society* (1991), they extend their project of retrieval to American sources from earlier in the twentieth century, especially Walter Lippmann and John Dewey.

Although Taylor and Bellah et al. are stringent critics of the individualism so deeply engrained in the liberal inheritance, in neither case do their critiques lead them to cross the line into socialism. Therefore, despite the deliberately progressive character of the politics they advocate, they are writing as reformers rather than as radicals.

Not only do the contemporary communitarian critics range across the map of current political philosophy, but the questions they raise have historical antecedents as old as the crisis of community itself. For example, Amy Gutmann begins her essay on the "Communitarian Critics of Liberalism" by contrasting communitarian positions today with those of a generation ago. "Whereas the earlier critics were inspired by Marx," she writes, "the recent critics are inspired by Aristotle and Hegel."[10]

The recent critics Gutmann has in mind are principally MacIntyre, Sandel, and Taylor. Being inspired by Aristotle and Hegel is not necessarily inconsistent with being inspired by Marx, but Gutmann argues that owing to their different sources, the "political implications of the new communitarian criticisms are correspondingly more conservative."[11] The sense in which the new communitarians are "more conservative" than their New Left counterparts is equivocal, however, inasmuch as Sandel's and Taylor's positions are not identical with MacIntyre's.[12] Sandel and Taylor are "conservative" only in the sense that neither is a Marxist or neo-Marxist, a new leftist, or a radical. In fact, in the assignment of labels, classical Europeans would call them "liberals" rather than "conservatives," for this nomenclature carries the implication that their versions of communitarianism are better understood as belonging to an intramural debate within the liberal tradition, rather than as an outright rejection of it.

If Gutmann finds an antecedent in the critics of the 1960s, Bellah and his colleagues reach still further back "into the earlier twentieth century for terminology that will put the issues in terms that [they find] helpful."[13] Ultimately, their reach is deeper still, to the orientation emblemized by Tocqueville's *Democracy in America*. Proximately, their reference is to a range of American responses to the English writer Graham Wallas's *The Great Society* (1915), especially those of Walter Lippmann and John Dewey, but also Josiah Royce, George Herbert Mead, Reinhold Niebuhr, Herbert Croly, John Courtney Murray, and others—social theorists who attempted to come to terms with the dynamic and cataclysmic events rocking the first half of the century whose "rise and fall" sets the historical stage of their work.[14]

This reflection on the various titles that summarize contending social visions is significant in the present context, which has the twofold aim of drawing Dewey into the contemporary communitarian debate, and of radicalizing his critique by bringing it into Marx's orbit. For Dewey contextualized his "search for the Great Community" in *The Public and Its Problems* (1927) within the problematic context of Wallas's "great society," to which Lippmann also replied; and although Bellah and his colleagues tend to blur the differences between them, Dewey wrote *The Public and Its Problems* precisely as a critical rejoinder to Lippmann's *The Phantom Public* (1925), an early argument on behalf of technocratic liberal elitism.

In *The Public and Its Problems*, Dewey's singular contribution to the development of a left communitarianism consists in two propositions: first, that "the cure for the ailments of democracy is more democracy"; and second, that democracy "is the idea of community life itself."[15] These claims permit us to focus a question about the main impediment to democracy so conceived. It is not, for Dewey, the complexity of modern societies in itself, but the political-economic problem of the private expropriation of socially produced wealth. Most pointedly, then, in *Liberalism and Social Action* (1935), under the misleading cover of a "renascent liberalism," Dewey explicitly endorses the socialism that had always attracted him from as early as his "left-Hegelian" support of "industrial democracy" during his tenure at the University of Michigan (1884–1894).[16]

In searching out the historical and spectral memories antecedent to our contemporary talk about community, Gutmann hearkens back to the New Left. Bellah and his coauthors hearken back to Lippmann, Dewey, and Wallas. Their nativism also draws them to Tocqueville. But to step historically further back is also inevitably to come to Marx, whose own "communitarian critique of liberalism" is archetypal.[17] For many of us on the Left today, the widespread sentiment is Ronald Aronson's, namely, that "Marxism is over, and we are on our own."[18] On the other hand, my working assumption here is just the opposite, that Marxism, both as a theory and as a practice, has never been more timely than it is today, in a world where the logic of capital has just begun to achieve in fact what it has always intended in principle: to be global, total, and even infinite.

While Aronson and other former Marxists preside at the graveside, the specter of Marx lives on, and Derrida's untimely turn to Marx's challenge may yet prove to be the more prescient clue to what our collective future holds in store. Derrida, whom it would be strange to call a "communitarian," advocates a "new International" that would be the most inclusive community of all, over against what we might call the "anticommunity" of the post–cold war "New World Order."[19]

The problem as I take it concerns how to go about being a "Marxist" in late capitalism and the regime of "flexible accumulation,"[20] and more particularly how to go about it in the context of contemporary American political life, where Marx's ideas and idiom have never taken deep root, and where he has never seemed more atavistic or irrelevant to more people than he does now. One possibility is that his voice can be brought into our public conversation through the communitarian opening that is still gathering momentum and allies; but it is doubtful that his ideas will have much cachet unless they can address characteristically American experiences. This Dewey can do, and he belongs to the communitarian movement with at least as assured a pedigree as any of its contemporary representatives.

If it should turn out that there are fundamental affinities between Dewey's thought and Marx's—an idea that Dewey's student Sidney Hook had sixty years ago[21]—then the time may be right to revive that project again, a stone's throw away from where West, for example, already is. The point in heading down this road in the first place hinges on the proposition that the crisis of community is the inevitable result of the relentless logic of the capitalist mode of production. Therefore, redressing the crisis requires us to understand it within its capitalist context. Conversely, as long as we fail to grasp that connection in its appropriate depth and breadth, we will continue to mystify social reality and misunderstand the deep logic of our current situation.

It might even be the case that the splintered, marginalized Left in the United

States of the 1990s—the dark night of the so-called Reagan Revolution in which even the term "liberal" has become an epithet—will be sidelined indefinitely until it directly confronts the heart of the beast, takes up a vigorous class analysis, and stands up for socialism without flinching. In fact, this is just what Dewey proposed, especially in *Liberalism and Social Action*, before military Keynesianism rescued capitalism from its near demise through the strategy of world war.

The postwar economic expansion that lasted into the early seventies had the economic and political consequence of softening and obscuring the sharp lines of class division that had been transparent in the United States of the thirties. This blurring, in turn, produced the further effect that most distinguished the "New Left" from the "old": namely, the eclipse and seeming irrelevance of a radicalized working class politics.

On the other hand, consciousness characteristically lags behind the dynamics of social reality, with serious implications for the development of communitarianism. For example, the authors of *The Good Society*, their disclaimer notwithstanding, are writing as and to middle class Americans of European descent.[22] They advocate "democratizing" the economy and an "increasingly social ownership of corporate wealth,"[23] but they are hazy about what that means, almost to the brink of incoherence (as I will argue below). They argue that a "more democratic economy cannot represent moral progress unless it also helps eliminate what has come to be called the underclass,"[24] but it is also clear that they are *not* the "underclass" and that what they mean by it, despite their liberal sincerity and compassion, is an objectified, alien other standing over and against themselves.

Hence, the coauthors of *The Good Society* worry about how "to keep the ghettos from turning into the police states they are beginning to resemble";[25] they are dismayed by "the polarization of our society, with the rich creating private enclaves...removed as far as possible from ecological and social breakdown";[26] and they reject "[this] feudal or Third World solution [as] unworthy of the American tradition."[27] But the "tradition" to which they refer and from which they take their orientation is white, middle-class, and to use the Marxist term, bourgeois. It is not surprising, then, to find their use of the term "class" placed in quotation marks.[28] That is, as communitarians, they fall short of achieving a serious and systematic class analysis, and their tacit assumption seems to be that the referent of "American society" is a broad and, in principle, inclusive middle-class majority to which Marxist categories do not apply.

This tacit assumption was arguably more plausible a generation ago in the context of the robust growth of the domestic economy, the heyday of liberal largesse and compassion. But the 20 percent decline in real income since 1973 noted by West is an index of the sea change that has taken place since then. The last years of the 1970s were marked by what economists then called "stagflation," which precipitated the draconian triumph of Marx's "free-trader Vulgaris" in the visage of the Chicago School, "Reaganomics," and the rediscovery of rapacious "free-market" principles that unleashed the ravages of finance capitalism on the domestic and global economy. If the eighties were the decade of the investment banker, the arbitrageur, corporate raiders and merger mania, the nineties are the decade of downsizing, outsourcing, massive layoffs, temporary and part-time work, the proliferation of menial, minimum-wage service sector jobs, the NAFTA, the GATT, and the virtually completed logic of the internationalization of capital. In this economic context, the coauthors of *The Good Society* can nevertheless see fit to write that "the old neoclassical [*sic*] categories of capital and labor no longer apply" and "no longer make as much sense as they once did."[29] These claims, undefended in the text, seem nearly perverse.

THE POSTMODERN DESTINATION OF LIBERAL SELFHOOD

If the broad social context of the communitarian critique of liberalism is the widely perceived crisis of community that saturates the "lifeworld," its narrow context in academia includes a series of issues in a debate that Peter Dews, in *The Limits of Disenchantment*, has recently triangulated among Derrida, Habermas, and Taylor.[30] All three share a common recognition that intellectually, we live in a post-Nietzschean, postmetaphysical universe of ideas. Therefore, it should not be surprising that deconstruction, the theory of communicative action, and communitarianism share certain premises in common even as they oppose one another.[31] First, the fact that each is writing "postmetaphysically" would seem to exclude both Marx and Dewey from their conversation, at least as equal partners, since neither Marx nor Dewey is "disenchanted." Marx still subscribes to historical materialism and a grand narrative of capitalism, while Dewey still subscribes to the metaphysics of humanistic naturalism and naturalistic humanism.

To be disenchanted in the relevant, post-Nietzschean sense is purportedly to recognize the contingency of all such narratives. The limit is marked by deconstruction. As Dews puts it:

> The dominant paradigm of hostility to meaning in recent European philosophy has undoubtedly been deconstruction, which initially appeared on the scene as a radicalization of Heidegger's overcoming of metaphysics. The thought of the early Derrida is marked by a determination to go beyond Heidegger which focuses on his mentor's refusal to abandon the philosophical quest for meaning, in the form of [the] *Seinsfrage*—the question of the 'meaning of Being'.[32]

Derrida's own "hostility to meaning" was never intended as nihilism, however, for "even in its initial phases" it was "driven by profound ethical impulses,"[33] impulses that may be broadly characterized as emancipatory.

Taylor and Habermas have turned out to be among the most assiduous critics of deconstruction because each has sensed that whatever Derrida's intentions were, nihilism would prove to be the deconstructive bottom line. Yet though they refuse the limiting case, their constructive alternatives are still articulated within the framework of disenchantment, within which Habermas wards off nihilism by recourse to the formal pragmatics of a communicative ethics, while Taylor wards it off by way of an ontological holism (linguistic rather than metaphysical, having to do with the ontological commitments of shared vocabularies, rather than the way things "really" are), which can bring into view the immediate, common, and irreducible goods that have dropped out of sight for procedural liberalism, but which nevertheless insist on being recognized by the "politics of recognition."[34]

Being post-Nietzschean, neither Taylor nor Habermas is what Taylor calls a "subjectivist, half-baked neo-Nietzschean," referring indirectly to Foucault and Derrida.[35] That is, neither one is "postmodern" in the sense of that term that strings together the names not only of Foucault and Derrida, but Lyotard and Baudrillard, and in an American context, John Caputo and Richard Rorty. And this is because they refuse to share what Dews calls the "hostility to meaning," particularly within the public, political domain.

Hence, Habermas's theory of communicative action centers on the discursive redemption of validity claims secured by a formal pragmatics that aims to be "universalistic" on the one hand without being "transcendental" on the other, but fallibilist, hypothetical, and empirically testable.[36] Despite his post-Nietzschean, postmetaphysical caveats, however, the "Kantian" character of Habermas's project has been frequently observed, which carries the main implication for our purposes that his formal pragmatics, arguably a type of proceduralism, replicates the Kantian disjunction between the "right" and the "good."

The disjunction between the "right" and the "good" is precisely what the respective communitarianisms of Sandel and Taylor call into question. The debate between Habermas and the communitarians is therefore reminiscent of an older debate between Kant and Hegel. In that spirit, we can say that Habermas's formal pragmatics is to Kantian *Moralität* what Sandel's and Taylor's communitarianism is to Hegelian *Sittlichkeit*. To the extent that this analogy has merit, Habermas's spiritually Kantian formalism would bring him into the orbit of Sandel's procedural republic and the unencumbered self (although Habermas's use of Mead in volume 2 of *The Theory of Communicative Action* effectively exempts him from Taylor's critique in "The Politics of Recognition" of the "monological ideal" of self-formation).[37] Or in other words, Habermas, in drifting away from Marx, may have come within the range of Walzer's "liberalism 1," and to the extent that this is so, he bears more than a passing resemblance to Rawls.[38] Accordingly, we might think that what the "ideal speech situation" is to Habermas, the "original position" is to Rawls.

But Rawls is no more attempting a transcendental deduction than Habermas is.[39] To avoid one kind of problem, however, they may well find themselves saddled with another—a problem Taylor exploits in his near (and finally mistaken) assimilation of Habermas to Rawls in "The Politics of Recognition." There Taylor identifies "two modes of politics, both based on the notion of equal respect," which "come into conflict."[40]

> For one, the principle of equal respect requires that we treat people in a difference-blind fashion.... For the other, we have to recognize and even foster particularity. The reproach the first makes to the second is just that it violates the principle of nondiscrimination. The reproach the second makes to the first is that it negates identity by forcing people into a homogeneous mold that is untrue to them.... The claim is that the supposedly neutral set of difference-blind principles of the politics of equal dignity is in fact a reflection of one hegemonic culture [and consequently] itself highly discriminatory.[41]

Taylor's point, which he wants to make "gently and gingerly,"[42] is that procedural liberalism may not be able to cope with the politics of difference,[43] and the proceduralists he has in mind are Rawls, Dworkin, and Habermas. The objection is that difference-blind proceduralism is also a form of particularism. This objection potentially could be met by defending some type of either metaphysical or epistemological "universalism," but Rawls does not, and Habermas's post-Nietzschean, postmetaphysical commitments block that road for him as well.

The critique that the politics of difference directs against liberalism "is the cruelest and most upsetting of all":

> The charge leveled by the most radical forms of the politics of difference is that "blind" liberalisms are themselves the reflection of particular cultures. And the worrying thought is that this bias might not just be a contingent weakness of all hitherto proposed theories, that the very idea of such a liberalism may be a kind of pragmatic contradiction, a particularism masquerading as the universal.[44]

Presumably because communitarianism is neither difference-blind nor the politics of difference (but in Taylor's version, the "politics of recognition" instead), it does not court the "pragmatic contradiction" into which proceduralism potentially falls.

As devastating as is the dilemma Taylor poses, however, liberalism still has a way out in Richard Rorty's "ironic" turn, just a short step away.

To see how close Rorty is, we can turn back to Sandel's critique of "The Procedural Republic and the Unencumbered Self." Sandel begins by laying out the "Kantian foundations" of the "liberal ethic," which "asserts the priority of right, and seeks principles of justice that do not presuppose any particular conception of the good."[45] For Sandel, Rawls is the contemporary philosopher who takes up Kant's project. Like Habermas, however, if Rawls is spiritually a Kantian, he is also post-Nietzschean and postmetaphysical, therefore leery of the "transcendental." As Sandel puts it,

> [Rawls] wants to save the priority of right from the obscurity of the transcendental subject.... And so [his] project is to preserve Kant's moral and political teaching by replacing Germanic obscurities with a domesticated metaphysic [*sic*] more congenial to the Anglo-American temper. This is the role of the original position.[46]

Sandel names the Rawlsian "self" in the original position "the unencumbered self," "the human subject ... installed as sovereign ... free to construct principles of justice unconstrained by an order of value antecedently given," radically "free to choose [her] purposes and ends unbound by such an order."[47] Such a self is "of course free to join in voluntary association with others, and so [is] capable of community in the cooperative sense," but belongs to no community in the "constitutive" sense and has no "constitutive ends."[48]

Once the radical contingency and heterogeneity of particularist conceptions of the good life are affirmed, then Rawls's "free and rational persons concerned to further their own interests," parties to the original position behind the veil of ignorance, therefore "unencumbered selves," might just as well be Rorty's "liberal ironists." Since, in MacIntyre's expression, "individuals *qua* individuals" are subjects of radical choice, each of them "author of the only moral meanings there are,"[49] unconstrained atoms swerving in the void, the only social responsibility incumbent on them is to avoid colliding with one another—"an equal right to the most extensive basic liberty compatible with a similar liberty for others."[50]

Since this argument turns both Rawls and Rorty into "libertarians," however, Rawlsians will be quick to object that its formulation fails to take account of the "difference principle," Rawls's *second* principle of justice. After rehearsing the reasoning that leads Rawls to the "difference principle" in the first place, Sandel rejoins, the difference principle, like utilitarianism, is a principle of sharing. As such, it must presuppose some prior moral tie among those whose assets it would deploy and whose efforts it would enlist in a common endeavor. Otherwise, it is simply a formula for using some as means to others' ends, a formula this liberalism is committed to reject. But on the cooperative vision of community alone, it is unclear what the moral basis for this sharing could be. Short of the constitutive conception, deploying an individual's assets for the sake of the common good would seem an offense against the "plurality and distinctness" of individuals this liberalism seeks above all to secure.[51]

If Sandel's communitarian argument against Rawls has merit—namely, that I can be morally bound to other people only in a constitutive community—then the difference between Rawls and Rorty vanishes, and the civic privatism that makes genuine community life impossible holds the field unchallenged in the procedural republic. We can then feel free to take Rorty's advice to *"[p]rivatize* the Nietzschean-Sartrean-Foucaultian attempt at authenticity and purity, in order to prevent [ourselves] from slipping into a political attitude which will lead [us] to think that there is some social goal more important than avoiding cruelty"; that is, colliding as privatized atoms.[52]

The truly startling outcome of these affiliations would be to find Habermas drawn into the same orbit, aside from Rorty's rapprochement toward him.[53] For these are the shoals on which critical theory may all too easily founder once we hew to a post-Nietzschean, postmetaphysical line.

If it can be pleaded that Rorty has already suffered enough abuse from certain quarters, why is it not tiresome to make him a whipping boy once again? Dews gives an answer:

> One might have thought that the disenchantment of the world classically described by Max Weber...would constitute a cultural trauma of such magnitude that philosophy could do little other than struggle to come to terms with it.... Yet ...many philosophers appear to have registered no turbulence at all. On the contrary, they are eager to drive the process of disillusionment further. Richard Rorty, for example, advocates a 'philosophical superficiality and light-mindedness' which 'helps along the disenchantment of the world' and which, he believes, will 'make the world's inhabitants more pragmatic, more tolerant, more liberal, more receptive to the appeal of instrumental rationality.' It is arguable, however, that Rorty can think thus only because he assumes that we can take *seriously* meanings which we know we have created, and which flimsily veil the indifferent universe of physicalism which Rorty—for all his hermeneutic gestures—regards as the ontological bottom line.[54]

In fact, one way of thinking about Rorty's project is that he has adapted deconstruction to the idiom of Anglo-American philosophy, and to repeat Dews again, deconstruction has been the "dominant paradigm of hostility to meaning in recent... philosophy."[55] Indeed, despite the liberatory uses to which deconstruction has been put, its potential nihilism has always made those of us who think of philosophy as part of a quest for meaningful lives uneasy.

The threat of nihilism has apparently made Habermas uneasy as well. Quoting from Habermas's essay, "Themes in Postmetaphysical Thinking," Dews notes how "Habermas acknowledges the continuing human need for contact with a transcendence which is more contentful and meaningful than the purely formal 'transcendence from within' to which we are exposed by the force of validity claims."[56] Recognition of a *material* need for self-transcendence in turn draws Habermas toward Taylor: "despite their ostensible disagreements in other respects," they agree that "the life of even the most democratic polity" (as if this were our present worry) "will degenerate into oppressive and purposeless routine unless the transcendent sources of ethical energy and moral inspiration are periodically renewed."[57]

But most surprising of all in Dews's triangulation is that there "also seems to be a certain convergence with the recent thought of Derrida."[58] Of course, Dews's reference is to *Specters of Marx*, the text in which Derrida finally gives his long-awaited answer to the question about the ethical and political import of deconstruction. The relationship between *this* Derrida and the author of *Of Grammatology*, and so forth, is complex, and fortunately, beyond the scope of this essay. Dews himself warns that many "commentators seem to assume that what has already come to be known as the 'ethical turn' in deconstruction represents an unproblematic extension of Derrida's earlier concerns, but in fact there is an extreme tension and torsion at work here."[59] He does not hesitate to criticize Derrida himself, making the more or less standard charge that deconstruction is self-referentially inconsistent.[60] But he concludes that, "[a]t its best, [Derrida's] recent thinking... attempt[s] to restore a sense of ethical orientation and political possibility, to defend what he terms an 'emancipatory desire' without the support of an objectivistic metaphysics."[61]

An emancipatory desire that is also a desire for self-transcendence is basic to the human task of creating a just and good society, a social order worthy of our human promise. In making his gesture to Marx, then, Derrida writes that "what remains irreducible to any deconstruction... is a certain experience of the emancipatory promise; ... an idea of justice— ... and an idea of democracy—*which we distinguish from its current concept and from its determined predicates today*."[62] The current concept and determined predicates of "justice" and "democracy" today are the fulfilled liberalism and liberal capitalism of the New World Order. Hence, Derrida proceeds to savage the "*neo-evangelistic* rhetoric of Fukuyama," author of *The End of History and the Last Man,* who celebrates the triumph of the New World Order.[63] Derrida mounts his assault on Fukuyama with a logocentric arsenal worthy of a logician, as if to expose that "philosophical superficiality and light-mindedness" that "helps along the disenchantment of the world" as the greatest enemy of humankind. For it would lull us all into the consumerist complacency of the liberal ironist, and lead us to "neglect this obvious macroscopic fact, made up of innumerable singular sites of suffering: No degree of progress allows one to ignore that never before, in absolute figures, never have so many men, women, and children been subjugated, starved, or exterminated on the earth."[64]

From the point of view of this essay, Derrida's untimely gesture in 1993 came just in time, although he assures the readers of *Specters of Marx* early in the book that for him, having lived with these questions for forty years, today they have the feel of a "tiresome anachronism."[65] For in the same year of the University of California, Riverside conference in which Derrida gave the plenary address that was to become this book, Zizek wrote:

> The fear of "excessive" identification is . . . the fundamental feature of the late-capitalist ideology: the Enemy is the "fanatic" who "over-identifies" instead of maintaining a proper distance toward the dispersed plurality of subject-positions. In short: the elated "deconstructionist" logomachy focused on "essentialism" and "fixed identities" ultimately fights a straw-man. Far from containing any kind of subversive potentials, the dispersed, plural, constructed subject hailed by postmodern theory (the subject prone to particular, inconsistent modes of enjoyment, etc.) simply designates *the form of subjectivity that corresponds to late capitalism.* Perhaps the time has come to resuscitate the Marxian insight that Capital is the ultimate power of "deterritorialization" which undermines every fixed social identity, and to conceive of "late capitalism" as the epoch in which the traditional fixity of ideological positions . . . becomes an obstacle to the unbridled commodification of everyday life.[66]

Unencumbered selves, transmuted into liberal ironists, disavow any "fixed identity" and maintain their proper distance from any constitutive meaning that might pledge them to some purpose larger than their own self-creation. The capital mobility requirements of flexible accumulation could hardly find better, more plastic subjects to engrave in capital's image: "the unbridled commodification of everyday life," a total colonization of the lifeworld.

The Insufficiency of the Communitarian Rejoinder

The communitarian critics of liberalism agree that the crisis of community is also a crisis of personal identity and meaning. Unencumbered, uncommitted selves, the Lockean individuals drawn in detail by Bellah and his colleagues, retreat to their lifestyle enclaves and maintain an ironic distance from the "dispersed plurality of subject-positions" they pass in the malls and skywalks. Made "more receptive to the appeal of instrumental rationality," all things become matters of calculation and contract, right down to intimacy, marriage, and family life. Displaced from constitutive communities, bereft of constitutive ends, undefined by the immediate, irreducibly common goods in the achievement and enjoyment of which we experience warm and vital human solidarity, they are the blank slates upon which the consumer society and advertising culture are free to inscribe their own semantically empty messages.

As Marx put it in his Paris Manuscript on "Private Property and Communism," this regime "has made us so stupid and one-sided that an object is only *ours* when we have it—when it exists for us as capital, or when it is directly possessed, eaten, drunk, worn, inhabited, etc.,—in short, when it is *used* by us."[67] Bellah et al. affiliate this more or less complete receptivity to the appeal of instrumental reason with our impoverished vocabularies of personal identity: "utilitarian individualism" at work, "expressive individualism" in leisure, romance, and family life.[68]

However, it is important to see that the crisis of community diagnosed by the communitarian critics is mainly apt within the narrow confines of what Taylor names the North Atlantic culture; and specifically in the United States, to the white bourgeoisie. Where it shows up elsewhere, in other regions, in decimated inner cities, or in the non-European communities to which capitalism comes from the outside, it might be best diagnosed as a colonial effect.

Decades before the new communitarians began to address the crisis today, Dewey grasped it in remarkably similar terms, and reading him today, it seems with an uncanny prescience. Perhaps this is in part because our situation in the Age of Reagan, the New World Order, and flexible accumulation shares traits in common with the America of 1930.

However, a more profound reason may be the one developed by Marx in the *Grundrisse* and elsewhere: The capitalist mode of production has emerged and developed historically through a long-term dissolution and breakdown of the economic foundations of precapitalist organic forms of community.[69] However one characterizes the emergence and development of modern societies from traditional ones—Karl Polanyi's *Great Transformation*, Weberian rationalization, and so forth—the crucial factor from a Marxist point of view is the economic context within which this ongoing revolutionary upheaval takes place. In keeping with the premises of historical materialism, the mode of production that prevails within a particular epoch will supply the key to understanding the forms of life that are materially based on it. Accordingly, whether this epoch is referred to as modernity (or postmodernity) or liberalism or by some other term, its material basis consists in the ongoing historical processes of dissolution that are integral to the capitalist mode of production.

Although Dewey writes social criticism as a professional philosopher rather than as a political economist, his virtue from a Marxist perspective is that he does grasp the crisis of community in a political-economic framework, that is, in relation to capitalism.

In coming to terms with the complementary relation between the breakdown of forms of community life and the potential collapse of personal identity and meaning, Dewey identifies "the lost individual."[70] He begins by observing that the "development of a civilization that is outwardly corporate—or rapidly becoming so—has been accompanied by a submergence of the individual."[71] Power in the corporate civilization is concentrated in the hands of an "industrial oligarchy," but the "power of the few is, with respect to genuine individuality, specious; . . . those outwardly in control are in reality as much carried by forces external to them as are the many."[72]

Expounding on these "external forces" in a later chapter, Dewey, who does not otherwise refrain from criticizing Marx, writes:

> Economic determinism is now a fact, not a theory. But there is a difference and a choice between a blind, chaotic and unplanned determinism, issuing from business conducted for pecuniary profit, and the determination of a socially planned and ordered development.[73]

Elsewhere Dewey criticizes Marxism for being a type of "economic determinism," which he interprets reductively. In general, he is the first to admit the poverty of his acquaintance with Marxist sources, and he is an unreliable guide to Marxist thought. In the passage just quoted, however, he implicitly concedes the Marxian point, which need not be made reductively.

Marx understands the capitalist mode of production as one in which the process of production has mastery over human beings, as opposed to being mastered by them.[74] In other words, capitalist production is organized by systemic imperatives that belong to the logic of the system as such, that appear to operate autonomously, and over which human beings do not exercise direct, conscious, collective, democratic, and planned control. The logical ordering of the system is what gives rise to the anarchy of the market, to which we seem subject as to a force of nature, which Dewey calls "a blind, chaotic and unplanned determinism." Although Dewey does not take up the rigors of Marxist value theory, he does identify the overarching imperative as "business conducted for pecuniary proft," the raison d'etre of capitalist production, and the singular imperative to which all other human, humane, and ecological imperatives are subordinated (or crushed when asserted too forcefully). The system itself is the locus of the externalized or alienated forces that dominate the lives of everyone who falls within its sway, regardless of class position. Dewey agrees with the Marxian assessment that capitalism oppresses us all, and not only the exploited working class.

Moreover, writing in 1930, Dewey understands that the era of laissez-faire capitalism is over, but this recognition does not prompt him to endorse a modified capitalism instead, the New Deal or the welfare state. Instead, in *Individualism Old and New*, he writes about a new capitalist corporatism, and in the same context from which I just quoted, he claims, "[w]e are in for some kind of socialism, call it by whatever name we please, and no matter what it will be called when it is realized."[75] Therefore, the choice he poses in this chapter, remarkably apropos of our present circumstances, is "between a socialism that is public and one that is capitalistic."[76] It is not oxymoronic to suggest that today, in the era of transnational corporations with revenues the size of the GDPs of several nation-states, we live in the "capitalistic socialism" Dewey envisioned—an economy planned by private interests according to the deep logic of the capitalist mode of production. Hence, Dewey writes, "[i]n reality, Karl Marx was the prophet of just this period of economic consolidation. If his ghost hovers above the American scene, it must find legitimate satisfaction in our fulfillment of his predictions."[77]

Dewey's socialist critique of corporate capitalism (or impending "capitalistic socialism") contextualizes his account of the "lost individual":

> . . . by it is meant a moral and intellectual fact that is independent of any manifestation of power in action. The significant thing is that the loyalties which once held individuals, which gave them support, direction and unity of outlook on life, have well-nigh disappeared. In consequence, individuals are confused and bewildered. It would be difficult to find in history an epoch as lacking in solid and assured objects of belief and approved ends of action as is the present.[78]

Dewey's "lost individual" is Bellah's "Lockean individual," Sandel's "unencumbered self," and MacIntyre's "individual *qua* individual," stripped of the "stable objects to which allegiance firmly attaches itself,"[79] and through which solid identity and personal meaning and purpose are attained.

Despite Dewey's broad descriptive agreements with the contemporary communitarians, then, what distinguishes his account from theirs is his unequivocal reference of the problem to its capitalist context and sources. By comparison, the account that Bellah and his coauthors develop in their chapter of *The Good Society* on "The Political Economy: Market and Work" is equivocal, ambivalent, and confused,[80] as I will briefly indicate by several points.

First, *The Good Society* does not fail to criticize capitalism; indeed, the chapter begins by comparing it to the Parker Brothers' board game, Monopoly.[81] It goes on to observe, if anemically, that "it has become clear that the market, left to itself, does not automatically result in human well-being."[82] The solution it proposes is "economic democracy,"[83] but the authors reassure the reader that "we are not arguing for an end to competition and achievement, any more than for an end to the market economy."[84] Hence, although they vaguely favor an "increasingly social ownership of corporate wealth,"[85] they fail to address the deep logic that will continue to produce just the opposite effect as long as it is in play.

Rather than develop a vigorous argument for a *real* economic democracy, then, the authors are intent to distinguish the laissez-faire form of capitalism from forms more amenable to public control. However, laissez-faire capitalism has been obsolete for most of the century, the Chicago School notwithstanding, so that attacking it is about like kicking a dead dog. Laissez-faire is long dead, but capitalism lives on. If it fails to be "economic democracy" anyway, then the task unmet in the authors' account is not to explain how unregulated, unplanned market competition, that is, something that does not exist, impedes the creation of a good society, but how its creation is impeded by the capitalism that does exist—the oligopolistic capitalism of transnational corporations, a capitalism that regulates and plans in spades, and which uses state instruments to do so (e.g., the NAFTA and the GATT).

Rather than focus on the logic of capital that leads from laissez-faire to flexible accumulation in the first place, *The Good Society* identifies the problem in what the authors call the "Lockean paradigm." Here they nearly glide into philosophical idealism: "Especially in the economic realm Americans find themselves under the pressure of market forces to which the only response seems submission. This is the ironic result of trying to live by the Locekan language of individualism in an institutional world it can no longer describe."[86] But neither the problem nor the solution is primarily a matter of linguistic reform, as Marx once had to remind his Young Hegelian contemporaries. Hence, the authors recognize that a "more active citizenship is not a matter of consciousness alone," but "requires the public will to reshape institutions." Having stated this exciting prospect, however, they blandly continue, "[w]e are all—corporations, workers, consumers —citizens in our economic life,"[87] as if the abstract category, "citizen," could neutralize the distinction between corporations and corporate interests on the one hand, and workers and working-class interests on the other, which belongs intrinsically to the logic of capital, and which we can find verified all around us every day. Only, neither the authors nor anyone else can verify it by disposing of the framework categories of "capital" and "labor," as the authors propose to do.

Finally, though the authors mention Marx by name once, rather than explore his critique of political economy, they are intent to rehabilitate the memory of Adam Smith.[88] No wonder, then, that they observe how "the French speak of American capitalism as ... 'savage capitalism,' "[89] as though French capitalism were somehow different in kind, as though a transnational capitalism owing no community allegiances at all had not arrived, and as though some other kind of capitalism were "civilized."

Bellah et al. will reply that after all, they never claimed to be Marxists or radicals, but reformers; that pointing this out to them hardly counts as critique; and that one need not be a Marxist or a socialist in order to criticize certain aspects of capitalism. On the other hand, like Dewey, they want to replace the "tyranny of the market" with "economic democracy,"[90] based on a new, communitarian paradigm in place of the Lockean, individualist one. This raises the question whether economic democracy can even be achieved within the framework of the capitalist mode of production. It is not a small point that Dewey did not think so, and it is this point that separates Dewey's from liberal communitarianism. An affirmative answer is dubious at best. *Real* economic democracy is really democratic socialism.

CONCLUSION

Marx and Dewey are philosophers of freedom, radical theorists of democracy, who understand democracy in communitarian terms. Although I do not argue the point here, radical democracy is inconsistent with any form of social oppression—including racism, sexism, heterosexism, or any other exclusionary, incipiently fascist form. Following Taylor, we could say that a communitarian democracy, far from being incompatible with a multiracial, multicultural society, is a "politics of recognition," neither "difference-blind," nor exclusivist and particularist. This point requires and deserves development beyond the scope of this essay.

Instead, my concern has been to argue that once we ask about the obstacles to radical democracy, we will inevitably come up against the capitalist mode of production and its totalizing logic. That logic gives both context and historical specificity to the particular forms oppression takes in the contemporary world.

A radically democratic theory, a genuinely left communitarianism, will confront the logic of capital directly, as distinct from a leftist postmodernism which, by sanctioning the dispersal of the subject, seems more to fulfill that logic than oppose it. Finally, by radicalizing the critical focus of the merely liberal versions of communitarianism, a left communitarianism, democratic socialism, may also have the potential to move us beyond liberal anguish, which laments the loss of identity and community but lacks the resources to redress it.

NOTES

1. Slavoj Zizek, *Tarrying with the Negative: Kant, Hegel, and the Critique of Ideology* (Durham, N.C.: Duke University Press, 1993), p. 216.

2. Cornel West, *Race Matters* (Boston: Beacon Press, 1993), p. 8.

3. Ibid., p. 5.

4. Ibid., p. 6.

5. Ibid., p. 5.

6. Ibid., p. 6.

7. Michael Sandel, "The Procedural Republic and the Unencumbered Self," *Political Theory* 12 (1984): 81–96.

8. Michael Walzer, in *Multiculturalism: Examining the Politics of Recognition*, ed. Amy Gutmann (Princeton: Princeton University Press, 1994), pp. 99–103. Here Walzer claims only to be "redescrib[ing]" Taylor's account in "The Politics of Recognition," included in the same volume, pp. 25–73.

9. Charles Taylor, "Cross-Purposes: The Liberal-Communitarian Debate," in *Liberalism and the Moral Life*, ed. Nancy Rosenblum (Cambridge: Harvard University Press, 1989), pp. 159–82, esp. pp. 171–72 and 179–82.

10. Amy Gutmann, "Communitarian Critics of Liberalism," in *Philosophy and Public Affairs* 14 (1985): 308.

11. Ibid., p. 309.

12. See Alasdair MacIntyre, *Whose Justice? Which Rationality?* (Notre Dame, Ind.: University of Notre Dame Press, 1988), esp. pp. 389–403.

13. *The Good Society* (New York: Random House, 1991), p. 6.

14. The second chapter of *The Good Society* is entitled, "The Rise and Fall of the American Century," pp. 52–81. As the authors explain, "By 'the Great Society,' Wallas meant the 'invisible environment' of communication and commerce that was linking the whole modern world in ever more coercive ways but was almost beyond human capacity to understand, much less to manage. For Wallas the great society was a neutral, indeed rather frightening, term for modernity" (p. 7). Wallas's account is not quite what Lyndon Johnson had in mind.

15. John Dewey, *The Public and Its Problems, in The Later Works, 1925–1953*, vol. 2, ed. Jo Ann Boydston (Carbondale: Southern Illinois University Press, 1988), pp. 327, 328.

16. John Dewey, *Liberalism and Social Action*, in *The Later Works, 1925–1953*, vol. 11, ed. Jo Ann Boydston (Carbondale, Ill: Southern Illinois University Press, 1991), pp. 5–65. With respect to Dewey's "left Hegelianism" and its bearing on his early support for "industrial democracy," Robert Westbrook, quoting Dewey's lecture notes, writes: "He told his students that the class divisions of industrial capitalism were incompatible with the ethics of democracy" (*John Dewey and American Democracy*, Ithaca, N.Y.: Cornell University Press, 1991, see esp. pp. 50–51).

17. For a *locus classicus*—one of many texts that could be cited—see Marx's introduction to the *Grundrisse*, trans. Martin Nicolaus (New York: Random House, 1973), pp. 82–85.

18. Ronald Aronson, *After Marxism* (New York: Guilford Press, 1995), p. 1.

19. Jacques Derrida, *Specters of Marx*, trans. Peggy Kampf (New York: Routledge, 1994). See esp. chap. 3, "wears and tears (tableau of an ageless world)," pp. 77–94. I readily concede that the sense in which Derrida's "new International" should be called a "community" is ambiguous. He does not mean by it an organized international working class movement, or a Sartrean fused group. He apparently intends something more protean, "made up of innumerable singular sites of suffering." (p. 85) Among his conclusions, he writes: "The name of new International is given here to what calls to the friendship of an alliance without institution among those who, even if they no longer believe or never believed in the socialist-Marxist International . . . continue to be inspired by at least one of the spirits of Marx or of Marxism." (pp. 85–86)

20. On "flexible accumulation," see David Harvey, *The Condition of Post-Modernity* (Cambridge: Basil Blackwell, 1989), and James L. Marsh, *Critique, Action, and Liberation* (Albany: SUNY Press, 1995), esp. pp. 291–312.

21. See Sidney Hook, *Towards the Understanding of Karl Marx* (New York: John Day, 1933); and "Why I am a Communist," *The Modern Monthly* 8 (1934): 143–65.

22. For the disclaimer, to the effect that the "we" and "you" of their text include everyone willing to "join [their] conversation," see *The Good Society*, pp. 17–18.

23. Ibid., p. 104.

24. Ibid., p. 105.

25. Ibid.

26. Ibid., p. 95.

27. Ibid.

28. Ibid., p. 106.

29. Ibid., pp. 94, 102. Why they call "capital" and "labor" "neoclassical" rather than "classical" categories, i.e., the ones developed by Smith, Ricardo, and Marx, is not explained in the text.

30. Peter Dews, *The Limits of Disenchantment: Essays on Contemporary European Philosophy* (New York: Verso, 1995), pp. 1–14.

31. In his essay on "Modernity, Self-Consciousness, and the Scope of Philosophy: Jürgen Habermas and Dieter Henrich in Debate," in ibid., pp. 169–93, Dews addresses a deep assumption that Habermas shares in common at least with his postmodern opponents (and perhaps we could also add Taylor). He writes, "One of the least noted features of the strife between Habermas and his postmodernist opponents over the 'philosophical dis-

course of modernity' is the number of assumptions which both sides share in common, despite the energy of the arguments between them" (p. 169).

32. Ibid., p. 2.

33. Ibid., p. 5.

34. For Taylor's account of "ontological holism," see "Cross-Purposes: the Liberal-Communitarian Debate," pp. 159–82; and for his account of the "politics of recognition," see "The Politics of Recognition," in *Multiculturalism: Examining the Politics of Recognition*, ed. Amy Gutmann (Princeton: Princeton University Press, 1994), pp. 25–73.

35. Taylor, "Politics of Recognition," p. 70.

36. See Habermas, *The Theory of Communicative Action: Reason and the Rationalization of Society* 1, trans. Thomas McCarthy (Boston: Beacon Press, 1984); and *Lifeworld and System: A Critique of Functionalist Reason* 2, trans. T. McCarthy (Boston: Beacon Press, 1987). Specifically on Habermas's strategy for fallibilistically establishing the "universal validity" of his formal pragmatics, see volume 1, pp. 137–41.

37. For Habermas's use of Mead, see *Lifeworld and System*, pp. 3–42. For Taylor's critique of the "monological ideal," see "Politics of Recognition," pp. 31–37. In particular, Habermas would agree with Taylor that "My own identity crucially depends on my dialogical relations with others" (p. 34).

38. Habermas's drift away from Marx is reflected, for example, in his "Excursus on the Obsolescence of the Production Paradigm" in *The Philosophical Discourse of Modernity*, trans. Frederick G. Lawrence (Cambridge: MIT Press, 1987), pp. 75–82. On the other hand, for an account that attempts to draw Habermas back to Marx, see Marsh, *Critique, Action, and Liberation*, esp. pp. 239–41 and chap. 13, "Is Late Capitalism Rational?," pp. 265–89. Marsh also criticizes the potential one-sidedness of Habermas's formalism, refuses the dichotomy between the right and the good, and argues instead for their dialectical mutuality and reciprocity in chap. 7, "The Right and the Good," pp. 113–24.

39. As Rawls once had to insist against his critics in "Justice as Fairness: Political Not Metaphysical," *Philosophy & Public Affairs* 14 (1985): 223–51.

40. Taylor, "Politics of Recognition," p. 43.

41. Ibid.

42. Ibid., p. 44.

43. Ibid., p. 61.

44. Ibid., pp. 43, 44.

45. Sandel, "Procedural Republic," pp. 83–85.

46. Ibid., p. 85.

47. Ibid., p. 87.

48. Ibid., pp. 87, 86. MacIntyre's critique of Rawls in *Whose Justice? Which Rationality?* parallels Sandel's, and it also traps liberalism in a dilemma very much like the one Taylor poses. See esp. chap. 17, "Liberalism Transformed into a Tradition," pp. 326–48.

49. Ibid., p. 87.

50. Quotations from *A Theory of Justice* (Cambridge: Harvard University Press, 1971) are from pp. 11 and 60 respectively.

51. Sandel, "Procedural Republic," pp. 89–90.

52. Richard Rorty, *Contingency, Irony, and Solidarity* (Cambridge: Cambridge University Press, 1989), p. 65.

53. Ibid., see p. 67.

54. Dews, *Limits of Disenchantment*, pp. 1–2. Dews's quotations of Rorty are taken from Richard Rorty, *Philosophical Papers Volume 1: Objectivity, Relativism and Truth* (Cambridge: Cambridge University Press, 1991), p. 193.

55. For a forcefully argued alternative view of the relationship between Rorty's project and Derrida's—one that seeks to disengage the latter from the former—see Bill Martin, *Humanism and Its Aftermath: The Shared Fate of Deconstruction and Politics* (Amherst, N.Y.: Humanity Books, 1995), esp. pp. 72–112. Martin persuasively insists that "it is simply not the case that Rorty's ironist theorizing represents a parallel to Derrida's work in analytic philosophy" (p. 101). If Rorty's path leads to a complacent liberalism, Derrida's definitely does not. The main text with which Martin works is *The Other Heading*. If anything, Derrida's *Specters of Marx* only strengthens Martin's reading.

56. Dews, *Limits of Disenchantment*, p. 10.

57. Ibid., pp. 10–11.

58. Ibid., p. 11.

59. Ibid., p. 6.

60. Ibid., pp. 6–7.

61. Ibid., p. 7.

62. Derrida, *Specters of Marx*, p. 59; emphasis added.

63. See ibid., pp. 56–75 for Derrida's scathing critique of Fukuyama. And see Francis Fukuyama, *The End of History and the Last Man* (New York: Macmillan, 1992). Fukuyama's book consists in an intepretation of Kojève's reading of Hegel's *Phenomenology of Spirit* grounded in the dialectic of master and slave, another version of the "politics of recognition." See "By Way of an Introduction," pp. xvi–xxiii.

64. Derrida, *Specters of Marx*, p. 85.

65. Ibid., pp. 13–14.

66. Zizek, *Tarrying With the Negative*, p. 216.

67. Karl Marx, "Private Property and Communism," included in *The Marx-Engels Reader*, 2d ed., ed. Robert Tucker (New York: W.W. Norton & Co., 1978), p. 87.

68. See Bellah et al., *Habits of the Heart: Individualism and Commitment in American Life* (Berkeley: University of California Press, 1985), esp. pp. 53–84.

69. Karl Marx, *Grundrisse*, see esp. pp. 483–514.

70. Dewey, *Individualism Old and New*, in *The Later Works, 1925–1953*, vol. 5, ed. Jo Ann Boydston (Carbondale, Ill: Southern Illinois University Press, 1988), pp. 41–123. His essay on "The Lost Individual," included here, pp. 66–76, originally appeared in *New Republic* 61 (1930): 294–96.

71. Ibid., p. 66.

72. Ibid.

73. Ibid., p. 98.

74. Marx makes this point, for example, in the fourth section of the first chapter of volume 1 of *Capital*, the famous section on the fetishism of commodities.

75. Dewey, *Individualism Old and New*, p. 98.

76. Ibid.

77. Ibid., p. 90.

78. Ibid., p. 66.

79. Ibid.

80. *The Good Society*, pp. 82–110.

81. Ibid., pp. 82–84.

82. Ibid., pp. 85.

83. Ibid., pp. 107 ff.

84. Ibid., p. 106.

85. Ibid., p. 104.

86. Ibid., pp. 85–86.

87. Ibid., p. 107.

88. Ibid., pp. 84–85, 92.

89. Ibid., p. 91.

90. Ibid., pp. 90–95, 107–110.

10

Antioppressive Politics and Group Hatreds

Frank Cunningham

W hen politics on the Left had only to concern itself with the *good* (the world's peoples) and the *bad* (their structural oppression on the basis of class, race, or gender) this was challenging enough. Now such politics is confronted as well with the *ugly*: violent ethno/national conflict of the sort which pervades eastern Europe. Of course, this is not the only place where conflict is sustained by group hatreds; nor is this a new phenomenon. But the explosions of violence in places like Bosnia, combined with their emergence from the background of socialism, make it less easy to categorize in traditional progressive terms. Moreover, the similarity of conflicts which divide populations in eastern Europe and the former Soviet Union to those between Jews and Arabs in the Middle East, Hindus and Muslims in South Asia, or Hutus and Tutsis in Central Africa, to mention some prominent examples, reinforces recent efforts of some progressive theorists to rethink these conflicts as well.[1]

In these situations there are persisting attitudes of mutual hostility, harbored by sufficiently large portions of a population to sustain aggressive, destructive, and self-destructive behavior of groups toward one another. While in all such conflicts there are undoubtedly villainous individuals and groups who commit terrible atrocities and hence deserve to be condemned, many if not all the conflicts involve participants who have gotten caught up in unjustified mutual enmity. Though each situation will have unique characteristics, they still exhibit similarities: appeal to real and mythical grievances, thirst for revenge, and blame on the part of each group for threats to one's standard of living, ethnic, national, or religious integrity.

One common approach to explaining such conflicts is that this is the "normal" human condition. Whether, as some of the sociobiologists would have it, xenophobia is a genetically inherited survival characteristic of human groups or group animosity is a cultural universal, as in René Girard's theory about revenge in human affairs, hatred-inspired conflict among groups should be expected; so the task is to explain how and why they are sometimes contained.[2] For adherents of this sort of approach, it is not surprising that ethnic violence followed the demise of socialism. The salient feature of that socialism (or of what went by this name) was its authoritarianism, which, like Hobbes' sovereign, forcibly restrained ethnic violence.

Such approaches face the same generic problem as do their Hobbesist analog. If a war of all against all is the natural human condition, then it is hard to see how nonaggressive behavior can ever be avoided. Accounts like the one appealing to authoritarian socialism can plausibly explain how this or that expression of antagonism is contained, but they do not get at the heart of the matter, which is to understand how *innately* hostile groups could ever coexist or even merge, for instance into common countries, long enough to generate solutions, whether authoritarian or something else. Neo-Hobbesists try to avoid this problem by viewing a state of war and the initial compact to contract out of it as hypothetical constructs useful for organizing thought about self-interest and cooperation. But in the case of violent group conflict, we are dealing with real historical processes. It is as if the Hobbesist needed to show it plausible that "ur-contracts" among warring individuals were actual events.

As to the authoritarian socialism explanation, a contrary case is that far from repressing ethnic hatreds, such socialism exacerbated or even caused them. Typically, this socialism set itself the task of obliterating the traditions of preexisting civil society (save specifically working class ones, and these selectively). The effect, however, was not to void people of ethnic, national, religious, regional, or other identifications but to drive them underground where desperation to preserve besieged identities became fanatic and the traditions' most intolerant dimensions were nurtured. It is true that in Yugoslavia overt commitment to different nationalities was permitted. However, this tolerance was artificial as long as it coexisted with a monopoly of state power on the part of the League of Communists. Also, socialist politics in the former Yugoslavia, especially after Tito's death, involved the manipulation of national loyalties in cynical and divisive ways that laid the basis for subsequent violent conflicts.[3]

Though this is not the place to prove it, I am inclined to believe that examination of the details of violent group antagonisms will always admit of an alternative account to the innate disposition one. If so, and in light of the generic consideration against an inherent human enmity thesis raised above, two alternative models recommend themselves. On one model the notion of innate or culturally universal tendencies to hostility is retained, but counteracting tendencies capable of compensating for them are also recognized. I favor another alternative model which is suspicious of claims to innate dispositions to anything as sociologically complex as group-identified hostility (or indifference or friendliness) and sees such attitudes as historically constructed. On either of these models, violent group conflict is viewed as a contingent affair. Whether a disposition to violence wins out over a counterdisposition or how enmity is constructed depend upon the constellation of circumstances within which groups find themselves.

Perhaps, then, ethnic or other instances of group violence are accidental. This is the view of Russell Hardin, whose *One for All* is among the few specifically philosophical efforts to address ethnic conflicts.[4] Hardin deploys rational choice theory to offer an alternative to accounts of such conflicts in terms of primordial hatreds. Central to Hardin's methodology is to distinguish among the identification of individuals with an ethnicity or nation, conflict among such groups, and violence in these conflictual interactions. Group identifications, according to him, are typically innocuous: It is rational for people to coordinate with a group in self-interested pursuit of goals they nonconflictually share with its members. The world's resources being scarce, however, groups find themselves in conflict. When conflict turns violent, enmity on the part of a group's members toward competing groups becomes itself a factor in their coordinating identifications with the tragic and self-perpetuating result of continuing violence. Whether or when conflict turns, or as Hardin puts it, "tips," into violence is a matter of historical accident.

Of course, if the alternative to being accidental is being genetically or historically fated, then rejection of the innate disposition thesis leaves only accident. The point of summarizing Hardin's view is to challenge such a dichotomy. He allows that, once started, violence can in turn affect people's identifications, seeing this as a "feedback" mechanism which complicates but does not compromise the basic analytic scheme within which primitive group identification is a matter of self-interest, neither benevolent nor malevolent in intent. Insufficiently treated, in my view,[5] is the relation between group identification and his second component, conflict. As is well known to students of class formation, race and racism, or feminism, class, race, and gender identities are always complexes involving both "inward"- and "outward"-looking dimensions in various admixtures within which the outward components often involve not just differentiation from groups defined by reference to alternate identities, but are also defensively formed in reaction to class, racial, and gender oppression. In the case of race, for example, it is plausibly argued by some that the very category is an oppressive construct.[6]

To the extent that conflict is thus implicated in group identities and is bred of oppression, neither identity formation nor violence is properly described as accidental. This follows from the systematic (or structural or systemic) nature of oppression. What makes the thwarting of people's aspirations, narrowing of their life options, or in general the imposition of unhappiness solely by virtue of their gender, race, or class especially pernicious is that this is not only or primarily due to the activities of individuals who happen to harbor prejudices or to be malicious or greedy. Rather, it results from structures and dynamics of domination. Counter-oppressive theorists have discovered some general features of such dynamics, as in Marxist explications of class oppression. Ongoing debates among antioppression theorists about the remote origins and workings of such dynamics and about the interaction of class, race, and gendered oppressions sometimes obscures the progress in research over the last decades in understanding how these oppressions are nonaccidental.

Individuals whose identities are partly formed in the midst of oppressive conflicts do not just happen to identify with some group to reap advantage from it, but find themselves unavoidably reacting to domination. The insidious violence of everyday oppression is already present in group conflicts, and even if the specific forms of more overt and organized violence are not predetermined, such quotidian violence provides a generally favorable climate for it. A sufficiently determined antinationalist or someone who thinks that ethnic identifications are always pernicious might want to classify national or ethnic chauvinism as themselves structurally oppressive, exhibiting dynamics analogous to those of class or gender oppressions. But successful defense of this contested orientation toward national and ethnic identities is not required to locate effects of structured oppression within ethnic or national conflicts. Sometimes these will be direct, as when racist attitudes fuel aggression. Class conflict is often proximately involved in the genesis of ethno/national strife, as is illustrated by the exacerbation of ethnic or national differences by imperialist forces—fine-tuned with devastating and lasting results, especially by British colonialism. Other times, oppressive dimensions of group conflicts are also remote, as for example in the subjugation of Palestinians by Israel, which has clear class-based features.

Success in finding elements of structured conflicts within ethno/national hostilities suggests a third orientation toward them, namely that they are nothing but effects or even disguised forms of the more obviously systematic subjugations. I know of nobody in recent years who is prepared so starkly to articulate this thesis, and I speculate that the reason for this is to be found in the recent history of polemics among antioppressive theorists. First, feminists successfully criticized class reductionism, and then antiracists exposed shades of a analogous reductionism among some feminists; the result has been a general suspicion of reductionism. Theorists like Eric Hobsbawm who claim that ethnic or national identities are largely "imagined"[7] could be viewed as providing part of an argument in support of such a reductionist position if it were further maintained that class or other interests entirely dictate what identities are in fact imagined into existence. But Hobsbawm himself does not advance such an argument. Nor does he deny that ethnic or national conflicts possess a life of their own.

I have, however, encountered a practical analogue of theoretical reductionism, sometimes quite strongly expressed, in discussions with some activists from conflict-ridden places. On the characterization of group hatreds sketched above, it was specified that hatred on the popular level, in addition to being generally destructive, is also mutually unjustified. A defense of practical reductionism can be constructed by challenging the applicability of this characterization in cases where one group is subject to structured oppression. The defense (which I shall frame in general terms because I believe that its actual proponents have been right to identify themselves as members of oppressed groups, and in criticizing them I do not want to give aid and comfort to apologists from oppressor groups) may adduce one or both of two grounds for justifying violent animosity.

When people are oppressed and when their oppression is partly sustained by popular level enmity on the part of members of a group which profits from their oppression, even if not all of them directly instigate it, then return hatred is not just explicable, but justified. Additionally or alternatively, it may be argued that in virtue of the defensively weak position which being an oppressed group involves, those wishing to resist or overcome oppression must and should make use of whatever limited number of weapons are at their disposal, and one such weapon is hatred of people from the oppressor group. In its most extreme form, such an argument supports terrorism. Short of this, one might appeal to a putative requirement of enmity for solidarity, maintaining in addition that it is sociologically unrealistic to expect such enmity to be selectively directed only toward individuals directly and knowingly complicit in oppression.

Now, it is within the grasp even of a North American, white, middle-class, male academic to understand how many people in circumstances quite foreign to the sheltered ones he enjoys could come to think in these ways. However, I shall take it that whatever counteroppressive results might come of such attitudes, they are massively outweighed by their negative effects. In the long term, perpetuation of enmity among people who must interact (and in a shrinking world this means more than just inhabiting shared or adjacent territory) can only be mutually detrimental. But enmity cannot be turned on and off like tap water, as is evidenced by the force of appeals among a populace to century-old animosities in current conflicts. In the short term, hatred as a weapon, in addition to its consequences for affected innocent victims, always backfires and becomes a sustaining cause of oppression, as when it impedes otherwise attainable negotiated resolutions or denies oppressed people allies from within an oppressor group. That the hostility of the oppressed which has this consequence is understandable just illustrates one more way that continuing oppression is systemic.

It must be allowed that group hatreds are not easily reversed, especially when they are sustained by oppressive relations and exacerbated by cycles of atrocity and revenge. South Africa offers hope that such reversal may nonetheless be possible. Here we have a situation where vengeful hatred of whites by blacks could most easily be comprehended: decades of economic deprivation, social degradation, and police brutality from which even ordinary minority white citizens so obviously profited that it is hard to see ignorance on their part as anything but willful. Yet despite fears of widespread vengeful malice, one sees instead what can only be interpreted as sincere efforts at reconciliation by the majority of blacks, and this not withstanding the retention of much privilege, at least by the wealthy whites. The relation between South African whites and blacks has been one of straightforward racist oppression and hence is not exactly the sort of conflict of concern in this essay; tribal and other conflicts within the black population or earlier ones between Anglos and Boers among whites are closer. This makes black determination to achieve reconciliation all the more remarkable.

For these theoretical and practical reasons, I believe the reductionist interpretation of the relation between structured oppressions and group hatreds should be avoided,[8] as should the opinion that violent group conflicts are fated by human nature or are matters of mere accident. Instead I suggest an orientation in which such conflicts and the enmity that fuels them are in a relation of mutual support with oppressions. The situation might be pictured as a triangle, involving antagonistic conflict between ethno/national groups, attitudes of animosity on the part of their members, and oppressive relations within and between groups, where each side of the "triangle" serves to support the other two sides. Such a picture is not difficult to substantiate: Hatreds spark or sustain violent conflicts, just as group conflicts breed mutual enmity. Class oppression at least exacerbates group conflicts, while (as dramatically illustrated on a large scale in the First World War) chauvinistic national or ethnic group attachments and antagonisms deny the unity required to counter class oppression. In addition to impeding class unity, racism and sexism feed group conflicts and hatreds, as when antagonists classify one another in racist terms and abuse of women is employed as a weapon of war, and in turn racism and sexism are reinforced by the conflicts.

I take these observations to be noncontentious. What is disputed are claims about the basic or ultimate relations among all these factors. Setting aside mono-causal accounts, with their unavoidably reductionist implications, two generic alternatives suggest themselves. Somebody might identify one or more features on one "side" of this triangle of factors as causally primary but subject to reactive influence by the other factors. For instance, Girard identifies mimetic desire as primary, or a version of psychoanalytic theory thus designates aggression, while in each case these are subject to modification or containment. Mainstream political-scientific conflict theory takes conflict between groups as primary. Class- or gender-based antioppressive theories typically identify one or more form of oppression as causally basic. Alternatively, yet deeper, underlying causes of the entire interactive complex might be adduced. Genetic explanations of sociobiology are sometimes framed in this way. A philosophical example may be seen in Hegel, who regarded such elements as interacting within a developing cosmic evolutionary process. (Whether Marx's theory was a secular version of this type of approach or one that takes one form of oppression as basic depends upon how he viewed the relation between working class oppression and overarching historical laws.)

Were a full account of the origin and nature of violent group conflicts being sought, I imagine that a stand on some version of one of these approaches (or of an alternative approach if someone disagrees that they and the monocausal theories exhaust the field) would have to be defended and applied to sufficient instances of the conflicts to make out a decisive case. Armed with such a theory, it might be possible to devise a strategy for eliminating violent group conflicts forever from all parts of the globe. (Of course, depending on its content, possession of this theory could instead be of limited use: A proven meteorological theory may tell you when to carry an umbrella, but it won't enable you to stop the rain.) A virtue of pragmatism was to indicate a way out of the impasse that in order to act one needed full knowledge at the most fundamental level. That such an impasse must be surmountable is indicated by the fact that successful practical projects—in science, technology, politics, and everyday social interactions—are regularly carried through based on limited knowledge. Regarding the interrelations of group hatreds and structured oppressions it seems to me that sufficient knowledge of the latter is available to suggest fruitful directions for one sort of practical task.

This task is to find resources within democratic practices, institutions and cultures to head off, confine, or reverse violent ethno/national conflicts. Pragmatic approaches are especially apt in the case of democratic politics if democracy is considered a process in which all aspects of human interaction are involved. On this conception, a radically foundationist approach according to which first some social or political theory is proven and then democratic politics are fashioned on its basis is doomed to backfire. One does not need to appeal to philosophical antifoundationism to substantiate this claim. One reason for suspicion of a foundationist approach to democracy is that it invites putting democracy on hold, so to speak, until its foundational guarantees are found. But, as political analogs of such a strategy have most unfortunately shown in the authoritarian socialist cases, once shelved, democracy is not easily invigorated. Suspicion is further vindicated if the pursuit of social or political theory is itself implicated in human interactions such that success requires openness to public input and is impeded by technocratic isolation of social theorists from such engagement.

At first sight, democratic solutions to the problem at hand might be regarded the least promising in light of the fact that the violent ethnic strife we see in the former Soviet bloc followed democratization, and in several conflict-ridden countries, political leaders who openly cater to chauvinistic sentiment have won elections. As an orienting hypothesis one might press a theory, also to be found in pragmatic theory at least as explicated by Dewey, and by some socialist theorists, most notably, C. B. Macpherson.[9] This hypothesis, which I call the "democratic fix," depends on some key features of the conception of democracy as a process.[10] One of these is that democracy is not something that a society either entirely has or lacks, but is, rather, a process admitting of degrees. This means that when a certain measure of public input to the constitution or conduct of government contributes to violence, it is at least conceivable that this is not due to excessive democracy but to insufficient measures and kinds of democratic participation.

For example, faced with the election of chauvinists, the democratic-fix thesis suggests that deficiencies in local electoral practices (the political party structure and nomination procedures, voter eligibility, media coverage, accountability, availability of extraparliamentary forms, and so on) impede the ability of those with pacifistic values from expressing their will. Chauvinists, once in political power, then contribute to a downward spiral with respect both to democracy and violence. Such a spiral, I submit, is just what has marked eastern Europe since 1989.

A practical recommendation following from this feature of the democratic-fix hypothesis is that formal and informal means allowing affected people in conflict-torn parts of the world to make their wills felt should be secured or strengthened. Certainly such empowerment would give voice to some who, in the grips of hatred, favor violent confrontation, but it is hard to see how this would make a difference to the current situations. On the other hand, empowerment of larger majorities could have pacifistic effects, as in the demonstrations in Bosnia which in 1992 forced peace negotiations. That the negotiations were short-lived illustrates not that people's commitment to nonviolence was weak, but that they had insufficient control over leaders bent on combat.

Other features of democracy relate more directly to the relation between ethno/national hatreds and group oppression. Democracy on the conception here being employed is unlimited. In terms of means, democracy is not confined to formal, electoral politics but is appropriate whenever people who share some social environment—a country, a city, a neigborhood, a family, membership in an organization or religious institution, and so on—attempt jointly to make the environment as much as possible conform to their wishes. This might be by means of party politics or formal voting, but it might also be by informal discussion and debate, by organization into social movements, or by mass actions such as demonstrations or strikes.

Moreover, the objects of democratic concern are not confined just to what is sometimes called the "public realm"—government policy regarding public services and the means to administer and finance them—but may be directed as well to the comportment and culture of groups and individuals in such "private" domains as the workplace, school, or family. Whatever stand one takes on the proper location of a line between the public and the private (or on whether there should be any such line), it can be agreed that democratic action is appropriate to each realm. Putting these two features of democracy together means that such things as campaigns of antiracist or women's movements to combat discriminatory practices and attitudes in popular culture are democratic campaigns.

The significance of this feature will be evident after summarizing a final aspect of democracy regarded as a process, namely that its effectiveness does not require decisiveness, but it does require openness. Those who view thoroughgoing consensus or realization of a Rousseauean General Will as the end of democracy are bound to be disappointed when it becomes clear that such universal consensus is perpetually elusive. A realistic aim of democracy is not to eliminate conflict but to make it possible to confront it nonantagonisticly. A "democratic ideal" may, and I think should, retain room for achieving consensus, but it must also keep open the possibility for reaching mutually acceptable compromises among groups or individuals in conflict.

Democratic confrontation of violent group conflicts is rendered feasible when it is recognized that one may have to be reconciled to living with conflict, so a main task is to find and maintain formal and informal channels and mechanisms for negotiation. However, access to such channels is to no avail unless contending parties wish to take advantage of them. Group hatreds are thus especially threatening to democracy because they do not admit of such compromise: only humiliation, dispersal, or obliteration of the hated group is acceptable. This means that democratic solutions cannot be sought without attention to the motives of those who are to take advantage of them.

One way to come at this problem is by interrogation of group identities. I assume that individuals importantly recognize themselves in terms of group identifications, but no individual identifies with (or, as theorists would have it, is constituted by) one group alone. Somebody may identify with any combination of an ethnicity, nationality, class, profession, religion, linguistic community, gender, generation, region, and so on, with varying and changing priorities. Groups comprised of people who share at least their highly prioritized identifications may have a range of attitudes toward other groups from friendly feelings to hostility, and conflicts over material or cultural resources may be peacefully negotiated or addressed with violence.

Whether the latter response is avoided will importantly depend upon what constellation of identifications jointly constitute the individuals involved. For instance, when people centrally integrate a religious identification with the state, the resulting theocratic identity will block avenues of negotiation about the sharing of state power, because such sharing would be threatening to the theocrat's very identity. Or when national or ethnic identifications are integrated with attachment to a territory, seeking ways that a land might be cohabited with those of another nationality or ethnicity will likewise be precluded. It is thus an important task to impede or avoid such integrations.

A tempting strategy, which I shall label "holistic," is to try dismantling the identifications that could come into pernicious combination and replacing them with universalistic ones. Militant humanistic secularism is a strategy of this sort regarding religion, as is internationalism of the World Federalist variety or versions of working-class antinationalism. Sometimes an ethos of overriding commitment to universal liberal-individualistic values is prescribed. An alternative strategy, exhibited in the work of left communitarian–leaning social theorists such as Michael Walzer or Charles Taylor,[11] advocates cultural politics from within existing identifications. Unless such a theorist thought that there exists some formula which, when applied to the values of any tradition, guaranteed weeding out its exclusionary dimensions, this strategy will be "piecemeal." It will work away at existing group identifications by various means, always with the aim of encouraging impulses conducive to accommodation and impeding those contrary to it.

I wish now to indicate how informal democratic politics with respect to race, class, and gender may contribute to this admittedly challenging task. Of course, antiracist, working-class, or antisexist politics may be carried on in more or less democratic ways, but the impulse behind such politics is of its nature democratic:

the effort significantly to enhance the control that large categories of people can have over their futures. Also, I believe it not difficult to show that when such antioppressive campaigns are themselves undemocratically pursued, this overall aim is subverted.

A clear model concerns racism, about which two observations are in order. First, racism supports violent ethno/national conflict. Despite the portrayal of murder and mayhem as a first resort to problems of human interaction in popular entertainment media, it is no small feat for a population to engage in or support the displacement, degradation, torture, or murder of other populations. Hence, it is no surprise that in most, if not all, situations of violent group conflict, opposing groups are characterized in a racist way. The dehumanization that racism entails makes otherwise inhuman acts possible. That Palestinians are regarded in a racist way by some Israelis or that Albanian Muslims are thus regarded by some Serbs or Croats when the similarities between the relevant peoples on any of the standard criteria of "race" (themselves of dubious objectivity) far outweigh their differences is no more than an extreme form of racist attitudes generally.

A second observation is that internal racism supports external racism. Without attempting to summarize a fully developed theory of racist culture[12] suffice it to note that racist attitudes provide those in their grips with a simple way of dividing a threatening social world. Like some other central orienting divisions, racism establishes boundaries between those worthy of inclusion in one's society and those to be excluded. Racist attitudes are unique dividers in regarding those to be excluded or combatted as threats to one's way of life and as somehow humanly inferior. Moreover, the markers of such aliens are invariably distinguished by their superficiality. It is this superficiality that makes for the attractive simplicity of a racist viewpoint. Thus skin color is the prototypical racist divider, to the extent that when attention to alternative markers, such as religious or national ones, takes on racist characteristics, it is not unusual for the racist to misperceive the skin pigmentation of the threatening others, as for example when Jews were regarded black in Medieval Europe.

Usually, if not always, racist viewpoints are "learned" at home, but their power in organizing one's local world makes it attractive to transpose racism to external threats (as in nearly all modern wars), and the flexibility allowed by the superficiality of racist markers enables the racist easily to expand markers initially attached to "enemies" within one's society to those without or to seize on new markers with the same desperate ferocity to which he or she had already been habituated. When societies interpenetrate, as in all the current eastern European cases, such transference is all the easier, and internally and externally directed racism reinforce one another. The evident conclusion to draw from this is that to the extent that group hatreds are supported by racism, local antiracist campaigns—including ones that do not have as their immediate concern racist attitudes involved in some specific group conflict—have the potential of removing or weakening at least this degree of support. I shall return to the significance of this claim after advancing some more hypotheses about class and gender based oppression.

Tensions between Anglo Canadians and Franco Quebeckers only rarely approach what could be called group hatred, and despite the seeming intractability of a perpetual constitutional crisis, the Bosnification of Canada can probably be avoided. But this will be no thanks to indigenous capitalists. As if to vindicate a conspiracy theory long abandoned by radical theorists, the largest Canadian capitalist enterprises have organized themselves into an association called the Business Council on National Issues (BCNI), which, working closely with the country's nearly hegemonic right-wing press, has energetically pursued a neoliberal campaign that in recent years has seen the entry of Canada into the North American Free Trade Agreement, the weakening of the trade union movement, regressive tax "reform," dramatic reduction in social services, and the election of Thatcher-type provincial governments. Recently, this association has overtly entered the constitutional debates by joining right-wing political leaders to push a solution to a vexing problem nearly everyone grants has plagued the country since Confederation.

A relatively strong central government has maintained cohesion and public services for a small Canadian population spread over a large land base. Because this population is divided into regions, roughly corresponding to provinces, each with special needs and more or less unique cultures, there have always been demands from each province for special powers to meet its needs. As in any such federation, a continuing problem is to find the right balance between decentralization of powers and maintaining the advantages of central governmental control. But in Canada the situation is more complex, because Confederation in 1867 brought together two national groups, the dominant Anglo communities and the Franco nation conquered by British forces in the previous century. This means that Quebec is not a province like the others. In particular, special efforts are required to protect its French language and attendant culture. Until recently, Quebec's economy had been dominated from Anglo Canada, thus breeding resentment, for instance over the fact that English was the unofficial language of work and that major industries, resources, and so on were owned by Anglo Canadians. A result is that Quebec has twice elected separatist governments and in 1995 a majority of its francophone population voted for sovereignty in a referendum.

This greatly exacerbates the centralization/decentralization problem: If Quebec is treated like all the other provinces, it will not have sufficient powers to conduct its affairs in a way that is satisfactory to its majority Franco population, but if Quebec is given special powers sufficient to this end, other provinces demand equal special treatment.[13] The BCNI's solution to this problem is radical devolution of powers both to Quebec and to the other provinces as well. In a publication of essays by radical philosophers I should not need to labor the point that this "solution" has very little to do with national interests and a lot to do with a current global neoconservative agenda. With devolution comes diminution of social services and weakened environmental, labor, health, and other regulations.

The BCNI does not disguise the fact that these will be the results of its plan, but maintains in a now-familiar way that they are required to free capital, attract investment, encourage competition, and other such things putatively to the long-range benefit of the country. Unfortunately, this plan is more than just the rhetoric of right-wing think tanks but is strongly endorsed by current conservative provincial governments, and devolution of powers with concomitant loss of services and central control has already been implemented by successive federal governments. So here we have class politics intersecting with national tensions.

To see how this relates to the question of democracy and group identities it will be useful to employ Macpherson's conception of possessive individualism. He described the evolution in nascent capitalism of a conception of human nature wherein people saw their powers as commodities to be bought and sold in the interests of accumulating other commodities in competition with each other. Against this image Macpherson pitted an alternative, vying with possessive individualism in liberal-democratic (and earlier) thinking, according to which a satisfying life consisted in the development of human powers for such things as friendship, learning, or the production and enjoyment of art and other cultural goods, for which people need not be in competition, but which can be enjoyed in common.[14]

Group identifications have the potential to support an antipossessive individualist culture because they have built into them the goal of common enjoyment and production of shared cultural goods. Of course, they also have destructive potentials, if part of the identification is enmity toward other groups: thus the problem central to this essay about how the later might be impeded. Hardin's solution is to encourage laissez-faire capitalism. Citing Adam Smith he avers that, "we make a better world by ignoring what kind of world we make and living for ourselves than if we concentrate first on the ethnic political structure of our world."[15] In promoting their individual self-interest people will turn away from such things as national identifications, which on Hardin's view are unavoidably exclusionary. Hardin's prescription is called into question by developments in postsocialist eastern Europe, where militant procapitalism, far from displacing exclusionary nationalism, has been coextensive with its proliferation. This suggests to me that

possessive individualist values can not only coexist with antagonistic group identifications, but might reinforce or cause them. If a project of voiding people of
self-defining group identifications is hopelessly unrealistic, then the question is
not whether they will thus identify but whether they will do so in a way that is hostile to others or not.

That the BCNI's recommendation for devolution is attached by it to demands
for provincial and regional autonomy contributes to the integration of possessive-
individualist values with provincial and regional identifications. The Quebec "distinctness" problem is to be solved by getting the federal government out of the way
of interregional and provincial participation in free-market capitalist competition.
The social psychology engendered by public forum advocacy of such a plan is both
to encourage people to think of the regional or national groups with which they
identify as necessarily, and indeed desirably, in competition with others, and also to
regard such group identification instrumentally as a tool for individual competition. This conclusion is reinforced by noting that just as this sort of psychology is
encouraged outside of Quebec by the likes of the BCNI, so a similar orientation is
developing in Quebec itself, where neoliberal business interests within the sover-
eignist forces have largely overwhelmed its social-democratic wing.

As in the case of racism, not all negative aspects of national or other group
identifications can be attributed to class-generated values like possessive individualism. Nor would the eradication of such values eliminate attitudes of group
enmity. However, if the story recounted above has any force at all, it illustrates
how combatting neoliberal projects such as those of the BCNI—that is, if I may
dare to put it this way, engaging in class struggle—can help to prevent pernicious
group values and thus facilitate confrontation of conflicts among groups in a
democratic way. Interprovincial negotiations and those between Quebec and the
rest of Canada would no doubt remain messy, but they would still be negotiations.

A distressing feature of nearly all ethno/national conflict that turns violent is
that they involve rape. What is more, the rape involved has an especially terrible character. Some soldiers in all wars take advantage of the situation they find themselves
in to rape women of conquered territory. This is bad enough, but in violent ethnic
conflicts, such as in Bosnia, rape is more planned and systematic, centrally including
public humiliation and degradation and always especially brutal.[16] Feminist theorists
have provided useful insights into the relation between war and gender oppression,
aiming to show not just that war carries with it violence against women during a war,
but that militaristic thinking in general is implicated in sexist conceptions of gender
and that these latter conceptions are themselves conducive to war.[17] Such research
invites speculation on the relation of gender to ethno/national violence.

One provocative theory in this regard is that of Rada Ivekovic, who challenges a theory held by many feminists that in war the aggressor nation symbolizes the aggressed-against nation as a woman to be violated. Ivekovic criticizes this view, not exactly for being wrong but for missing a prior implication of gender in the construction of nationalism. At least the "radical nationalisms" of the former Yugoslavia, on her view, are born of a male attempt to achieve self-sufficiency by denying men's dependence on women. (The nation is falsely regarded an original and self-sufficient entity and defined as essentially opposed to other nations in a way that is modeled on hostility of men toward women for threatening their own self-sufficiency.)[18] Whatever its merits as a theory about the origins of nationalism, this thesis is suggestive in focusing on the relation between sexist and nationalist conceptions. In particular, it suggests to me that the unique characteristics of rape in ethno/national conflicts can be explained by reference to an integration of gender and nation or ethnicity in the group identities of its perpetrators.

This rape is intended to humiliate the opposing national or ethnic group in degrading its women. But if one can degrade "their nation" by degrading "their women," this must mean that they could degrade "our nation" by similarly degrading "our women" (and, indeed, often the attacks are reciprocal). In both cases, the actual women of each national or ethnic group are reified and regarded just insofar as they are taken to represent the group, and this, moreover, in a sexist, possessive way. Were women of each group viewed as full human beings, each herself a complex individual whose own identity is constituted by diverse identifications, perhaps including her national or ethnic group but perhaps not and in any case also including other identifications, among them ones she shares with women and men of other ethnicities or nationalities,[19] this would no doubt constitute a large step toward dismantling sexist attitudes toward women in general.

In addition this would have two consequences specific to the group hatreds problem: It would render pointless the "strategy" of national humiliation by rape, and it would call into question the exclusionary aspect of an ethno/national identification. This aspect depends upon an assumption by members of a national or ethnic group that all of them share commitment to the group as a top or at least as a nonsacrificable priority; those suspected of not harboring this value are ostracized or marginalized. It would be threatening enough to an exclusionary identification to allow that a large part of the population, and moreover its women, who are supposed to be guardians of tradition at the hearth, shared loyalties with people of other groups. It would be devastating to recognize that some of them genuinely identify with the group at the same time. Such recognition is challenging to the monolithic character of hatred-prone group identifications, that is to the very characteristic which makes such things as sharing a territory or state power unthinkable from within them.

I have taken the example of rape as one instance of sexist oppression implicated in violent group conflicts, albeit an especially prevalent and terrible one. No doubt there are other examples, just as racism and class oppression may reinforce group hatreds in several ways as may other forms of structured oppressions not treated in this paper. I hope the examples offer reason to believe that in all such cases structured oppressions reinforce group violence. For those who wish to extricate their societies from group hatred driven violence, or to support those embarked on such an effort elsewhere, or to avert group conflicts from turning to violence in their own societies (and nobody should be complacent on this score), I hope that I have also given reasons for taking structured oppressions as seriously as the group hatreds themselves.

The practical consequence of such a stance is to resist a temptation to prioritize, that is, first to seek an honorable peace (or any kind of peace) and then turn to problems of sexism, racism, or class oppression in one's own and others' national or ethnic group. Even if structured oppressions do not cause group hatreds, they reinforce them in such a way that confronting the hatreds, and especially confronting them in a democratic way, is at the very least immeasurably assisted by confronting these oppressions at the same time. Between combatting the bad and the ugly one need not and should not make a choice.

NOTES

1. Some examples among many are Svetozar Stojanovic, *The Fall of Yugoslavia: Why Communism Failed* (Amherst, N.Y.: Prometheus Books, 1977); Iftikhar Malik, *State and Civil Society: Politics of Authority, Ideology, and Ethnicity* (New York: St. Martin's Press, 1997); and the essays in Doug Allen, *Religion and Political Conflict in South Asia* (Westport, Conn.: Greenwood Press, 1992). I discuss this topic in a general way in "Group Hatreds and Democracy," in *Squaring the Circle*, ed. Daniel Avnon & Avner de Shallit (New York: Routledge, 1998).

2. A representative sociobiological argument is that of Richard Alexander, *Darwinism and Human Affairs* (Seattle: University of Washington Press, 1979); René Girard's classic text is *Violence and the Sacred* (Baltimore: Johns Hopkins Press, 1979; French language original, 1973).

3. See the account of Stojanovic, *The Fall of Yugoslavia*.

4. Russell Hardin, *One For All: The Logic of Group Conflict* (Princeton: Princeton University Press, 1995).

5. I have criticized Hardin's approach in a review essay of his book in *The Canadian Journal of Philosophy* 27, no. 4 (Dec. 1997): 571–94.

6. Among the many who argue this are Étienne Balibar and Immanuel Wallerstein, *Race Nation and Class* (London: Verso, 1991); see the chapters of part 1.

7. Eric Hobsbawn, *Nations and Nationalism since 1780* (Cambridge: Cambridge University Press, 1990).

8. Chapter 9 of my *Democratic Theory and Socialism* (Cambridge: Cambridge University Press, 1987) argues against reductionism in general and "practical" reductionism in particular.

9. The most pertinent work of Dewey is *The Public and Its Problems* (Denver: Alan Swallow, 1927); Macpherson's fullest statement of his view of democracy is in *Democratic Theory: Essays in Retrieval* (Oxford: Calendon Press, 1973).

10. That democracy is a process with the features claimed for it is argued for by me in *Democratic Theory and Socialism and in The Real World of Democracy Revisited and Other Essays on Democracy and Socialism* (Amherst, N.Y.: Humanity Books, 1994).

11. Pertinent works by Charles Taylor are *Reconciling the Solitudes: Essays on Canadian Federalism and Nationalism* (Montreal and Kingston: Queen's-McGill University Press, 1993) and "The Politics of Recognition," in *Multiculturalism,* ed. Amy Gutman (Princeton: Princeton University Press, 1994); among pertinent works of Michael Walzer are his *The Company of Critics: Social Criticism* and *Political Commitments in the 20th Century* (New York: Basic Books, 1988) and *Thick and Thin* (Notre Dame: University of Notre Dame Press, 1994).

12. David Goldberg's *Racist Culture: Philosophy and the Politics of Meaning* (Oxford: Blackwell, 1993) provides a good survey and critique of various viewpoints (chapter 4). I adopt his focus on "exclusion" as essential to racism, but for the purpose at hand I focus on the superficiality of racism and specify that those excluded are regarded as a threat.

13. A good recent treatment of the dilemma Quebec poses for Canadian Confederation is by Kenneth McRoberts, *Misconceiving Canada: The Struggle for National Unity* (Toronto: Oxford University Press, 1997.)

14. Macpherson, *Democratic Theory*, pp. 52–57.

15. Hardin, *One for All*, p. 179.

16. See the essays in Alexandra Stiglmayer, ed., *Mass Rape: The War against Women in Bosnia-Herzegovina* (Lincoln, Neb.: University of Nebraska Press, 1993).

17. Useful texts are Miriam Cooke and Angela Woolacott, eds., *Gendering War Talk* (Princeton: Princeton University Press, 1993) and Jean Vickers, *Women and War* (London: Zed Books, 1993).

18. Rada Ivekovic, "Women, Nationalism and War: 'Make Love Not War,'" *Hypatia* 8, no. 4 (fall 1993): 113–26.

19. See the testimony by Bat-Ami Bar On, "Meditations on National Identity," *Hypatia* 9, no. 2 (spring 1994): 40–62.

11

Prisons, Profit, Crime, and Social Control

A Hermeneutic of the Production of Violence[1]

Stephen Hartnett

"The first man who, having enclosed a piece of land, thought of saying 'This is mine' and found people simple enough to believe him, was the true founder of civil society. How many crimes, wars, murders; how much misery and horror the human race would have been spared if someone had pulled up the stakes and filled in the ditch and cried out to his fellow men: 'Beware of listening to this impostor. You are lost if you forget that the fruits of the earth belong to everyone and that the earth itself belongs to no one'."
—Jean-Jacques Rousseau, *A Discourse on Inequality*, 1754[2]

"Rage is indeed the only form in which misfortune can become active . . .[yet] rage is not only impotent by definition, it is the mode in which impotence becomes active in its last stages of despair."
— *Hannah Arendt, On Revolution, 1963*[3]

I t is painfully evident that the correctional-industrial complex (1) has not proven effective at rehabilitating prisoners, (2) has not lowered crime rates and in fact bears no relationship to crime rates, (3) has coincided with the most profound escalation of violence among poor young men aged sixteen to twenty in our national history, and (4) has pursued imprisonment patterns that indicate deeply racist practices.[4] Despite these obvious failures, the correctional-industrial complex has nonetheless become one of the most heavily capitalized sectors of the U.S. economy. For example, the National Council on Crime and Delinquency estimates that state and federal expenditures on prisons over the next ten years will amount to $351 *billion.*[5] Given the dramatic failures mentioned above, and considering that even despite these failures the correctional-industrial-complex continues to expand at an historically unprecedented rate, it would appear that a legitimate question is "on what grounds can our society legitimate prison?"

The available data demonstrate clearly that this question cannot be answered via appeals to rational discourse regarding either judicial or criminological premises. Indeed, the Bureau of Justice Statistics reports that while imprisonment rates have doubled since 1980,[6] "the level of violent crime [considering all age groups] in 1992 did not differ significantly from the number measured in 1981."[7] Thus Hans Henrik Brydensholt (Chairman of the European Council Study Group on Crime) notes that "[t]here is no direct relation between the level of crime and the number of imprisonments."[8] It is painfully evident, then, that pursuing the question "On what grounds can our society legitimate prison?" obliges concerned scholars to engage in a hermeneutic of both the historical and psychological roots of our concepts of justice, crime, and punishment. My suspicion is that a historical examination of the roots of our notions of justice, crime, and punishment might reveal that prison was never intended either to end crime or to enhance justice per se, but rather, that prison—like all other forms of state-sanctioned violence—was created *to contain certain volatile forms of violence so that other, more focused, more productive forms of violence might proceed uninhibited.*[9]

In order to address these suspicions, I engage in the following four moves. First, in order to consider the question from two related philosophical perspectives, I address Jean-Jacques Rousseau's *Discourse on Inequality* and Hannah Arendt's *On Revolution* and "On Violence," each of which explore the relationships among property, crime, law, and the production of violence. Second, in order to consider the question from a criminological perspective, I address Cesare Beccaria's *On Crimes and Punishments*, perhaps the first study to demonstrate that the emergent disciplinary techniques of early-modern criminology are among the foundational movements simultaneous with the Enlightenment. Third, in order to consider the question from an economic perspective, I examine Peter Linebaugh's *The London Hanged*, in which he documents how late-eighteenth-century Britain's rapidly changing imperial needs (as both a military and economic power) forced a dramatic reconsideration of cultural practices regarding property, workers' rights, crime, and state-sponsored violence. These first three sections demonstrate that philosophers, criminologists, and economists have long been aware that the historical function of prisons has been neither to prevent crime nor to deter violence, but rather, to reinforce hierarchies of class privilege and political power. Finally, in order to demonstrate some of the consequences of these claims from the perspective of a contemporary American prisoner, I recount the story of how my friend Big Will sought fiery retribution in the Indiana Reformatory, a maximum security prison.

A PHILOSOPHICAL CONTEXT: ROUSSEAU, ARENDT, AND THE PRODUCTION OF VIOLENCE

Part 2 of Rousseau's 1754 *Discourse on Inequality* offers a scathing critique of "civil society" in which the rising infrastructure of early modernity, rather than signifying the culmination of a majestic unfolding of progressive waves of refinement, civilization, and leisure, in fact demonstrates little more than the successful production and then defense of the concept of private property. Hence Rousseau's claim that, "[i]f we follow the progress of inequality... we shall find that the establishment of law and the right of property was the first stage, the institution of magistrates the second, and the transformation of legitimate into arbitrary power the third and last stage."[10]

Furthermore, as argued in the quotation that serves as one of the epigraphs for this essay, Rousseau believes that a considerable amount of the "crimes, wars, murders" and "misery and horror" involved in this "transformation of legitimate into arbitrary power" may well have been averted had someone, or some group, refused to accept either the original designation or the ensuing defense of private property.

As in all of Rousseau's speculative, proto-anthropological works, his overwhelming sense of romanticism forces us to question the deeper psychological drives behind such nostalgic claims for a prehistoric culture that thrived without private property.[11] Nevertheless, in a passage less well-known than the one mentioned above, Rousseau makes a startling observation regarding the relationship of crime and law:

> The more violent the passions, the more necessary are laws to restrain them; but the disorders and crimes which these passions cause every day among us demonstrate well enough the inadequacy of laws to achieve this end; and what is more, *it would be worth considering whether these disorders did not arise with the laws themselves.*[12]

The rough narrative stretching from the foundational "this is mine" to the ensuing institution of "civil society" to its subsequent "crimes, wars, and murder" thus requires the imposition of laws that, rather than deterring the various crimes resulting from "passions," actually serve the function of enabling the ruling elite to construct politically useful categories of "disorderly" conduct.[13] Henceforward, under this imposing regime of violence and crime-producing "law":

> One will see oppression increase continually without the oppressed ever being able to know where it will end, nor what legitimate means remain for them to halt it. One will see the rights of citizens and the freedom of nations extinguished little by little, and the protests of the weak treated as seditious noises.[14]

The law then, for Rousseau, is but a rhetorical facade behind which we find the interests of private property and political privilege.[15] Writing some two hundred years later, surveying the wreckage of the French Revolution and Robespierre's 1793 Reign of Terror, Hannah Arendt observes that the imposition of such arbitrary law leads to what she calls "delirious rage." The historical problem with such "delirious rage," however—as the gruesome example of Robespierre demonstrates—is that rage does not prompt the slow, meticulous negotiations that lead towards "the foundation of freedom," but rather, the impulsive, explosive violence necessary to "liberate man from suffering."[16] Indeed, citing the fact that over seventeen thousand citizens were guillotined between 1792 and 1794 alone, Jean Bethke Elshtain observes along with Arendt that the indiscriminate rage released by the French Revolution amounted to little more than an "orgy of repetitive destruction."[17] Rightly terrified by the prospect of such sweeping bloodletting in the name of some abstract higher cause, and perhaps wary of the "delirious rage" simmering within American culture at the time of her writing,[18] Arendt argues that unfettered rage, left to its own cathartic yet imminently destructive impulses, can do no more than "liberate the devastating forces of misfortune and misery."[19]

Rousseau and Arendt thus propose three related points: (1) that there is a trajectory from private property to the need for laws protecting property; (2) that these property-protecting laws in turn enable the production of politically useful notions of "deviance" that not only bear little resemblance to actual criminal behavior, but in fact go a long way towards creating the category of "the criminal" in the first place; and (3) that the psychological residue of living a life of oppression (which follows from neither owning property nor gaining equal access to the privileges of law and public conversation, let alone finding oneself imprisoned) in turn creates an explosive and powerful—although not necessarily constructive—sense of "delirious rage" that manifests itself not in the "foundation of freedom," but rather, in violent outbursts that seek the immediate destruction of existing powers. Thus, while sporadic eruptions of "delirious rage" may threaten the status quo in an immediate, temporarily disturbing way, it is readily evident that the law, even when administered with gross impunity, manages with remarkable dependence to protect the property rights and political privileges for which it was instituted in the first place.

That such "delirious rage" proves to be little more than an "impotent" expression of "the last stages of despair"[20] follows from the fact that "violence," for Arendt, is generally a last-ditch response of those (either citizens or entire governments) who lack genuine political "power." Indeed, in "On Violence" Arendt argues that whereas "power" is the fundamentally creative "human ability to act in concert" while pursuing freedom, "strength" is but "an individual entity;" "violence," then, is the "instrumental" use of "strength" to counteract the legitimate "power" that follows from collective, public action.[21] Put in its most simple terms, "the loss of power becomes a temptation to substitute violence for power."[22] Fear of the mute brutality of the masses' "delirious rage" in the face of their "loss of power" explains, on the one hand, Arendt's preference for the American Revolution's relative calm compared to the French Revolution's explosive violence.[23] On the other hand, elected governments too may succumb to the abuse of "violence" when they have lost genuine "power." For example, the manner in which America waged the Vietnam War (the subject of Arendt's elegant essay, "Lying in Politics"[24]) demonstrates to Arendt that the American government has lapsed into a form of "terror," or more specifically, "[t]he form of government that comes into being when violence, having destroyed all power, does not abdicate but, on the contrary, remains in full control."[25]

Arendt's *On Revolution* and "On Violence" thus offer important insights for our contemporary debates regarding prisons, crime, and their relationship to democracy, for the correctional-industrial complex operates in such an arbitrary, racist, wasteful, and violent manner that it is hard to view its machinations as anything other than what Arendt describes as "terror." The inability of citizens to counteract the correctional-industrial complex in turn means that many Americans feel absolutely powerless in the face of what (whether correctly or not) looks more and more like a conscious attack on their democratic rights; this perhaps explains the startling and ominous multiplication of C-rate conspiracy theories, violent revolutionary fantasies, and half-baked secessionist manifestoes that litter our ghettos and prisons, for in the face of the paralysis of actual democratic "power," various violence-based alternatives come to look more and more tempting, even necessary.[26] Indeed, Arendt's work suggests that in the absence of genuine democratic "power," it is logical to assume that alienated individuals will manifest their "strength" in the historical forms available to them: "violence" and "delirious rage" thus mark the perceived impossibility of collective, democratic action. The correctional-industrial complex amounts then, following Arendt's conceptual framework, to *a massive institutional machinery for producing violence* that wrenches us ever closer to Rousseau's chilling prophecy that with the accelerated disempowerment of citizens, "*all individuals become equal again because they are nothing.* . . . Here everything is restored to the sole law of the strongest, and consequently to a new state of nature . . . [that is] the fruit of an excess of corruption."[27]

A CRIMINOLOGICAL CONTEXT: BECCARIA'S APPEAL TO THE SOCIAL CONTRACT OF MODERNITY

Cesare Beccaria was one of the leading members of the *Accademia dei Pugni* (roughly translated as the Academy of Fisticuffs), a group of young, alienated Italian aristocrats who, according to Piers Beirne, sought "to create a model bourgeois society that combined spiritual and moral regeneration through the material advantages of economic growth."[28] *On Crimes and Punishments* (originally published in Italian in 1763, in French in 1765, and in English in 1767) is accordingly considered not only one of the first and most important documents of early-modern criminology, but also, in Franco Venturi's glowing language, "[t]he most famous book of the Italian Enlightenment."[29] Put simply, Beccaria and his colleagues were among the generation of late-eighteenth-century intellectuals—including Rousseau, Smith, and Jefferson, just to name a few[30]—who attacked the existing monarchical, aristocratic, and theological order of favors, privileges, and arbitrary rule with the imminently modern, bourgeois logic that a free marketplace and a formalized judiciary would accelerate the pace of scientific, political, and economic development.[31]

When Beccaria speaks of the "necessity to curb and control the domestic turbulence of particular interests,"[32] or when he argues that "[t]he first laws and the first magistrates arose out of the need to remedy the harms produced by the physical despotism of every individual,"[33] it is accordingly understood that he is referring to those nobles who, under the protectorate of church and king, act with impunity in both economic and political matters. The emerging world of early-modern capitalism, on the other hand, requires a smooth system of equivalences, efficient transportation, individual investment, and, above all, a respect for private property that transcends familial, theological, or even national affiliations. Indeed, in part 2 of his landmark essay on "Capitalism and the Origins of the Humanitarian Sensibility," Thomas Haskell observes that "[a] growing reliance on mutual promises, or contractual relations, *in lieu of relations based on status, custom, or traditional authority* comes very close to the heart of what we mean by 'the rise of capitalism'."[34] Situating the Enlightenment within this early-modern bourgeois assault on what Haskell calls "status, custom, and traditional authority" perhaps explains Beccaria's high praise for "the printing press," as it "makes the general public, and not just a few individuals, the repository of the holy laws."[35] Further-more, Beccaria notes that the printing press "drives out the shady propensity to cabal and intrigue, which vanishes when confronted with enlightenment and knowledge."[36] An enlightened, modern republic, then—for Beccaria in *On Crimes and Punishments* as for Madison in *The Federalist* and for Kant in his famous essay "What is Enlightenment?"—requires the diffusion of power through a labyrinth of citizens who are able to engage in public discourse due in large part to the aid of emerging public presses.[37]

In addition to facilitating public discourse (and thus short-circuiting secret "cabals"), the press serves another, more important political function for Beccaria, as he argues that "[p]unishments should be so selected as to make the most effica-cious and lasting impression on the minds of men with the least torment to the body of the condemned."[38] Early-modernity thus involves (1) a normalized public sphere free from the "despotism" and "turbulence of particular interests" and "cabals" that act secretly to peddle influence and favors, (2) a celebration of Enlightenment principles that promise both increased political rights and acceler-ated economic exchange, and (3) a movement towards a sense of social control based on *essentially semiotic principles*. Indeed, while Beccaria is a vocal critic of the barbarity of capital punishment, it would also appear in the passage cited above that the question of physical versus semiotic punishment is not concerned with justice so much as with the utilitarian calculus of which form of punishment will produce "the most efficacious and lasting impression" on the minds of other potential criminals.[39] In fact, while arguing in favor of the long-term deterrent effect of penal servitude over the short-term spectacle of capital punishment,[40] Beccaria argues that "[i]t is not the terrible but fleeting sight of a felon's death which is the most powerful brake on crime, but the long-drawn-out example of a man deprived of freedom."[41] Furthermore, Beccaria is clear that public executions simply provide opportunities for "fanatical demagogy which arouses the volatile emotions of curious crowds,"[42] whereas proportionate sentences handed down by duly appointed courts, and discussed publicly in the popular press, convey a more measured (and less volatile) sense of the state's authority.

This shift from a form of social control based on the violent spectacle of often arbitrarily assigned bodily torture to "rational" discourse grounded on a formal-ized and universal set of laws indicates a dramatic transformation in the exercise of political authority from a dependence on outright terror to what we call today "ideology." For example, Beccaria observes that:

> Verdicts and the proof of guilt should be public, so that *opinion, which is perhaps the only cement holding society together*, can restrain the use of force and the influence

of the passions, and so that the people shall say that they are not slaves but that they are protected, which is a sentiment to inspire courage and as valuable as a tax to a sovereign who knows his true interests.[43]

This is a remarkable passage, for Beccaria clearly aligns the role of the courts and the press in constructing "opinions" that serve the interests of the sovereign; executions are not wise, then, because they stir "passions" that prompt thoughts of "slavery," whereas publicly discussed prison sentences "inspire" both allegiance to the crown and fear of the overwhelming retribution awaiting future felons. The end of bodily executions in favor of a semiotic coalition between the courts and the public press (forging what Foucault calls "a whole learned economy of publicity"[44]) is therefore integral to the construction of a new, *modern* political world run not by outright terror, but rather, by "opinions" that—via their wide distribution by new means of printing technology—act as the "cement holding society together."[45]

The importance of Beccaria's *On Crime and Punishments*, then, is not only that it provides one of the first rigorous studies of the politically useful functions of criminology, or that it initiates the long process of rationalizing new, increasingly semiotic technologies of "reform," but that it demonstrates so completely the relationships among early-modern notions of crime, punishment, justice, and mass-produced "opinion" with the larger philosophical and political imperatives of the Enlightenment itself.[46] Indeed, Beccaria—much like his influential contemporary, Rousseau—understands clearly that state-sponsored violence in the name of punishing crime represents not a response to irrational outbreaks of inexplicable lawlessness, but rather one of the foundational maneuvers in establishing the hierarchies of wealth and power upon which early modernity rests.

AN ECONOMIC CONTEXT: "CUSTOM" AND CAPITALISM AT THE HEART OF IMPERIALISM

It would be difficult to overstate the importance of Peter Linebaugh's *The London Hanged: Crime and Civil Society in the Eighteenth Century*[47] for the study of how premodern notions of crime, punishment, justice, and private property were finally wrenched into their fully modern, bureaucratized version in the late eighteenth and early nineteenth centuries. Remarkably, many of the life stories that Linebaugh reconstructs from his immaculate archival research speak to similar historical crises as those addressed by Rousseau, Arendt, and Beccaria. For example, in a passage typical of the wide-ranging scope and detail of Linebaugh's project, he notes that

John Dixon was at the taking of Havana in 1762 when a third of the Spanish fleet was destroyed and the loot was allotted according to rank, an admiral receiving £122,000 and a common seaman £3. John Ward, a gauze-weaver, a married man, often in the workhouse, took part in the lucrative seizure of Senegal in 1758 when plunder valued at more than £250,000 was taken. He was hanged for stealing a watch.[48]

And so the British Royal Navy plunders Havana and Senegal in the name of God and king (and Linebaugh later discusses India as well), while John Ward, one of Albion's dogged foot soldiers, has his neck snapped for petty theft on the docks of London. Thus, adding historical depth to Beccaria's observations that "disorder grows as the boundaries of empires expand,"[49] Linebaugh demonstrates that there is a dialectical relationship between the international expansion of the empire (as a military and economic power) and the domestic need to redefine popular notions of crime and property—hence Beccaria and Linebaugh both place imperialism at the heart of their discussion of modern notions of crime and punishment.

The most volatile example of the impact of imperialism and capitalism on concepts of property and crime involves London's dockworkers and shipbuilders. Indeed, as England expands its increasingly international scope of military and economic activities, the need for more battleships, more warehouse space for appropriated goods, and increased efficiency in loading and unloading cargo places, London's shipbuilders and dockworkers literally at the heart of imperialism. Historically, prior to the universal institutionalization of wage payment, London's shipbuilders and dockworkers were paid in species only twice a year, and even then the payment of wages was frequently "several years in arrears."[50] Workers managed to survive, however, because of two primary factors: (1) Since no one in the larger dock economy was paid regularly, the exchange of goods and services among workers and local merchants depended on barter and the generous extending of credit and favors among fellow workers, and (2) workers were traditionally entitled (by what Marx refers to as "custom") to large amounts of the raw materials of their trade, which they then either integrated into their lives as useful materials, or bartered for the goods they could not buy with actual money.[51] For example, Linebaugh notes that the scrap wood left over from shipbuilding, known as "chips," was "an essential part of the dockworkers' ecology—in housing, in energy, in cooking, in furnishings," and that workers appropriated "chips" equivalent to "between a third and half of weekly earnings."[52] According to Linebaugh, customary access to perquisites (the etymological root of what we call today "perks") was so widespread that up to 60 percent of a given timber order for building a war ship actually ended up circulating as "chips" within the dockworkers' premoney economy.[53]

One of the primary goals of both the leading British capitalists of the late eighteenth century and the Royal Navy, then, was to increase production and lower labor costs—hence improving both profits and battle readiness—by denying workers their "customary" perquisites. To put this as simply as possible, *the new political-economy of capitalism and imperialism required a redefinition of both property and crime*: thus, what had previously been a customary raw material of working class life was now someone's *private property*; accordingly, what had previously been a customary right to materials now became a *crime*.[54] This redefinition of the daily activities and materials of life in the dockyards not only serves obvious political and economic goals, but, as Paul de Man observes in his analysis of the role of property in Rousseau's *Social Contract*, significant semiotic goals as well. Indeed, de Man notes that such early-modern redefinitions of notions of property and possession enact "a principle of functional identification between the owning subject and the owned object," and that "[t]he fascination of the model is not so much that it feeds fantasies of material possession . . . but that it satisfies semiological fantasies about the adequation of sign to meaning seductive enough to tolerate extreme forms of economic oppression."[55] In short, redefining the traditional materials of perquisites as private property, and the taking of traditional "custom" as crime, enabled not only new levels of production (and hence profit) for the emergent bourgeoisie, and new levels of efficiency for the Royal Navy's imperial ambitions, but it also contributed to the semiotic rationalization of what had previously been sites of cultural contestation. Henceforth, under this now-rationalized system of semiotic "adequation," the ambiguous and subtle work patterns of the docks and ship yards would be governed by an institutionalized language of legitimate ownership and illegitimate crime.

In addition to this rationalizing of previously contested forms of daily life, Linebaugh demonstrates that attempts to enforce these new definitions of property and crime were the driving impulses behind many of the technological innovations and workplace changes that propelled British shipping into a new era of unprecedented productivity.[56] For example, Samuel Bentham (the younger brother of Jeremy Bentham),[57] upon his appointment as inspector general of naval works in 1795, launched an all-out war on workers' "customary" privileges to "chips" by instituting modern methods of workplace management, including tighter "inventory" of materials, better "fortification" of the docks, more thorough training of "security personnel," more selective worker "recruitment," increased dependence on "task" labor, and, when these innovations failed, the aggressive "criminalization" of anyone who still persisted in taking their customary perquisites.[58] Thus, by the summer of 1802, when the West Indian Merchants Committee opened its stunning new dockyards—which were capable of handling over six hundred ships, were fully fortified, were built to streamline production, and were monitored by well-paid police—Bentham's war against customary perquisites had lowered shipping costs by 40 percent.[59] In short, Britain's capitalist elite produced phenomenally enhanced profits by criminalizing the behavior of the dockyard workers and shipbuilders.

Finally, while His Majesty's soldiers were paid three shillings per week to fight for God and king, the police monitoring the West Indian Merchants Committee's new behemoth dockyard were not only paid five shillings *per day*, but were also responsible for handling the pay of all workers,[60] hence functioning both as a disciplinary force and as the go-between from capitalists to laborers. Popular conceptions of the police as little more than stooges for the political and business elite are thus rooted in hard historical fact, for as Linebaugh demonstrates, the police were instituted for two reasons: to protect the new, modern definition of private property, and to insure the smooth functioning of the empire's naval dockyards.[61]

A PRISONER'S CONTEXT:
JOE PAYNE, BIG WILL, AND BURNING 'EM ALIVE

At 9 P.M., Thursday, 7 November 1996, Joseph P. Payne Sr., an inmate in the Virginia Reformatory, was scheduled to be executed by lethal injection for the murder of David Dunford, a fellow inmate. However, to the surprise of everyone awaiting Payne's execution, Republican Governor George F. Allen, acknowledging a lack of evidence on the part of the prosecution, offered a last-minute commutation in which Payne, in exchange for his life, accepted both a life sentence *without the possibility of parole*, and a deal in which any monies made from book, film, or television representations of his story go directly to a state-sponsored victim's assistance program.[62] Preempting Payne's possible future profits from tabloid renditions of his story is an astute move, for in addition to the obvious narrative drama generated by such last-minute stays of execution, the 3 March 1985 murder for which Payne was sentenced to die involved a horrific, wonderfully sensational, made-for-TV scenario in which Payne, using pilfered paint thinner, burned Dunford alive in his cell at the Powhatan Correctional Center.[63]

I was immediately drawn to Payne's story because it reminds me so clearly of a story told by my incarcerated friend and student, Big Will. In one of his many essays written for our collaborative ethnography project at the Indiana Reformatory (a maximum security prison outside Indianapolis), Big Will tells the story of how he was approached by three young, recently incarcerated members of the Vice Lords, who informed him that as of the next payday, they would be collecting half his monthly wages for their "strong box." Aside from standing six-foot-two and weighing well over 275 pounds, Big Will is an older, peaceful, well-educated, and highly respected prisoner who has served most of his adult life behind bars; he was thus understandably amused by yet apprehensive about this attempted muscle job by his conspicuously smaller, younger, yet aggressively gung-ho house-mates, as he commented that "I've been in prison since these wannabe hoodlums were in the second grade!" To make a long story short, Big Will understood that the Vice Lords' threat put him in a nonrational situation, in which measured rea-soning and negotiation were irrelevant, and that the only way to defend himself from the grandstanding violence of these young predators was thus "to embarrass, humiliate, and destroy them in one fell swoop." Big Will accordingly decided that deterring the Vice Lords' promised future violence—which would take the form either of extortion or outright bodily harm—required a definitive demonstration of his resolve not to be pushed around by hoodlums. He thus began to plot the ultimate prison version of what Arendt calls "delirious rage": burning enemies alive in their cell.

The grace-saving twist to Big Will's story is that after pouring two gallons of gasoline into the cell of his would-be intimidators (who had gathered for their nightly illegal card game), Big Will stood in front of their cell, lighter in hand, and extended his about-to-die victims a last-minute opportunity for appeal. Big Will notes with more than a little satisfaction that the previously strutting and trash-talking Vice Lords "pleaded for their lives like the frightened little boys they really were." Big Will then told the boys to strip, and after flinging their clothes over the second-tier rail, leaving them naked, groveling on their knees in gasoline, trem-bling for their lives, and thus properly humiliated in front of their tough-guy peers, he simply walked away. By demonstrating his ability to kill while simulta-neously maintaining the moral high-ground of not having to kill, Big Will taught the Vice Lords that he was not a man to be toyed with; he thus walked away from the terrified gangsters a free man, under the threat of extortion no more.[64]

Big Will's remarkable story is indicative of some of the paralyzing paradoxes of living amidst the "delirious rage" of a prison environment where intimidation, extortion, and the threat of deadly violence are the inescapable facts of everyday life. The politico-economic pretext to Big Will's story, however, is that the over-whelming saturation of contemporary prison culture with violence has been con-clusively linked to two factors: (1) warehousing young offenders in overcrowded prisons leads to increased prison violence (between individual prisoners, between members of rival gangs, and between prisoners and guards), and (2) prison vio-lence is frequently the end result of intentional, violence-producing, divide-and-conquer strategies of prison administrators who believe that keeping inmates fighting amongst themselves is in the best interests of prison security. The first of these claims has been addressed persuasively in recent research essays by, among others, Bohlen, Holmes, Purdy, and Rasmussen and Benson, and in prisoners' autobiographical accounts by, among others, Rideau, Wikberg, and Frazier.[65] Regarding the second of these claims, consider the unfolding scandal of California's Corcoran State Prison, where prisoner testimonies, FBI investigations, and even former Corcoran guards have all corroborated the charge that, taking full advantage of existing gang and racial tensions, guards carefully orchestrated prisoner-on-prisoner violence both to entertain and enrich themselves (by running profitable numbers games on staged fights) *and* to prevent the formation of transgang and/or crossracial prisoner unity.[66] Furthermore, as James Marquart's daring participant-observer research in Texas prisons demonstrates, "the internal institutional order" of prisons is based significantly on "the use of physical coercion" by guards to "maintain control and order," to "maintain status," to pursue "upward mobility" within the officer corps, and to "build solidarity" among guards. In fact, Marquart's study demonstrates that "guard *violence is neither idiosyncratic nor a form of 'self-defense',*" but rather, *"a socially structured tactic of prisoner control that is well entrenched in guard culture."*[67] The point here is that the macrological, structural, and politico-economic realities of *who the state chooses to imprison*, in tandem with the micrological, institutional, and policing realities of *how the state chooses to imprison*, combine to foster a prison culture geared towards *the production of violence.*[68] "Delirious rage," then, is not an inexplicable aberration within an imminently logical judicial system, but rather, one of the structural components of a punitive system geared towards the reinforcement of economic and political privilege.

After close to twenty years in prison, Big Will has come to understand that this dual-pronged production of violence (at both the macrological, structural, and politico-economic level *and* the micrological, institutional, and policing level) has fostered a prison culture based primarily on a rhetoric of terror. Hence, armed with a sophisticated understanding of both the force of semiotics and the role of "delirious rage" in prison culture, Big Will successfully produced a persuasive rhetorical gesture by performing a nonviolent version of the "burn 'em alive" tactic. Payne clearly acted less consciously (and certainly with less restraint) when he allegedly torched Dunford, yet the fact remains that his action, much like Big Will's, was not a bizarre eruption of inexplicable violence, but rather a painfully definitive example of the structuring principle of prison life: In a world geared towards the production of "delirious rage," where any genuine political power, using Arendt's definition of the term, is impossible, and where arbitrary physical coercion, as Marquart's essay demonstrates, is "a socially structured tactic of prisoner control,"[69] the instrumental use of violence becomes nothing less than a logical response to the foreclosure of other modes of action.

The commutation of Payne's imminent death into *an irreversible life sentence* (a deal that one would be hard-pressed to describe as anything less than Faustian) thus raises provocative questions regarding the relationships among prevailing concepts of crime and justice, the larger historical function of prisons, and the political-economy of the administration of violence in democratic culture. To put the issue in its truly baffling form, Payne was about to be killed legally because he had killed illegally someone who also had killed illegally, yet the only reason he killed illegally this other illegal killer was that the legal killers who run the prison had not provided adequate protection of his life; hence Payne was locked in an environment where had he not killed illegally the other illegal killer, then he quite probably would have been killed illegally himself—and so, by killing illegally in order to deter his own illegal killing, he incurred the wrath of a state that decided to kill him legally. This assumes, of course, that Payne (like Big Will) torched Dunford for essentially rational, instrumental reasons: That is, I am assuming that even incarcerated criminals don't burn people alive unless they have been irrevocably provoked by the threat of imminent violence. To reframe the issue in a different light: In order to deter the onslaught of anticipated violence, Payne committed an illegal act of violence-deterring violence; likewise, in order to deter the onslaught of anticipated violence, the state decided to commit a legal act of violence-deterring violence; and so on. The story takes on an even more numbing tone when we note that there were fifty-six state-sponsored executions last year (marking a record of death not matched since 1957), with another 3,054 prisoners languishing on death row.[70]

CONCLUSION

In terms of thinking about the historical role of prisons and punishment in America, it is important to remember that many of the first settlers of the "New World" were actually British, Scottish, Irish, French, and Dutch prisoners sold into indentured servitude. In fact, in *Bound for America*, A. Roger Ekirch estimates that "[c]onvicts represented as much as a quarter of all British emigrants to colonial America during the eighteenth century."[71] Indeed, selling prisoners to the various companies exploring the Americas lowered the cost of maintaining European prisons (since they could remain relatively small), enabled European elites to rid themselves of potentially troublesome agitators from the "dangerous classes," and provided the cheap labor necessary for the first wave of colonization.[72] Historically, then, social control, prisons, and imperialism go hand in hand with peonage, forced labor, and slavery. For example, in 1825 (in Frankfort, Kentucky) Joel Scott, who was unable to pay for high-priced slaves, instead paid $1,000 for the rights to Kentucky's prison laborers for one year. After winning this contract, Scott built his own private 250-cell prison to house his new "workers."[73] Or consider the example of San Quentin's founder, James Madison Estill, who throughout the first half of the 1850s, operating San Quentin prison under a private labor lease with California, (1) sold escape "passes" to prisoners who could afford them, while (2) forcing those who could not afford such "escapes" to labor for his profit, while (3) simultaneously making tidy profits off of prison sales of alcohol and prostitutes, all the while (4) (and this was certainly the most profitable activity) selling his black prisoners to pirate slave traders.[74]

Scott in Kentucky and Estill in California were not alone, however, in recognizing the potential of using the state's prisoners as a form of privately appropriated (and less culturally odious than slavery) forced labor. In fact, according to J. T. Sellin in *Slavery and the Penal System*, the postwar "Reconstruction" period saw prisons replace slavery as a less controversial means of controlling the labor of both blacks and poor whites:

> Burdened with heavy taxes to meet the expenses of rebuilding the shattered economy, and committed to the traditional notion that convicts should, by their labor, reimburse the government for their maintenance and even create additional revenue, the master class, drawing on its past experience with penitentiary leases, reintroduced *a system of penal servitude which would make public slaves of blacks and poor and friendless whites.*[75]

This dramatic claim is repeated in *The Wheel of Servitude: Black Forced Labor after Slavery*, where Daniel Novak observes that reconstruction "convict labor practices were the most brutal of all the devices used to restore 'order' to Southern labor."[76] Noting that 95 percent of leased convicts were black, and that many states prohibited leasing agents from contracting white convicts, Novak accordingly argues that the leasing of convict labor amounted to little more than a formal reworking of previous slave practices.[77] Thus, while reconstruction was based in large part on the rhetoric of a modernizing marketplace driven by free labor,[78] Novak notes that traditional plantation notions of privilege and hierarchy were reproduced by figures such as "U.S. Senator Joseph Brown, of Georgia, [who] had a twenty-year lease guaranteeing him three hundred convicts per year, for which he paid the state the munificent sum of seven cents per man per working day."[79]

Much like slavery, the conditions of leased prison labor were atrocious. For example, Novak notes that the death rate of prisoners leased to railroad companies between 1877 and 1879 was 45 percent in South Carolina, 25 percent in

Arkansas, and 16 percent in Mississippi.[80] Conditions in the labor camps of the Texas State Penitentiary in Galveston were so bad that 62 prisoners died in 1871 alone.[81] Finally, it is important to note that the profitability of convict leasing both during and after Reconstruction in turn produced sentencing practices that made a mockery of the law. For example, according to U.S. District Court Judge Emery Speer's analysis of court records in Bibb County, Georgia (*circa* 1905), "more than 149 people (almost all black) had been sentenced to a total of nineteen years at labor for crimes no more serious than walking on the grass or spitting on the side-walk."[82] This is not the place for a full overview of the history of punishment in America;[83] I mention these few examples simply by way of demonstrating that, his-torically, the correctional-industrial complex is rooted in forced convict labor, inhumane (and even deadly) working conditions, the perpetuation of racial for-mations based in slavery, and the perversion of the law in favor of the interests of private capital.

Given this perspective, the current trend of privatizing prisons and prison labor may be seen not so much as a recent reaction of the "lock 'em up" genera-tion, but rather, as recreating one of the fundamental historical links between cap-italism, prison, and slavery.[84] The question "On what grounds can our society legit-imate prison?" needs to be answered then not with reference to enlightened judi-cial or criminological premises, but rather—as Rousseau, Arendt, Beccaria, Linebaugh, and each of the historical examples addressed in this essay demon-strate—with straight talk regarding the protection of private property, the contin-uation of racial stereotypes, the defense of entrenched political privilege, and the production of politically useful forms of state-sanctioned violence.

NOTES

1. An earlier draft of this essay was presented at the Radical Philosophy Association National Conference, Purdue University, West Lafayette, Indiana, 14–17 November 1996. For assistance in researching the political economy of prison, I thank Danny Postel. For working through many of the historical and criminological materials contained in this essay, I thank my students at the Indiana Reformatory, the Indiana Correctional Industrial Facility, and San Quentin Prison.

2. Jean-Jacques Rousseau, *A Discourse on Inequality* (1754), trans. Maurice Cranston, (New York: Penguin, 1994), p. 109.

3. Hannah Arendt, *On Revolution* (New York: Penguin, 1963), pp. 110–11.

4. For an extended examination of these claims, see Stephen Hartnett, "Lincoln and Douglas Engage the Abolitionist David Walker in Prison Debate: Empowering Education, Applied Communication, and Social Justice," *Journal of Applied Communication Research* 26,

no. 2 (May 1998): 232–53, and "Prison Labor, Slavery, and Capitalism in Historical Perspective," *Dark Night Field Notes* 11 (winter 1998): 25–29. For up-to-date reports on each of the topics listed above, contact The Sentencing Project, 918 F Street, N.W., Suite 501, Washington, D.C. 20004.

5. "NCCD Analysis Finds," *Corrections Digest* 25, no. 5 (9 Mar. 1994): 1–4. On the question of what such expenditures indicate about America's continued inability to grapple with issues of race, class, and empire, see Ward Churchill and J. J. Vander Wall, ed., *Cages of Steel: The Politics of Imprisonment in the United States* (Washington, D.C.: Maisonneuve Press, 1992).

6. Bureau of Justice Statistics, *Jail Inmates 1992*, and *Prisoners in 1992* (Washington, D.C.: Department of Justice, 1993).

7. Bureau of Justice Statistics, *National Crime Victimization Survey Report: Criminal Victimization 1992* (Washington, D.C.: Department of Justice, 1993), and *National Crime Victimization Survey: Young Black Male Victims* (Washington, D.C.: Department of Justice, 1994).

8. Cited in Nils Christie, *Crime Control as Industry: Towards Gulags, Western Style* (London: Routledge, 1994), p. 34, emphasis added. Regarding the thesis that notions of "crime" have more to do with political expediency than actual judicial concerns, see the essays collected in David Greenberg, ed., *Crime and Capitalism: Readings in Marxist Criminology* (Philadelphia: Temple University Press, 1993).

9. Regarding the political manipulation of both violence and images of violence, see David Brown and Robert Merrill, ed., *Violent Persuasions: The Politics and Imagery of Terrorism* (Seattle: Bay Press, 1993), and Noam Chomsky, *The Culture of Terrorism* (Boston: South End Press, 1988).

10. Rousseau, *Discourse on Inequality*, p. 131.

11. Hence Bernard Yack's observation in *The Longing for Total Revolution: Philosophic Sources of Social Discontent from Rousseau to Marx and Nietzsche* (Princeton: Princeton University Press, 1986) that "[t]here are good reasons to doubt Rousseau's interest in the historical specificity of individuals and institutions." (p. 73) A more productive reading follows from Paul de Man's thesis that Rousseau's speculative work in part 1 needs to be read against the political observations of part 2 as a metaphorical critique of the possibilities of language itself; see de Man's remarkable comments in *Allegories of Reading: Figural Language in Rousseau, Nietzsche, Rilke, and Proust* (New Haven: Yale University Press, 1979), pp. 135–301. The definitive example of this type of deconstructive examination of Rousseau's philosophy of language remains Jacques Derrida, *Of Grammatology*, trans. Gayatri Spivak (Baltimore: Johns Hopkins University Press, 1976), pp. 101–268.

12. Rousseau, *Discourse on Inequality*, p. 102; emphasis added.

13. For a recent study that substantiates this thesis with excellent historical information, see Marie-Christine Leps, *Apprehending the Criminal: The Production of Deviance in Nineteenth-Century Discourse* (Durham: Duke University Press, 1992). In terms of applying this thesis to our contemporary correctional-industrial complex, see Clarence Lusane, "Congratulations, It's A Crime Bill," *Covert Action Quarterly* 50 (fall 1994): 14–22, and Stephen Hartnett, "Imperial Ideologies: Media Hysteria, Racism, and the Addiction to the War on Drugs," *Journal of Communication* 45, no. 4 (autumn 1995): 161–69.

14. Rousseau, *Discourse on Inequality*, p. 133.

15. For a sophisticated analysis of Rousseau's understanding of how the rhetoric of law strives to present itself as a nonrhetorical, literally authorless entity, see Neil Saccamano, "Rhetoric, Consensus, and The Law in Rousseau's *Contrat Social*," *Modern Language Notes* 107, no. 4 (Sept. 1992): 730–51.

16. Arendt, *On Revolution*, p. 111.

17. Jean Bethke Elshtain, "Hanna Arendt's French Revolution," *Salmagundi* 84 (fall 1989): 208.

18. On Arendt's experiences in America around the time of her writing *On Revolution* and *Crises of the Republic*, see "America in Dark Times," in Elisabeth Young-Bruehl, *Hannah Arendt: For Love of the World* (New Haven: Yale University Press, 1982): 383–437.

19. Arendt, *On Revolution*, p. 112.

20. Ibid., pp. 110–11.

21. Hannah Arendt, "On Violence," in *Crises of the Republic* (New York: Harcourt, Brace & Jovanovich, 1969), pp. 143–45.

22. Ibid., p. 153.

23. See Elshtain, "Arendt's French Revolution," and Margie Lloyd, "In Tocqueville's Shadow: Hannah Arendt's Liberal Republicanism," *Review of Politics* 57, no. 1 (winter 1995): 31–58, and "Practicing Political Theory Otherwise," in Frederick Dolan, *Allegories of America: Narratives, Metaphysics, Politics* (Ithaca: Cornell University Press, 1994), pp. 170–99.

24. "Lying in Politics," published in Arendt's *Crises of the Republic*, focuses in particular on the labyrinthine world of deception exposed by *The Pentagon Papers*.

25. Arendt, "On Violence," p. 154.

26. I do not want to belabor this point, but by way of example, consider this fantasy revenge scenario from a poem circulating around prison: "perhaps they will find you after their release/ you who would treat another as less than a fellow human/ lessons of cruelty are often well learned." This same collection contains a poem depicting a future post–civil war America in which all lawyers, policemen, stoolies, prison guards, and even "the rude woman who worked at City Hall" have been massacred by a vengeful "people who had been long oppressed."

27. Rousseau, *Discourse on Inequality*, pp. 134–35; emphasis added.

28. Piers Beirne, "Inventing Criminology: The 'Science of Man' in Cesare Beccaria's *Dei Delitti e Delle Pene*," *Criminology* 29, no. 4 (1991): 785.

29. Franco Venturi, *Italy and the Enlightenment*, trans. Susan Corsi (New York: Longman, 1972), p. 154.

30. For example, the effect of Rousseau on Beccaria was so great that Beccaria named his first daughter, Giulia, born in 1762, after Julie, the central character in Rousseau's influential *La Nouvelle Heloise*. See Richard Bellamy's excellent commentary in his "Introduction" to *Beccaria: On Crimes and Punishments and Other Writings*, trans. Richard Davies (Cambridge: Cambridge University Press, 1995).

31. Along this line of thought, consider Fredric Jameson's argument in *The Political Unconscious: Narrative as a Socially Symbolic Act* (Ithaca: Cornell University Press, 1981) that

"[t]he Western Enlightenment may be grasped as part of *a properly bourgeois cultural revolution*, in which the values and the discourses ... of the *ancien regime* were systematically dismantled so that in their place could be set the new conceptualities, habits and life forms, and value systems of a capitalist market society." (p. 96; emphasis added)

32. Beccaria, *On Crimes and Punishments*, p. 14.

33. Ibid., p. 27.

34. Thomas Haskell, "Capitalism and the Origins of the Humanitarian Sensibility, Part Two," originally published in *The American Historical Review* 90 (June 1985), and cited here as it appears in the remarkable collection, *The Antislavery Debate: Capitalism and Abolitionism as a Problem in Historical Interpretation*, ed. Thomas Bender (Berkeley: University of California Press, 1992), p. 144. For a brilliant reading of the inherently fictional character of such Rousseau-like "mutual promises" in forming the social contract of early modernity, see "Promises (*Social Contract*)," chap. 11 of de Man's *Allegories of Reading*, pp. 246–77.

35. Beccaria, *On Crimes and Punishments*, p. 17.

36. Ibid., p. 18. On the repression of the emergent intelligentsia in Milan, which forced Beccaria and his colleagues to publish much of their work secretly—hence explaining Beccaria's aversion to "cabal and intrigue"—see the comments in Beirne, "Inventing Criminology," pp. 784–87.

37. Beccaria's aversion to "cabals" is echoed in Madison's November 1787 *Federalist #10*, where he too argues that the rise of early modernity, in this case seen in the diffusion of power through an extensive system of representation, is based on "guarding against the cabals of the few" (*The Federalist*, ed. Jacob Cooke [Middleton: Wesleyan University Press, 1961], p. 63). In his September 1784 essay, "An Answer to the Question: What is Enlightenment?", Kant argues that the enlightenment depends on "the freedom to make a *public* use of one's reason" (cited here as the essay appears reprinted in *Practical Philosophy*, trans. and ed. Mary Gregor [Cambridge: Cambridge University Press, 1966], p. 17). While I am not aware of any evidence that Kant studied Beccaria, it has been established that Jefferson, Adams, and Madison (among others) all read Beccaria closely. See the comments in Venturi, *Enlightenment*, pp. 160 ff. and Beirne, "Inventing Criminology," p. 781 ff.

38. Beccaria, *On Crimes and Punishments*, p. 31.

39. The utilitarian nature of Beccaria's argument prompted Jeremy Bentham to gush: "Oh my master, first evangelist of Reason!" (cited in David Young, "Cesare Beccaria: Utilitarian or Retributivist," *Journal of Criminal Justice* 11, no. 4 [1983]: 318). Also see "Bentham and Beccaria," chap. 3 of H. L. A. Hart, *Essays on Bentham: Studies in Jurisprudence and Political Theory* (Oxford: Calendon Press, 1982), pp. 40–52.

40. For a blistering critique of Beccaria's position regarding penal servitude, see Graeme Newman and Pietro Marongiu, "Penological Reform and The Myth of Beccaria," *Criminology* 28, no. 2 (1990): 337–39.

41. Beccaria, *On Crimes and Punishments*, p. 67.

42. Ibid., p. 29.

43. Ibid., p. 36; emphasis added.

44. Michel Foucault, *Discipline and Punish: The Birth of the Prison*, trans. Alan Sheridan (New York: Vintage Books, 1995; French original in 1975), p. 109.

45. Again, it is fascinating to observe that Beccaria's appeal to "opinions" was later repeated by Madison in *Federalist #49*, where he noted (2 February 1788) that "[a]ll governments rest on opinion" (*Federalist*, p. 340). *The Federalist Papers* then, in both content (a rational debate about the construction of a democratic apparatus of government) and form (a barrage of essays launched by enlightened citizens in the popular press in order to further debate regarding the recently proposed Constitution [17 September 1787]) amounts to precisely the kind of public, communicative rationality called for by Beccaria.

46. The definitive study of the entwining of the enlightenment and "reform" remains Foucault's *Discipline and Punish*, for the purposes of this essay, see in particular the chapter entitled "The Gentle Way in Punishment," pp. 104–31. It is important to note that such "reforms" prompted considerable backlash from traditional elites. Regarding the vicious attacks on Beccaria (including Father Facchinei's accusing Beccaria of "six charges of sedition and twenty-three charges of irreligion"!) see "Beccaria and His Treatise," chap. 4 of Marcello Maestro, *Voltaire and Beccaria as Reformers of Criminal Law* (New York: Columbia University Press, 1942), pp. 51–72. Also see Beirne, "Inventing Criminology," pp. 781–83.

47. Peter Linebaugh, *The London Hanged: Crime and Civil Society in the Eighteenth Century* (Cambridge: Cambridge University Press, 1991).

48. Ibid., p. 262.

49. Beccaria, *On Crimes and Punishments*, p. 19.

50. Linebaugh, *London Hanged*, pp. 375, 376.

51. This helps to explain Marx's argument in "The Law on Thefts of Wood," where he states: "We reclaim for poverty *the right of custom*, and moreover a right of custom which is not a local one but which is that of poverty in all lands" (originally printed as an editorial in *Rheinische Zeitung*, 1842; cited here as it appears in *Karl Marx: Selected Writings*, ed. David McLellan [Oxford: Oxford University Press, 1977], pp. 20–22; emphasis added).

52. Linebaugh, *London Hanged*, p. 379.

53. Ibid., p. 380.

54. A parallel form of redefinition—also triggered by dramatic changes in the structure of political economy—was occurring in America at this time as well, as paupers were transformed from family and neighborhood obligations into anonymous menaces to society that required institutionalization. As David Rothman explains it, "he who had once been an accepted part of the community now became an odd and even menacing figure" (p. 161). See Rothman's excellent historical material in *The Discovery of the Asylum: Social Order and Disorder in the New Republic* (Boston: Little, Brown, & Co., 1971).

55. de Man, *Allegories of Reading*, p. 262.

56. Regarding the relationship between the modernization of production and disciplinary culture, see Dario Melossi and Massimo Pavarini, *The Prison and the Factory: Origins of the Penitentiary System* (London: Macmillan, 1981; Italian original in 1977), and J. J. Tobias, *Crime and Industrial Society in the 19th Century* (New York: Shocken Books, 1967).

57. Jeremy Bentham is known to many scholars via Foucault's discussion of his work in the "panopticism" chapter of *Discipline and Punish*, pp. 195–228. However, by situating Jeremy's ideas regarding "panopticism" in relation to Samuel's work as manager of the

Imperial Shipyards of Russia (circa 1779–1786; where he used slave labor) and as inspector general of Britain's Naval Works (where he attacked successfully the taking of "chips"), Linebaugh provides a view of the Bentham brothers that situates their work more squarely within the larger politico-economic needs of modernizing capital and expanding imperialism (cf. *London Hanged*, pp. 373–94)—his is a significant contribution towards a more thoroughly historical·understanding of the bases of "panoptic" discipline.

58. Linebaugh, *London Hanged*, pp. 390–94.

59. Ibid., p. 425.

60. Ibid., p. 430.

61. See Sidney Harring, "Policing a Class Society: The Expansion of the Urban Police in the Late Nineteenth and Early Twentieth Centuries," and Steven Spitzer, "The Political Economy of Policing," both in *Crime and Capitalism*, pp. 546–67 and 568–94, respectively.

62. Mike Allen, "Virginia Prisoner Receives Rare Mercy on Death Row," *New York Times*, 10 Nov. 1996, p. A10, and Peter Finn, "On Execution Day, Allen Grants Clemency," *Washington Post*, 8 Nov. 1996, pp. A1, A13; both note that Payne's assumed guilt is based on information garnered in a dubious plea bargain with another prisoner. Nonetheless, as if on cue, the *Post* immediately ran an editorial in which the first paragraph, while supporting Allen's granting of clemency, stresses that "*The Governor is no soft touch* when it comes to prisoner cases," and that Allen has "a history of support for the death penalty." See "Governor Allen's Clemency," *Washington Post*, 9 Nov. 1996, p. A26; emphasis added.

63. While the deal with Payne thus suggests the prevalence of prisoners magically making money off of the state, in fact the reverse is more accurate. Indeed, many states now bill prisoners not only for medical care and legal fees, but for their room and board as well; Michigan, for example, collected over $1,000,000 from its prisoners in 1994 alone. For an introduction to this growing trend, see Christian Parenti, "Pay Now, Pay Later: States Impose Prisoner Peonage," *Progressive* (July 1996): 26–29.

64. Big Will's remarkable story is part of a larger series of essays on the violent socialization processes of the Indiana Reformatory, a maximum security prison outside Indianapolis. I collected hundreds of such essays as part of a collaborative ethnography project (in conjunction with Ball State University) at the reformatory, January 1994–May 1996, and hope to publish a study of these writings in the future.

65. Wilbert Rideau and Ron Wikberg, ed., *Life Sentences: Rage and Survival Behind Bars* (New York: Times Books, 1992), and Mansfield Frazier, *From Behind the Wall: Commentary on Crime, Punishment, Race, and the Underclass by a Prison Inmate* (New York: Paragon House, 1995); both offer broad firsthand insights into the role of violence in prison culture. Also see any issue of *The Prisoner News Service*. Celestine Bohlen, "Bursting Population Overwhelms Italy's Prisons," *New York Times*, 28 Feb. 1995, p. A3, notes that overcrowding in Italy's prisons has led to an unprecedented rise in prison suicides. Steven Holmes, "Inmate Violence is on Rise as Federal Prisons Change," *New York Times*, 9 Feb. 1995, pp. A1, A8, observes that in conjunction with the decreasing age of prisoners locked in increasingly overcrowded prisons, inmate-on-inmate violence from 1994–1995 has risen by 18 percent, while inmate-on-staff violence for this same period has risen by 27 percent. Matthew

Purdy, "Even in a Season of Peace, Rikers Stands on the Razors Edge," *New York Times,* 15 May 1995, p. B11, notes that the steady rise in violence in the eight facilities on Rikers Island correlates with decreasing staff/inmate ratios, one of the most obvious results of overcrowding. David Rasmussen and Bruce Benson, *Economic Anatomy of a Drug War: Criminal Justice in the Commons* (Lanham, Md.: Rowman and Littlefield, 1994), note that in Illinois' Graham and Centralia facilities, inmate population increases of 33 percent led to an overall increase in disciplinary reports of 63 percent, and a 120 percent increase of inmate-on-staff violence (pp. 25 ff.). There is no question, then, that overcrowding young prisoners creates more violence.

66. See Reynolds Holding, "Accusations of Prison Cover-up," *San Francisco Chronicle,* 28 Oct. 1996, pp. A1, A6, and A7; and Corey Weinstein, "Brutality at Corcoran," *Prison Focus* 1, no. 1 (winter 1997): 4–5 (This excellent magazine is available from the California Prison Focus, 2489 Mission Street #28, San Francisco, CA. 94110). Regarding the guard-sanctioned (and even encouraged) culture of violence at New York's State Prison at Dannemora, see Matthew Purdy, "An Official Culture of Violence Infests a Prison," *New York Times,* 19 Dec. 1995, pp. A1, A17. On the political economy of guards and disciplinary technology, see Fox Butterfield, "Political Gains by Prison Guards," *New York Times,* 7 Nov. 1995, pp. A1, A13, and Mike Zielinski, "Armed and Dangerous: Private Police on the March," *Covert Action Quarterly* 54 (fall 1995): 44–50.

67. James Marquart, "Prison Guards and The Use of Physical Coercion as a Mechanism of Prison Control," *Criminology* 24, no. 2 (May 1986): 342, 363, and 348. Marquart arrives at his conclusions after serving as a guard (although doing so to gather research) at a Texas prison. Not surprisingly, surveys of guards demonstrate that they refuse to acknowledge their use of force in public. For example, John Hepburn's survey of over 360 guards at five different prisons concludes that "[g]iven the uniformly low degree of importance assigned by guards to coercive and reward power, it appears that legitimate power is the remaining vestige of guards' positional power" ("The Exercise of Power in Coercive Organizations: A Study of Prison Guards," *Criminology* 23, no. 1 [Feb. 1985]: 160). For a case study of how guards' public denials of prisoners' accusations of guard-violence leads to incommensurable legal, political, and ethical claims, see Stephen Hartnett, "Behavior Modification or Rights Violation?" *Nuvo Newsweekly,* 1 June 1994: 10.

68. The definitive study here is Jeffrey Reiman, *The Rich Get Richer and the Poor Get Prison: Ideology, Class, and Criminal Justice* (New York: Macmillan, 1979). For additional analysis of the historical roots of this claim, see Christie, *Crime Control as Industry,* for a study of how the technology of disciplinary violence has become big business; see Anne-Marie Cusac, "Stunning Technology: Corrections Cowboys get a Charge Out of Their New Sci-Fi Weapons," *Progressive* (July 1996): 18–22.

69. Marquart, "Prison Guards," p. 348.

70. See Bureau of Justice Statistics, *Capital Punishment, 1995* (Washington, D.C.: U.S. Department of Justice, 1996) and "56 Executions This Year Were the Most Since 1957," *New York Times,* 30 Dec. 1995, p. A10. For a concise overview of the political and legal issues surrounding the recent barrage of state-sponsored executions, see Bryan Stevenson, "The Hanging Judges," *Nation* 263, no. 11 (14 Oct. 1996): 16–19.

71. A. Roger Ekirch, *Bound for America: The Transportation of British Convicts to the Colonies, 1718–1775* (Oxford: Clarendon Press, 1987), p. 27.

72. In fact, Ekirch notes that convicts sold into service in the New World generally cost plantation owners around L13, whereas slaves cost as much as L 35 to L 44 (*Bound for America*, pp. 124–26).

73. See the discussion in David Shichor, *Punishment for Profit: Private Prisons, Public Concerns* (Thousand Oaks: Sage, 1995), pp. 34–35.

74. See Ward McAfee's excellent essay, "San Quentin: The Forgotten Issue of California's Political History in the 1850s," *Southern California Quarterly* 62, no. 3 (fall 1990): 235–59.

75. J. T. Sellin, *Slavery and the Penal System* (New York: Elsevier, 1976), p. 34.

76. Daniel Novak, *The Wheel of Servitude: Black Forced Labor after Slavery* (Lexington: University of Kentucky, 1978), pp. 32–33.

77. Ibid., pp. 32 ff.

78. The definitive text remains Eric Foner, *Reconstruction: America's Unfinished Revolution, 1863–1877* (New York: Harper and Row, 1988).

79. Novak, *Wheel of Servitude*, p. 145.

80. Ibid., p. 33.

81. Shichor, *Punishment for Profit*, p. 38.

82. Novak, *Wheel of Servitude*, p. 35.

83. For such an overview, the reader would do well to begin with Rothman's *Discovery of the Asylum*, Adam Hirsch's *The Rise of the Penitentiary: Prisons and Punishment in Early America* (New Haven: Yale University Press, 1992), and Lawrence Friedman's *Crime and Punishment in American History* (New York: Basic Books, 1993).

84. The best extended analysis of this issue is David Shichor's *Punishment for Profit*. For shorter essays, see Reese Ehrlich, "Workin' for The Man: Prison Labor," *Covert Action Quarterly* 54 (fall 1995): 58–63, and Christian Parenti, "Making Prison Pay," *Nation* 262, no. 4 (29 Jan. 1996): 11–14.

12

The Debate About the End of History and Global Democracy[1]

Gabriel Vargas

In connection with the fall of the so-called truly existing socialism in eastern Europe and the Soviet Union (1989–1991), we have seen a complex worldwide recomposition. This recomposition has been geographic, with the rise of new nations heretofore present in latent form behind the USSR, Yugoslavia, Czechoslovakia, and the two German republics; economic, with the adoption of market economies by ex-socialist countries; political, with the introduction of liberal democracy; and ideological, with the decline of Marxism/Leninism as an official ideology, the recuperation of neoliberalism, and the resurgence of nationalist and religious movements. The collapse of those societies, however, also implied in capitalism the resurgence of old ideologies[2] such as neoliberalism, the growth of new ideologies such as postmodernism (especially in versions by Lyotard, Baudrillard, or Vattimo), and the updating of other ideologies such as the "end of history," all of which presented themselves as interpretations of the crisis and of its attending global recomposition. In this paper I will discuss the "end of history" proposed by Francis Fukuyama and the notion that liberal democracy is the only possible horizon.

The conception of the "end of history" offered by Fukuyama in his famous article and in his book[3] has its antecedents both in the erroneous thesis of the "end of ideologies" by Daniel Bell[4] and in ideas about the "end of Marxism," "the end of philosophy," and the "last man," which, as Jacques Derrida says,[5] constituted the daily bread of the 1950s. In those times, philosophers like Hegel, Marx, Nietzsche, and Heidegger were seen, in fact, as classics of the end. But the difference between those conceptions of the "end of history" and the current proposal is that the former represented a Weberian disenchantment with the consequences of modernity,[6] while the latter, Fukuyama's, represents an inexplicable regress and a surprising optimism with regard to a concept of modernity that seems not to have assimilated the terrible experiences suffered by humanity in the twentieth century.

Now, what does it mean, in general, to speak of the end of history? The "end of history" requires us first of all to clarify the terms "end" and "history." The concept "end" takes us to those of "telos" (in Greek) and "finis" (in Latin). These terms mean "to bring about" or "realize" but also a "border" or "limit" or "termination." "End" is the completion of a process, its fulfilling, but also its border or horizon. On the other hand, when one speaks of history, one can distinguish between the actions in which people engage in a given situation, with or without consciousness of them, and the explanation of such actions from a philosophical or scientific point of view.

Therefore, with the "end of history" one might understand the following: (1) a prediction for the future, as we see in the classic philosophies of history (Augustine of Hipona, Voltaire, Herder, Kant) or in the Judeo-Christian tradition, (2) a form of understanding the past (Hegel), or (3) a termination or exhaustion of a stage or period of history. The meaning used by Fukuyama is the last, but with the additional sense that there will be nothing new in spite of the fact that things will continue to happen. In fact, according to his idea, after the extended battle between liberalism and socialism during the nineteenth and twentieth centuries, liberalism and its conception of democracy triumphed in 1989 and became the only horizon for the future. In Fukuyama's own words, liberal democracy may be "the endpoint of the ideological evolution of humanity," "the final form of government," and as such it would indicate "the end of History."[7]

This idea already prompts two objections. The first seems obvious: How is it possible to maintain that after all the social and theoretical evolution observed throughout history, suddenly things will come to a halt and there will be nothing new? If we attend to past experience, it is impossible to think that in the future there will be no new realities and new theories to modify or even take the place of the liberal model. The second is that the relationship between liberalism and democracy has been and is conflictive, not only because democracy has a longer history than liberalism but also because there are numerous contradictions between the two models, models that are presented in Fukuyama as unproblematically complementary. Norberto Bobbio argues in his book *Liberalismo y democracia* that while it is true that liberalism and democracy have as their starting point the individual, liberalism begins with an atomistic conception while democracy is organicist.[8] There can be a relationship between the two, but it is "merely possible, not necessary."[9] This nonnecessity is seen in the fact that if democracy goes so far as to touch upon the vital interests of the market economy, the former tends to be overcome. (The clearest example that we have in Latin America is the overthrow of Salvador Allende in Chile.) There would be a third objection, but its analysis would be digressive, and that is that the events of 1989–1991 might not be the triumph of liberal democracy, but rather its liquidation. This is the thesis of Jean-Marie Guéhenno in his book, *La fin de la démocracie*.[10] I do not agree with that thesis, which is but another idea of the end, simply in the opposite sense of that proposed by Fukuyama. My thesis is that the crisis of bureaucratic socialism implies the necessity of democracy, but in a new and radical sense: economic, political, and cultural.

Fukuyama continues his argument by asserting that if there have been injustices or problems in the stable democracies such as the United States, France, or Switzerland, these are due to "incomplete application of the twin principles of liberty and equality, upon which modern democracy is founded, rather than due to a failing of the principles themselves."[11] Derrida, in his incisive critique of Fukuyama's book in *Spectres of Marx*, says that the author conveys an evangelical message (the good news being the union between liberal democracy and the "free market") that is based on severe logical contradictions. Fukuyama has the audacity to contend that the series of horrors, oppressions, and genocides that have occurred in the name of democracy are merely empirical phenomena that have little to do with the ideal. "As such, as the telos of a form of progress, such an orientation would have the form of an ideal finality. Everything that seems to contradict it would proceed from historical empericity, as massive and catastrophic and world-wide and multiple and recurrent as it may be."[12] But in connection with this idea, Fukuyama insists that "while the earlier forms of government are characterized by grave defects and irrationalities that led to their possible collapse, liberal democracy is free from these fundamental internal contradictions."[13]

This idea is also a *petitio principii* for the following reasons. Firstly, in liberalism itself there has been the contradiction, since the beginning, between political ends and economic ends. In this sense, Bobbio has demonstrated how liberalism has two souls: a political soul that represents the quest for liberties of expression, organization, and representation, and another that belongs to the market economy. These two souls are in permanent conflict. Secondly, liberal democracy reduces its action exclusively to the political sphere and does not permit democracy in the economic and cultural spheres, as C. B. Macpherson has demonstrated.[14] Thirdly, there exists an ongoing contradiction between democracy internal to the nation-state and the consequences of its decisions upon other countries, as has occurred with the

Helms-Burton ruling on Cuba. (David Held, in his book *Models of Democracy* has examined the consequences of such processes, proposing "democratic autonomy."[15]) And finally, in the fourth place, there are the great limitations and paradoxes that democracy has encountered in the contemporary world, which Bobbio has called the unfulfilled promises of democracy, and which have been examined recently by Claus Offe and Philippe C. Schmitter.[16] In summary, it can be said that contemporary democracy has encountered great obstacles such as: oligarchic power, the invisible power of technocracy, the controlling power of the media which creates biased information, and the great corporate powers, among others. All of these have generated apathy and disillusionment in the citizenry.

How is it possible then that such a series of problems can be ignored when they are of such obvious relevance? Fukuyama says that his thesis does not refer to the end of events, but rather of history (taking into consideration the experience of all peoples in all ages) understood as a "unique, evolutionary, coherent process."[17] According to him, this conception is attributable to Hegel and Marx. In the case of Hegel, interpreted through Alexander Kojève, we can accept that he did intend to portray history as an optimistic and rational process, although it is subject to interpretation whether or not there exists a speculative closure of the evolution in the Prussian state, or, as others think, the process is an open one. But in the case of Marx, the interpretation is simply false.

Hegel was the first thinker to conceive of history as a rational process from the point of view of political economy.[18] In almost all his work, but especially in his *Lessons on the Philosophy of Universal History*,[19] he argued that history should be understood as the process of self-knowledge by the spirit, through which in different phases it would overcome its alienation. For that reason he said that "[w]e should seek in history a universal end, the ultimate end of the world, not a private end of the subjective spirit or of the will. And we should learn it through reason, which cannot be interested in any private and finite end, but only in the absolute end."[20] It is not a question of the reason of a particular subject, but of divine and absolute reason. From this central idea, Hegel employs the categories of variation, rejuvenation, reason, idea (in relation to liberty), spirit of people, ethnicity, state, etc. The end of the spirit is its self-knowledge, in itself and for itself. In Hegel's words, "the end is that there may be a spiritual world in accordance with its self-concept, that may fulfill and realize its truth, and produce religion and the state in such a way that they conform to its concept. Such is the universal end of the spirit and of history."[21] This process is realized through phases whose determined logic the philosophy unveils. The process of the spirit's realization culminates in the rational state. The state is not only its political aspect but also the spirit of a people, its ethicity (*Sittlichkeit*).

In this conception of history there are many positive aspects, but also problems. Advances include the explanation of history as a process, the dialectic form employed in such explanation, and the reflection on the state as a whole, which implies the tripartite structure formed by the family, the civil society, and the state and which impugns the dichotomy proposed by natural rights theory. Nevertheless, critics since Marx have criticized Hegel's idealistic conception and the identity between rationality and spiritual fulfillment in his argument,[22] as well as the fact that it amounts to a legitimization of the historical moment in which Hegel lived. Others have criticized his logocentrism, his eurocentrism, and his ambiguity when he says, on the one hand, that "Europe is absolutely the fulfillment of universal history,"[23] and on the other that "America (i.e. the USA) is the country of the future."[24]

Although one can detect the pretension of a historical culmination in Hegel, the truth is that historical evolution is an open process that never ends and its conception is far from that of a liberal democracy.

In the case of Marx, he rejects throughout his writings Hegel's teleological notion of the "end of history" even though he holds on to other meanings. For Marx, history does not come to a predetermined end; it is not guided by a transcendent or immanent subject, nor is the rationality of history determined by its finality. But through Marx's works we can discover many aspects of the concept of history. In brief summary, I would say that they are the following:

(a) In the *Economical-Philosophical Manuscripts* of 1844,[25] Marx considers history as a realization of a human essence generated by work. "All of the so-called universal history is no more than the generation of a man by means of human labor. Concerning the genesis of nature for man, we see in it the tangible and irrefutable proof that man has been born of himself."[26] This concept of human essence was interpreted by some authors in a teleological way, but in reality it implies a critique, albeit speculative, of alienated existence. In spite of that, Marx already distinguishes in this work, in contrast to Hegel, between alienation and objectivation.[27] This speculative essence is "the sum of social relations."

(b) In *The German Ideology*[28] we already find a concept of open history as a product of praxis, although this praxis may be conditioned by previous social relations. "This conception reveals that history does not end by dissolving itself in 'self-knowledge', as a 'spirit of the spirit' but that in each of its phases there is a material result, a sum of forces of production, a historically determined behavior towards nature and between individuals, which each generation transfers to the succeeding one, a mass of productive forces, capitals and circumstances which, although partially modified by the new generation, nevertheless dictates to it, its own conditions of living, which determine a certain development, a special character. Therefore, circumstances make the man, while in the same measure man makes his circumstances."[29] There is not, therefore, a previous direction for history; instead, humans have to go about constructing such a direction. This open conception of history remains in all his subsequent works.

(c) Beginning with the famous "Prolog" to *Contribution to the Critique of Political Economy* of 1859,[30] there arise many erroneous interpretations, with an enormous following through schematic and dogmatic versions of Stalinism and post-Stalinism, especially involving the erroneous idea that Marx held a linear conception of history.

Such an interpretation is clearly denied by a previous manuscript, "Pre-capitalist Economic Formations,"[31] in which it is shown that Marx considers history to be a complex, irregular, and combined process. The idea is reaffirmed when Marx explicitly refuses to formulate a philosophy of universal history. That is the thrust of a letter written to "Otiéchestviennie Zapiske" (Annals of the Nation), at the end of 1877:

> ... to my critic this is of a little import. He at every turn endeavors to convert my historical outline about the origins of capitalism in western Europe into a historical-philosophical outline about a general trajectory to which all peoples find themselves fatally subjected, no matter what the historical circumstances that may attend them, while at the same time the greater impulse of productive forces, of social labor, assures the development of man in each and every one of its aspects. (In this you do me too much honor, and at the same time, too much scorn).

Marx adds that he "does not want to construct a philosophy of history."[32]

But in the famous "Prolog," Marx also affirms that "bourgeois relations are the last antagonistic form and with this social formation *concludes*, therefore, the *pre-history* of human society."[33] This phrase recalls Hegel's conception in his *Lessons of the Philosophy of History* in which he speaks for the begging of history. In fact, for Hegel, the only moment worthy of philosophical reflection is the beginning of the state, which also is that of rationality—not where it is still a possibility but where it is already consciousness, will, and action. In this sense, Hegel says:

Peoples can live a long life without a State, before obtaining that determination. And they can without a State obtain an important development, in certain directions. This pre-history however falls outside our purview, as has already been shown, even though the development has been followed by a real history or the peoples may not have managed to form a state.[34]

For Marx, on the other hand, prehistory concludes with the end of relations of exploitation, in a first socialist phase with the extinction of the state, and in a second with communism, according to his *Critique of Gotha's Program*. Today, in light of what has occurred in the twentieth century, the proposition of such a self-regulated society, the disappearance of alienation, the extinction of the state and, therefore, the overcoming of a prehistory of humanity has become, in spite of the desires of Marx and Engels, a utopia. But if we consider that the social contradictions that engendered his idea of the end of prehistory not only continue to exist, but have become aggravated, then we should not understand utopia as a coming of "the kingdom of God" so much as a critique of the status quo, a pre-being-itself in the sense of Ernest Bloch (*Das Prinzip Hoffnung*)[35] and a process that should develop out of a new sense of history. We would admit that, against Marx but also with Marx, his utopia continues to have force even though there may be a need for Marxism to develop new theories about the transition between the old and the new societies.

Be that as it may, in Marx, it is not a question of an overcoming of prehistory that must necessarily come to pass, but rather of the necessity of beginning a more just and rational way towards the self-realization of the human species. In spite of what has been said, the conception of history in Marx was interpreted, in the so-called "truly existing socialism," as a teleology. Such an interpretation set the stage for his most prominent detractors to impugn such a model, going so far as to find a formulation of a "new historicism," for example by Karl Popper in his book, *The Poverty of Historicism*.[36] There Popper conducted an interpretation of Marx that was hardly serious or rigorous, not considering the different meanings that history acquires in Marx's works nor the openness he gives it. His critique misses the mark because it seems to focus more on Soviet manuals from the 1950s than on the texts by the authors he criticizes.

From all this I conclude that the ideology of the "end of history" has no consistency whatsoever. It will hold for a time, only to be taken over by a new ideology, answering to the incessant necessity that the system has desperately to maintain social cohesion in the face of disintegration. But why do this model and others in similar vein acquire any credibility? I find three causes.

The first is that, in fact, two processes have reached their end: one was the soviet model and the other, the productivist and optimist modernity sought by the

Enlightenment. The Soviet model not only fell because of external contradictions but also for internal reasons.[37] The second is that a form of capitalist modernity has reached its end, and that a new phase is beginning whose characteristics are not yet clear. It requires formulating a new critical conception of modernity. And the third is that, after the collapse of so-called socialism, an alternative concept of the political and economic orders is needed for our societies. The formula that liberal democracy has offered us, to make compatible liberty and equality, is in crisis.

Finally, a few words about Latin America. In Latin America in general and Mexico in particular we have lived, through all these years, the struggle between capitalism and socialism. In Mexico in the 1930s, in fact, there was a play to construct a Keynesian state derived from specific conditions of the Mexican Revolution of 1910. But in the 1980s, our country, like all Latin America, fell into one of the most profound crises in its history. While the governing powers implemented neoliberalism and the North American Free Trade Agreement as solutions, the progressive movements have struggled to implant an authentic democracy. In other sectors, for example, the Zapatista movement, an autonomous democracy is advocated. Neoliberalism intends to export its specific form of democracy (limited and legalistic) as a legitimate form of globalization. The analysis of the characteristics and consequences of liberal democracy, initiated in the highly developed countries, is necessary for us because it shows in what measure it is necessary to avoid the repetitions of history. As one of the classics has said, history repeats itself first as a tragedy and then as a farce.

NOTES

1. Translated by Paul Dixon.
2. Here I am talking about "ideology" only in one of the senses of the concept: like fallacy, mystification.
3. Francis Fukuyama, "The End of History?" *National Interest* 16 (summer 1989); and *The End of History and the Last Man* (New York: Free Press, 1992).
4. Daniel Bell, *The End of Ideology: On the Exhaustion of Political Ideas in the Fifties* (Harvard: Harvard University Press, 1988). With the "end of ideology," Bell proposes another ideology: "instrumental reason" in the sense of Adorno and Horkheimer.
5. Jacques Derrida, *Specters of Marx: The State of the Debt, the Work of Mourning, and the New International,* trans. Peggy Kamuf (New York: Routledge, 1994).
6. Perry Anderson, *A Zone of Engagement* (London: Verso, 1992).
7. Fukayama, *End of History,* p. xi.
8. Norberto Bobbio, *Liberalismo y democracia,* trans. José F. Fernández Santillán (México: Fondo de Cultura Económica, 1989).

9. Ibid., p. 51.

10. Jean-Marie Guéhenno, *La fin de la démocracie* (Paris: Flamarion, 1993).

11. Fukayama, *End of History*, p. xi.

12. Derrida, *Specters of Marx*, p. 71.

13. Fukayama, *End of History*, p. 11.

14. C. B. Macpherson, *The Political Theory of Possessive Individualism* (Oxford: Claredon Press, 1962), and *The Life and Times of Liberal Democracy* (Oxford: Oxford University Press, 1977).

15. David Held, *Models of Democracy*, 2d ed. (Standford: Stanford University Press, 1977).

16. Claus Offe and Philippe C. Schmitter, "Las paradojas y los dilemas de la democracia liberal," *Revista Internacional de filosofía política* 6 (1995).

17. Fukayama, *End of History*, p. 12.

18. See Georgy Lukács, *El joven Hegel y los problemas de la sociedad capitalista*, trans. Manuel Sacristán (México: Editorial Grijalbo, 1963).

19. G. W. F. Hegel, *Lecciones sobre la Filosofía de la Historia Universal*, trans. José Gaos (Madrid: Revista de Occidente,1974).

20. Ibid., p. 44.

21. Ibid., p. 67.

22. See, e.g., Iztvan Mészáros, *Beyond Capital* (Londres: Merlin Press, 1995), esp. p. 9.

23. Hegel, *Lecciones*, p. 201.

24. Ibid., p. 177.

25. Karl Marx, *Economic and Philosophic Manuscripts of 1844*, trans. Martin Milligan (New York: International Publishers, 1968).

26. Ibid., p. 90.

27. See Adolfo Sánchez Vázquez, *Filosofía y economía en el joven Marx* (México: Ed. Grijalbo, 1978).

28. Karl Marx and Fredrich Engels, *The German Ideology*, in *Collected Works,* vol. 5 (New York: International Publishers, 1974–1986).

29. Ibid., p. 39.

30. Karl Marx, *A Contribution to the Critique of Political Economy*, in *Marx and Engels Selected Works in One Volume* (New York: International, 1968).

31. Karl Marx and Eric J. Hobsbawm, *Formaciones económicas precapitalistas*, trans. José Aricó (México: Cuadernos de Pasado y Presente, 1971).

32. Karl Marx and Friedrich Engels, *Escritos sobre Rusia, II. El porvenir de la comuna rural rusa*, no. 90, ed. J. Aricó, trans. Felix Blanco (México: Cuadernos de Pasado y Presente, 1980), pp. 64–65.

33. Marx, *Contribution to the Critique*, p. 78; my emphasis.

34. Hegel, *Lecciones*, p. 136.

35. Ernest Bloch, *El principio esperanza*, trans. Felipe González Vicen (Madrid: Editorial Aguilar, 1979).

36. Karl Popper, *The Poverty of Historicism* (London: Routledge, 1961).

37. See Gabriel Vargas Lozano, *Mas allá del derrumbe* (México: Siglo XXI Editores, 1994).

Contributors

John Brentlinger is professor emeritus of philosophy at the University of Massachusetts at Amherst. He is the author of *The Best of What We Are: Reflections on the Nicaraguan Revolution* and *Villa San Miedo: Presente* (with photographer Mel Rosenthal). He is presently writing on Marxism, politics, and spirituality.

Frank Cunningham is professor of philosophy at the Unversity of Toronto. He teaches political philosophy and is author of *The Real World of Democracy Revisited* and *Democratic Theory and Socialism.*

Stephen Hartnett is assistant professor of speech communication at the University of Illinois in Champaign-Urbana. For the past ten years he has been teaching college in prisons in Indiana and California, and working as an activist campaigning against the death penalty, the war on drugs, and the correctional-industrial complex.

Thomas M. Jeannot is associate professor of philosophy at Seattle University. A member of the RPA, his interests include Marxism, classical American philosophy, hermeneutics, and social analysis.

Joel Kovel, MD, is a trained psychiatrist and psychoanalyst. He is currently Alger Hiss Professor of Social Studies at Bard College, Annandale-on-Hudson, New York. He received a Guggenheim Fellowship in 1987. His principal works include

White Racism, The Age of Desire, History and Spirit, Red Hunting in the Promised Land, and the just-completed *The Enemy of Nature.* A longtime activist, Kovel ran for the United States Senate on the Green Party ticket in 1998.

Xiaorong Li is research scholar at the Institute for Philosophy and Public Policy, University of Maryland, College Park. She has written articles about international justice, human rights, "Asian values," and feminism. She is currently at the Institute for Advanced Study at Princeton.

Steve Martinot worked for fifteen years in heavy industry, mostly as a machinist. He has a master of arts in creative writing from the University of Colorado and a Ph.D. in literature from the University of California, Santa Cruz. He teaches interdisciplinary studies from time to time in the Bay Area and has published numerous articles on Sartre, Derrida, and Heidegger. He is also involved in research in the field of critical white studies, an antiracist critique and deconstruction of the structures of white supremacy and white identity. He recently published a translation from French of Albert Memmi's latest book, *Racism.*

Charles Mills is associate professor of philosophy at the University of Illinois at Chicago. He works in the general area of oppositional political theory, and has recently published two books on race: *The Racial Contract* and *Blackness Visible: Essays on Philosophy and Race.*

Patrick Murray is professor of philosophy and chair of the philosophy department at Creighton University in Omaha, Nebraska. He is the author of *Marx's Theory of Scientific Knowledge* and the editor of *Reflections on Commercial Life.* His research interests center on the relationship between capitalism and modern philosophy and include the British empiricists, Hegel, Marx, and the Frankfurt School.

Richard Peterson is professor of philosophy at Michigan State University. He has published *Democratic Philosophy and the Politics of Knowledge* as well as articles on various themes in social and political thought. He is working on a book on the intersection of race, intellectuals, and modern politics.

David Roberts is a Ph.D. student in philosophy at the University of Alberta. He received his M.A. in philosophy from the University of Montana with a thesis on ethical naturalism. He is the coauthor, with Andrew Light, of "Toward New Foundations in Philosophy of Technology: Mitcham and Wittgenstein on Descriptions" in *Research in Philosophy and Technology,* volume 19, and was assistant editor of *Philosophy and Geography* from 1996 to 1998.

Jeanne Schuler is associate professor of philosophy at Creighton University in Omaha, Nebraska. Her research interests focus on the history of modern and nineteenth-century philosophy (especially Kant and Hegel), critical theory, and feminism. She has written on Hume, Kant, Hegel, Kierkegaard, Adorno, Arendt, de Beauvoir, Baudrillard, Benhabib, postmodernism, urban geography, and moral luck.

Tony Smith is professor of philosophy and political science at Iowa State University. He is the author of *The Logic of Marx's Capital, The Role of Ethics in Social Theory, Dialectical Social Theory and Its Critics,* and *Capital and Technology in the Age of Lean Production* (forthcoming). His current research project is a comparative study of competing theories of globalization.

Gabriel Vargas teaches in the philosophy department of the Universidad Autnoma Metropolitana in Mexico City. He teaches political philosophy and philosophy of history. Lozano has published several books and articles, both within and outside his country, including *Que hacer con la filosofa en Amrica Latina?* and *Mas all del derrumbe.*